AQA GCSE DRAMA

Joy Morton   **Ron Price**   **Rob Thomson**
Consultants: Jon Taverner, Russell Whiteley

D0493564

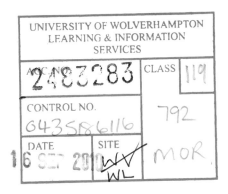

Heinemann

Heinemann is an imprint of Pearson Education Limited,
a company incorporated in England and Wales, having
its registered office at Edinburgh Gate, Harlow, Essex, CM20 2JE.
Registered company number: 872828

Heinemann is a registered trademark of Pearson Education Limited

Text © Ron Price, Joy Morton and Rob Thomson 2001

First published 2001

ISBN: 978 0 435186 11 1

10 09
10 9 8 7 6

Produced by Gecko Ltd, Bicester, Oxon
Original illustrations © Heinemann Educational Publishers 2001
Illustrations by Beccy Blake, Abigail Conway, Andrew Quelch and Nick Schon
Printed in China (CTPS/06)

Acknowledgements
We, the authors, would wish to express our thanks to the following for their various contributions towards this book:
Sian Benyon, David H. K. Berezan, Claire Bowen, Tim Browning, Adam Clarke, Nicola Cutcher, Peter Dawkes, Peter Ging, Oli Grey, Laura Hare-Winton, Jake Howell, Alex Hurle, Claire H. B. Jackson, Marianne Jones, Ricky Keeley, Anita Liley, Fiona McKenzie, Laura Middleton, Naomi Richards, Lucy Stoneham, Nichola Tuttle, Sam Wilson; and to all our readers.

Special thanks go to The Emmbrook School, Wokingham, and its students; to Millthorpe School, York, and its students; to Studio Carr Ltd. Wokingham, Berkshire for the photographs; to Emma Dickson,
Jon Taverner and Russell Whiteley for their support, encouragement and advice throughout the whole process; and most particularly to Shirley Wakley, our Editor, for all her patience, enthusiasm, guidance and good humour!

The publishers gratefully acknowledge the following for permission to reproduce copyright material. Every effort has been made to trace copyright holders, but in some cases has proved impossible. The publishers would be happy to hear from any copyright holder that has not been acknowledged.

Hear Hear from *All I Ever Wrote* by Ronnie Barker, published by Essential Books Limited, reprinted with permission of Essential Books Limited; Extract from 'AQA Examination material' reproduced by permission of the Assessment and Qualifications Alliance; Extract from *Find Me* by Olwen Wymark, first published by Samuel French Limited © Olwen Wymark 1920, reproduced by permission of The Agency (London) Limited. All rights reserved and enquiries to The Agency (London) Limited, 24 Pottery Lane, London W11 4LZ fax 0207 727 9037.

The publishers would like to thank the following for permission to reproduce photographs on the pages noted:
Cover: Craig Lovell/CORBIS (puppets); CORBIS (mime artist); Robbie Jack (woman holding baby/*Caucasian Chalk Circle*); Robbie Jack/CORBIS (three men)
Inside: Hulton-Getty (children emigrating, p65); PYMCA (homeless teenager, p69); CORBIS (refugees, p110); CORBIS (lighting box, p189); all other photographs – Studio Carr Ltd

Forewords

I was delighted when asked to write a Foreword to this book. Having spent many years writing reports to centres on GCSE Drama, detailing strengths and weaknesses, I became aware that there was little published material available aimed specifically at candidates. In particular, there was very little material that offered comprehensive advice and guidance; which explained drama and theatre techniques in depth; and which demonstrated their uses through exercises that instructed and motivated the reader.

Here, though, is a book which I believe does all these things and more. Not only are the requirements of the AQA course discussed very clearly but, most importantly, it gives students of all abilities the opportunity to realise their potential. It offers structured exercises on a range of responses in which the appropriateness to style, genre and audience is explored alongside the identification of potential problems and workable solutions.

It provides, I feel, excellent and exciting practical work based on all the Performance and Technical Options and it explains coherently how to plan and structure written material for both Coursework and the Examination.

I am certain that students will find all of the information contained of immense value and easily accessible and that they will thoroughly enjoy learning and developing their skills while responding to the activities and mini-projects.

Jon Taverner, Chief Examiner

This book is not merely a support for the AQA Drama Specification, it is a very useful and instructive resource for the study of approaches to, and the development of skills for, dramatic presentation in general at GCSE and post 16 level.

The journey through development to application of essential techniques is graduated carefully and the exercises provided ensure that both rehearsals and performances are investigated creatively and in depth.

The mini-projects are initially designed to provide students with detailed stimulus material and outline many and various approaches to the themes and texts being explored. These will be very useful as students embark on courses in Year 10. The later projects, with their more skeletal outlines, ensure that students have to develop their own artistic responses to the themes and build on the earlier development of their skills base.

The various practical Options are also investigated in depth and the requirements of the AQA Examination are described in very user-friendly language. The sections on faults and pitfalls will be welcomed and applauded by teachers and moderators alike for their clarity and common sense.

The advice regarding the Written Paper is detailed, sensible and supportive. The practical points made regarding answering questions accurately and with detailed justification will not only be invaluable for the Drama paper but should also provide a useful guide for approaching other written examinations.

I consider that this book is long overdue. I am convinced that it will be welcomed eagerly by both students and teachers who will immediately recognise and appreciate the expertise of the authors who have created an extremely accessible and exciting Coursework book.

I look forward to seeing Drama Examination results going through the roof as more candidates become inspired and motivated by the encouragement, wisdom, detailed practical investigation and well-considered exploration of the AQA specification contained in this publication.

Russell Whiteley, Chief Examiner

Contents

Forewords by Jon Taverner and Russell Whiteley   iii
Introduction   vi

A
Developing your skills   1

A1   Preparation techniques   1

A2   Rehearsal techniques *(The Body in the Bedroom)*   5

A3   Personal performance techniques *(The Audition)*   17

A4   Group performance techniques
      (The Ruined Abbey and *The School Staff-Room)*   28

A5   Techniques for styles/genres/types   37

A6   Technical techniques *(The Accused)*   46

A7   Written techniques *(Find Me)*   52

B
Applying your skills through mini-projects   63

B1   Mini-projects   63
    1   Rehearsal techniques: Exporting children   65
    2   Performance techniques: Runaways   69
    3   Group performance techniques:
       The Ruined Abbey or *The School Staff-Room*   73
    4   Theatre-in-Education: Healthy eating for Year 7   77
    5   Script – performance: *The Last Hurdle*   81
    6   Script – technical: *The Last Hurdle*   86
    7   Musical stimulus: Cats   90
    8   Dance/Drama: The burying of Pompeii   94
    9   Developing originality: Soap Opera!   98
   10   Building on other cultures: *The First Kangaroo*   102

B2   Outline mini-projects   107
   11   Refugees   110
   12   The Billumbungles   111
   13   Proud of us!   112
   14   The weather   113
   15   Can you hear me? *Hear Hear*   114
   16   Music   116
   17   What's in a name?   117
   18   The truth about teenagers!   118
   19   'Age cannot wither'   119
   20   The Witches: *Macbeth*   120

B3   Possible sources for further project work   122

section C

Succeeding in the Options 123

Option requirements at a glance 123

C1 Requirements for performance options 124
Option 1: Devised thematic work 134
Option 2: Acting 138
Option 3: Improvisation 142
Option 4: Theatre-in-Education 145
Option 5: Dance/Drama 149

C2 Requirements for technical options 153
Option 6: Set 160
Option 7: Costume 164
Option 8: Make-up 169
Option 9: Properties 173
Option 10: Masks 177
Option 11: Puppets 181
Option 12: Lighting 185
Option 13: Sound 190
Option 14: Stage management 194

section D

Preparing for the Written Examination 199

D1 Getting to know the written paper 199
Macbeth by William Shakespeare, Act 5 Scene 1 205

D2 Set plays – performance questions 207

D3 Set plays – design questions 211

D4 Response to live productions 218

Appendices 229

Introduction 229

1 Assessment guidelines 231
2 Rehearsal log-sheet 233
3 Performance self-assessment sheet 235
4 Technical self-evaluation sheet 237
5 Audience evaluation sheet 239
6 Response to live performance 241
7 Lighting cue-sheet 247
8 Sound cue-sheet 248
9 Make-up design sheet 249
10 Costume design sheet 250

Introduction

We have written this book to give you as much help as possible to achieve a good result in your examination. We suggest that you read carefully the requirements for the overall examination and for each option or paper. In each section of the book we have outlined a process that you can follow, provided you with suggestions on how you might fulfill the requirements, and given you tasks to build your skills and increase your knowledge. Remember that this examination seeks to assess your work as a creative performer or designer and your understanding of how effective theatre is created.

GCSE Drama is an exciting and creative course and we hope that this book helps you to enjoy the many challenges that lie ahead.

How to find your way around the book

Section A introduces you to, or reminds you of, various techniques which will help you to provide an effective presentation. Section B gives you some mini-projects for practising and reinforcing the necessary techniques. Section C gives you advice on each of the Coursework Options which you can offer for assessment. Section D takes you through the techniques needed for the written examination.

Joy Morton
Ron D. Price
Rob Thomson

Developing your skills

A1 Preparation techniques

Using this section of the book

These techniques will help you to make sure that you prepare in a productive and purposeful manner. On pages 63–122 you will find some mini-projects through which you can link the various techniques together, and create a detailed and impressive piece of work.

Under each of the headings below you will find a description of the technique and how it may be relevant to your performance work. There are also activities for you to try before applying the techniques to the mini-projects and later to your assessed pieces of coursework.

Research

This is finding information from a variety of sources, to help both your understanding and the development of your piece of work.

Among other things, for Acting you would **research** the time and place in which the play is set; for Devised thematic work, the theme; and for Theatre-in-Education, the needs of your chosen audience. Information can come from many places including the Internet, CD Roms, newspapers and magazines, the school and local libraries, interviews with people, historical sources, or a questionnaire that you create yourself.

Good **research** is a useful, and often essential, preparation technique for all performance options. It is also worth remembering that you gain marks in both your coursework options for your **research**.

A1.1   activities

1   Find five articles from newspapers, magazines or books which you think a group could turn into interesting improvisations. Discuss how you might bring the articles to life.

2   If you were performing a scene on the subject of 'The Creation' you might want to research and compare stories from different religions and different tribal myths; compare Darwin's Theory of Evolution with the 'Big Bang' Theory; and see how various painters and composers have interpreted the subject. Make notes of where you might look for the necessary information.

For the future

When you are given a presentation task, think carefully about the topics that need **researching**, identify the best sources of the information you need, and make notes on what you find out!

Breathing exercises

These are exercises to help your breath control, which in turn affects the clarity and projection of your voice and the efficient use of your body in movement.

Breathing out is the power that creates sound, so your lungs must be able to breathe out for long enough to be able to speak long phrases with comfort. As with singing, when your breath runs out before the end of a phrase or line it is because there is no more air left in your lungs to produce any sound. So the more air which the lungs can collect, the stronger the sound you can produce. Good **breathing** also has an effect on the control, strength, pace and quality of your movement: if you don't have enough air in your lungs, your movement becomes weak and meaningless. A good supply of air also gives confidence. Repeat various **breathing exercises** frequently to improve your lung capacity and your vocal sound.

Obviously **breathing exercises** are particularly useful in any performance option where you are using speech, but they can also be vital for movement and for Dance/Drama.

A1.2 activities

1 Take as large a breath as you can, and then breathe out as slowly as possible, counting aloud all the time. How far can you get before you have to breathe in again? You probably start with a good, firm sound, but as you run out of breath, the sound becomes rasping, quieter and more of a mumble – the lack of air causes lack of tone, lack of projection and lack of clarity.

2 This time you need to stand some distance away from your partner. Breathe in and out naturally several times. Then control your breathing: breathe in, and say 'one' as you breathe out. Breathe in and say 'one – two' as you breathe out. Breathe in and say 'one – two – three' as you breathe out. Continue, until it becomes a bit of an effort to speak, then stop. Can your partner still hear you by the end? Try to get a little further each time you do this exercise.

For the future

These should not be isolated exercises. If you want to improve your breath control, and therefore the quality of your voice and movement, you need to do these and/or other **breathing exercises** you know on a regular basis. Many actors do a few each time they 'warm up'.

Movement exercises

These are methods by which you practise particular movements, or series of movements.

Movement exercises can be used to experiment with possible movements for a character or a situation; to help you to perfect a particular movement or key moment; or to help you to understand how one movement flows into the next. You need to analyse the needs for that moment, character or situation, breaking down exactly how and where your body should move; and then practise until it becomes completely natural to you.

Movement exercises can be a very useful preparation technique for all performance options, and may be used throughout the rehearsal period.

A1.3 activities

1 In threes, depict a scene on a park bench, where nine or ten totally different people come. Each of you will play at least three characters each, concentrating on making sure that the movement for each is totally different from any of the others portrayed. At no time will the bench be empty.

2 It is your first day at a new school. Show your feelings at various times through the way you hold your body, and the way you move. How do you feel just before you leave home? When you go through the school gates? When you meet other pupils of your age? When you are approached by older pupils? When you meet the Headteacher? Each time you want to show a change of feeling, make sure you change your movement.

3 If you are familiar with Laban's eight efforts, produce a sequence of elements where you are using a different pace or a different tension from your partner. Notice which combinations are particularly effective visually.

For the future

These should not be isolated exercises. If you want to improve the quality of your movement, you need to do these and/or other **movement exercises** you know on a regular basis. Many actors do a few each time they 'warm up'.

How might you develop the aggressive movement suggested in this picture without using violence?
Notice how individuals differ in posture and gesture

Actor objectives

These are what you, as the actor, want to achieve in communicating to the audience.

For example, the **actor objective** might be to make the audience feel sorry for your character, or to communicate the fact that your character is sly and secretive. Whatever performance you prepare, you must have clearly in your own mind what you want to achieve, both with the piece as a whole and with your intended character.

These **objectives** will give your work a clear focus, and will affect the whole way you prepare, rehearse and polish your work.

The decisions about **actor objectives** are of great importance in all performance options.

A1.4   activities

1　Try an improvisation with a partner. In this improvisation of someone visiting a friend who is in hospital, try the scene with the actor objective of the visitor being to horrify the audience at their lack of sensitivity. The actor objective of the patient is to make the audience feel sad at how ill they are.

2　Try this same scene using as much as possible the same dialogue. But this time change the objective of the visitor to making the audience aware of how close the two people are. The patient's objective could be to give the audience a surprise or shock at the end of the scene.

For the future

You need to be clear in your own mind what your **actor objectives** are, and remind yourself before you start each rehearsal, so that you can focus on the most relevant rehearsal techniques to use during that particular session.

Examiners' tip

Spend time preparing properly. In-depth research and decisions about objectives are essential to an effective production. Knowing clearly, right from the start of rehearsals, exactly what you wish to communicate will save you hours of wasted time, and will result in a much more successful final presentation.

Preparation techniques at a glance

	General help	Help with character	Help with movement
Research	■	■	■
Breathing exercises	■		■
Movement exercises	■	■	■
Actor objectives	■	■	■

A2 Rehearsal techniques

Using this section of the book

These rehearsal techniques will give you the tools with which to perform in a successful manner: all are essential to good performance work. After you have done your preparation work and you are into the rehearsal period you can apply these techniques to develop and communicate a characterisation, although they will not all be essential every time. Learn to experiment to find your best ways of doing things.

Under each of the techniques listed below you will find activities to try. By doing these you will improve your performance skills and be able to select those you will need when you try the mini-projects (pages 63–122), and later when you create your pieces for actual assessment.

Some of the activities in this section are based on *The Body in the Bedroom*, printed below.

The Body in the Bedroom by Joy Morton

Characters: ALEX: businesslike, practical, able to think in an emergency
             LOL: flippant, unkind, enjoys irritating people
             TUKET: rather nervy and unsure, always keen to do the 'right thing'
             A.J.:   rather authoritarian, likes to take control

There is a bloodcurdling scream in the darkness, a loud thud as someone falls to the floor, and then silence. The lights go up to reveal a body on the floor. ALEX *knocks at the door and enters, sees the body, stops, hurries over and kneels down beside it.*

ALEX   Oh no. Joe, can you hear me? Joe . . . Joe . . . (*Puts ear to* JOE's *chest; then fumbles for a pulse.*) Oh dear.

    LOL *enters.*

    LOL   Got a problem then?
    ALEX   Yes. It seems that Joe's dead.
    LOL   Dead?
5   ALEX   He's not answering me. He looks a terrible colour. And I can't find a pulse.
    LOL   Move up then, Alex. Let me have a feel. (*Tries to find a pulse.*) No, no pulse.

    TUKET *enters.*

    ALEX   We'd better call the ambulance just in case. (*Hurries off.*)
    TUKET   Oh, how terrible. Poor soul!
    LOL   Poor soul? He was a horrible man. No one liked him.
10 TUKET   Lol, you mustn't speak like that of the dead! It's not right, you know.

    A.J. *enters.*

    LOL   Why not? It's the truth.
    A.J.   Well, you're not exactly top of the popularity list you know!
    LOL   So? What is that supposed to mean? You know we all hated Joe: so why pretend it was any different?
15 TUKET   (*moving closer*) Shouldn't we be giving him the kiss of life or something?
    LOL   Too late for that, my dear.

	A.J.	Let's have a look then: see what's what. If he's dead, there must be a reason for it.
20	LOL	Obviously! But what makes you think that you can tell more than we can. You're not a doctor.
	A.J.	No, Lol, I'm not. But there are always supposed to be clues, which might be helpful.
	TUKET	Oh! A.J., don't! You speak as if it was murder . . . talking about clues.

ALEX returns.

25	ALEX	Murder? Surely not? There's nothing to suggest it's murder, is there?
	LOL	Well, why not? Perhaps it was . . .
	TUKET	Well, A.J. has started 'looking for clues'.
	ALEX	For goodness sake, we don't even know for sure that he's dead. The ambulance will be here in a few minutes.
30	A.J.	Well, I think he's dead. And I think we should take a look around.
	LOL	Come on, everybody. Do what Chief Inspector A.J. says. You never know, it might amaze us what we can find. Just like 'Hunt the Thimble' when we were kids!
	ALEX	Stop it all of you. That's just how you're beginning to behave – like a lot of
35		kids. Just because Joe has collapsed you're letting your imaginations run away with you. Things are getting out of control.
	A.J.	Perhaps that's what has happened already, Alex. (*pointedly*) Someone . . . has lost control.

They all look at A.J. As the meaning registers, they move away from each other.

	TUKET	Are you trying to say that if it is murder, then one of us must have killed him? (*Sits down suddenly on the end of the bed.*)

Lights fade.

Off-text improvisation

This is when you use your imagination to create short scenes that do not appear in the actual scenario of your piece.

You can use **off-text improvisation** to increase your understanding of the characters, and to explore them in a number of different situations. You may also explore scenes from the past or the future, or what may be happening in the next room to where the play is taking place. It may be interesting to create scenes from the history of the characters, such as when they first met.

The use of **off-text improvisation** is a useful rehearsal technique for all Scripted Acting, Improvised, Devised and Theatre-in-Education work.

A2.1 activities

1   In groups of five, read the extract from *The Body in the Bedroom*. Go back in time to when the characters (including Joe) were at school together. Produce an improvisation that shows what they were like as children and shows how their same basic characters could be seen even then.

2   In your groups, again take the extract from *The Body in the Bedroom*. This time, create a new scene that happens either just before the known story begins or tells us what happens to the characters after the known story ends.

For the future

It is always worth doing some **off-text improvisation** in order to increase your understanding of the characters and their relationships. It is obviously useful to do early on, but you may need to come back to it later in the rehearsal time, especially if you feel that relationships are not coming across clearly enough.

On-text improvisation

This is simply performing the scripted text using your own words and actions rather than those that are set down in the script itself.

On-text improvisation can help you to understand difficult words, speeches and ideas, such as you find in Shakespearean English; it can help you to experiment with the pace of the performance; and it can allow you to experiment with the content of the scene, which might suggest new ways of performing the scene or character.

On-text improvisation is a rehearsal technique that is useful when you are working with any script in the Acting or Devised options.

A2.2 activities

1   In groups of four, read the extract from *The Body in the Bedroom* again. Briefly discuss the scene and how the characters feel. Put the script away and perform the scene in your own words.

2   Each of the characters in this extract has something different to hide about his/her relationship with Joe. Joe could be related to one; Joe could have been blackmailing one; Joe could have been having an affair with one of their partners. Decide what this is and how it would affect their reactions during this scene. Try the improvisation again, and notice how these changes affect your performance.

For the future

It is always worth doing some **on-text improvisation** in order to increase your understanding of the scene you are doing. It is obviously useful to do right at the beginning of rehearsals, but you may need to come back to it later, especially if you feel that you are not communicating your objectives clearly enough.

Character modelling

This is creating living statues. One or more partners stay(s) frozen in a plain or neutral position while another moulds them into positions or attitudes.

Character modelling can be very helpful when you are deciding on the posture and gesture of your character. Being modelled by others, or modelling classmates into your character, is a good way of getting more ideas for your role. It can also be used alongside tableaux to create greater detail. The posture of a good model may also help you with a starting point for making decisions about movement.

Character modelling can be used during the preparation period for all the performance options.

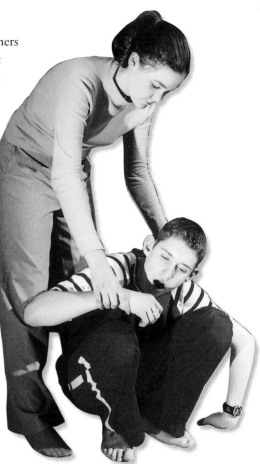

She is modelling him as an animal. What animal?

A2.3 activities

1 Create models of famous people or well-known stereotypes. Can others in the class guess who it is that you have modelled?

2 Choose one or two characters from *The Body in the Bedroom*, and try character modelling them. What more do you discover about them from the exercise?

For the future

It is always worth doing some **character modelling** in order to increase your understanding of your character. It is obviously useful to do early on, but you may need to come back to it later, especially if you feel that you are not showing enough depth to your character. It may be that someone else can add something extra for you.

Character objectives

Although this sounds similar to the actor objectives, this time you are deciding what the *character*, rather than the actor, wants to achieve by what they say and do.

If you are working from a script the **character objective** may be in the words and stage directions; or it may be left for you to decide yourself. But, whether in scripted or improvised work, you should be aware of what your character wants to communicate to the audience.

Decisions about **character objectives** will benefit all performance options, in every role that you create.

A2.4   activities

1 Try a short devised improvisation of a door-to-door salesperson trying to persuade a homeowner to buy replacement windows. The character objective of the salesperson could be to be very charming but persistent, while the homeowner's objective is to rescue food that is cooking on the stove.

2 In this activity use mime only. Your scene is based on a train. Both characters have the same objective – to get as much space as they can for themselves.

For the future

You always need to identify your **character objectives** if you are to be successful in communicating your character to the audience. This needs to be done early on, so that you can focus your performance clearly, but you also need to keep reminding yourself throughout the rehearsal period.

Hot-seating

This is when one actor sits in the centre of a circle, as the character they are playing, and the rest of the group (not in role) ask him/her questions about that character.

Questions can be about the character's past, their feelings, their relationships with other characters, their attitudes and beliefs. The actor in the middle must answer in role, as they believe their character would do. **Hot-seating** is a valuable rehearsal activity as you can explore different aspects of your character and begin to create your 'history'. It is also very useful for exploring the characters in plays that you may be studying for the written examination. It can be done with just two people but it is better with a group.

Hot-seating is a preparation technique that you can use for all the performance options.

Angry Ethel answers questions

A2.5 activities

1 Gather a group of classmates who all watch the same Soap Opera. Choose a character and a recent incident in the series. Take questions from the group and answer as that character.

2 Choose to be an ambulance driver who attended an incident at a concert. Take questions about your job, about what you did and how you felt regarding this incident, and about how the onlookers behaved.

3 Take one of the characters from *The Body in the Bedroom*. Take questions from the group about your history, character, life, feelings towards the others, etc.

For the future

It is always worth doing some **hot-seating** in order to increase your understanding of your character. It can be done at any time during the rehearsal period when you feel you need to know more about your character.

Emotional memory

This is where you try to use your own experiences to help you create an emotion.

By tapping in to your own experiences and memory of emotions, and adapting them to the needs of your character, you can convey the emotion you want more realistically. It may be that the emotion you have to produce is one that you yourself have not encountered; in which case you have probably observed someone else in this position either in real life or in a drama or movie you have seen. In all performance work, emotion must be considered: it can be very difficult to communicate feeling, but it is vital if the performance is to be successful.

Emotional memory is an extremely important rehearsal technique for any performance option where you want to communicate emotion to your audience.

A2.6 activities

1 Everyone has at some time been lost and anxious. Try to remember when this happened to you. How did you feel? How did this affect you physically? Once you have gathered and remembered these memories apply these to a solo mime of a small child lost on a beach and unable to locate his/her family.

2 Try to remember the last time you were really angry with another person. Use this memory to create with a partner an improvisation where a parent is angry with his/her child who has stayed out too late and made them very worried.

For the future

It is always worth using your **emotional memory** for any scene where you want to convey emotion. Usually you will need to come to a reasonable understanding of your character before you can show the emotion, so this technique will probably be more useful later in the rehearsal period.

Internal dramatic dialogue

This is when, in your head, you turn the thoughts of your character into words which you only think and do not say aloud.

Quite often there will be a section of the performance when you have nothing to say, although you are still on stage. Even if you have no dialogue you must not just 'switch off' and stop acting. This technique helps you to respond to the situation your character is in and to remain 'in role' throughout. By using **internal dramatic dialogue**, you are likely to show your thoughts and feelings in your face, posture, movement and gesture. However, be careful not to overdo it and distract from the main dialogue or action: your **internal dramatic dialogue** must help, not hinder, communication.

The use of **internal dramatic dialogue** will help you to portray your characters in all performance options.

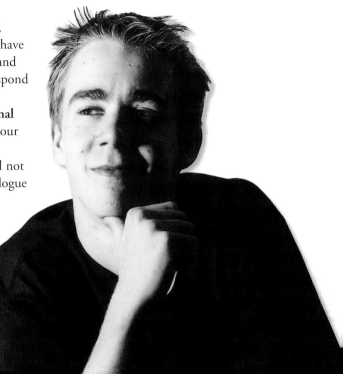

The smug expression of a character who is enjoying watching someone else get the blame for his actions

1   On your own, imagine that you are a teacher inspecting the scene of an arson attack on your primary school. You have no words to say, but in your head say the thoughts of the character as you pick through the sad debris of your children's work and toys. Notice how it affects your face, body and movement.

2   Look again at the extract from *The Body in the Bedroom*. Identify points where the characters might need to be using internal dramatic dialogue to communicate their feelings, thoughts or characters.

For the future

It is always worth considering your **internal dramatic dialogue** for any scene where you want to convey thoughts without actually speaking. Usually you need to come to a reasonable understanding of your character within the scene before you can show your thoughts of what is happening around you. So this technique will probably be more useful later in the rehearsal period, especially if you feel that you are not managing to show your thoughts and feelings clearly enough.

Tableau (plural = Tableaux)

This is a still image or a moment frozen in time (a freeze-frame). It is like a picture made up of people (a still image).

A group of students rehearsing 'Exporting children' mini-project 1 page 65

Tableaux can be a springboard into the improvising process; a way of using the images created by your research; and a useful way of finding an effective start or end to a scene. They can also help you to use the performance space fully and imaginatively. A good **tableau** uses different levels and has depth to the image. It may also have a focus point to which you want to draw the audience's eyes.

A tableau is a useful technique for all the performance options including Dance/Drama: and the linking of tableaux is particularly useful in developing a structure.

A2.8 activities

1   Take a traditional or well-known story and see if you can communicate to the rest of the class what it is through five tableaux of key moments.

2   For *The Body in the Bedroom* identify two places where tableaux would aid the communication of a message to the audience. Discuss what message you mght want to convey at those points.

For the future

It is always worth doing some **tableau** work when you have got your basic ideas, as it can give you the framework for successful development of storyline and character. So this is a technique which can well be used very early in the rehearsal period; but also at any time you want to make the group positioning clearer.

Thought-tracking

This is speaking the thoughts of your own character at a particular moment in time, or speaking the thoughts of another character as seen by their posture and expression.

What thoughts could each character have at this moment?

Thought-tracking is usually done at a moment when the action is stopped, as in a tableau. It gives you the chance to hear the thoughts of various characters at that moment in time, and it helps to develop your understanding of both your own role and the relationship your character has with others. **Thought-tracking** also develops your ability to show your thoughts and feelings through your body and face, because it makes you realise what you need to do.

Thought-tracking can be useful during the rehearsal of all performance options.

A2.9 activities

1 Improvise spontaneously a short family scene at the dinner table. Ask someone outside the scene to freeze the action at frequent intervals: and then to speak the words which they think each character is thinking. How close can they get? How can the actors improve their communication of their thoughts?

2 In the extract from *The Body in the Bedroom*, thought-track all the characters at the final moment of the extract.

For the future

> It is always worth trying some **thought-tracking** for any scene where you want to convey your thoughts. Usually you will need to come to a reasonable understanding of your character within the scene before you can show your thoughts about what is happening around you. So this technique will probably be more useful later in the rehearsal period.

Mime

This is acting and communicating without the use of speech, and obviously relies greatly on your movement and gesture techniques. However, it does not mean that you have to remain silent: the use of vocal noises such as sighs, laughter and grunts can be revealing and useful.

Mime helps you to give greater detail to any gesture, mannerism, expression or emotion that you may be using. And it helps to explore the movement of the scene so that the piece does not become static or visually dull. Running through a scene in **mime** can also help to identify the pace of different units.

Mime can be an extremely useful rehearsal technique for all performance options, and especially for Dance/Drama.

A2.10 activities

1 Working in pairs, each of you decides on a number of roles, such as a traffic warden or a librarian, and creates a mime that will communicate this character to your partner.

2 Create a mime that shows through movement alone a location such as a school, a role like a teacher, and an emotion such as anger. Create your own combinations. Can your partner guess all three correctly?

3 Create an improvised mime on *The Body in the Bedroom.* Try to communicate to the audience any feelings the characters show, as well as the storyline. How closely can you keep to the script itself?

For the future

> It is always worth doing some **mime**, as it helps you to focus on how your body can communicate something extra. It can be used at any time during the rehearsal period, especially when you feel that your movement, action, gesture and/or facial expression need more variety.

Units

This is about breaking up your play or dance into smaller sections. A unit is simply a small section of your piece.

Breaking the piece into **units** can help you to become familiar with the play or scene. Some may be small, even just one word such as 'No'. Others may be quite long, such as an explanation, a set of directions, or a conversation about a single event.

Taking each **unit** in turn during the rehearsal process stops you from trying to do too much at once, and can give greater focus and detail to your work.

Breaking up your performance piece into **units** is a useful technique for all performance options.

A2.11 activities

1 Look again at the extract from *The Body in the Bedroom*, and break it up into units. Choose the units by selecting changes in the action or movement of the characters.

2 Taking the same text, this time decide upon the units by the introduction of a new important fact which might act as the climax to each unit.

3 In a group of three, improvise a short scene of three robbers planning *The Perfect Crime*. Decide on a sequence of about three or four units that depend on changes in emotion, e.g. comradeship to anger to sulking to forgiveness. Make sure that you really identify and develop the right emotion in each of the units.

For the future

> It is always worth breaking up your piece into **units**, as it helps you to focus on the purpose of what you are doing at different stages of the piece. You should be aware of it throughout the rehearsal period.

Blocking/stage choreography

This is when your group makes decisions about the positions of actors at key points in your scene.

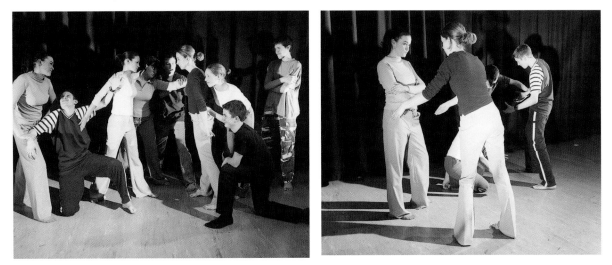

Which shows the greater understanding of blocking/stage choreography?

When you start working on how your performance piece will appear to an audience you must think about how to create visual interest. When all the characters just sit on chairs and talk to each other, the piece becomes unexciting and boring! You may want to use all the space, and **blocking** will make sure that the audience can see what they need to at all times. You may want to make sure that important action is placed in a prominent or strong position on your set or stage. You might work out the **blocking** of your actors by using a series of tableaux, plotting major pathways, or by creating a storyboard where you show the actors' movements in diagrams of key moments. If your group finds difficulty in remembering what was agreed in rehearsal, the storyboard can be used as a method of recording and will save valuable time.

Blocking is an essential preparation technique for all performance options.

A2.12 activities

1 In a group of four, work on the blocking of a comedy scene about three dreadful removal workers who are giving a homeowner a house move they will never forget. Start by working out five or six tableaux. Then create a storyboard that shows the progress of the action. Once you have completed this, try to create the action of the whole piece.

2 Look again at the extract from *The Body in the Bedroom*. Work through it in action, and identify the points where you need to make decisions about the positioning or movement of your actors, so that no one is blocked by anyone else.

For the future

It is always worth **blocking** your work, as it helps you to focus on the positioning of the group, especially at key moments. You obviously need to ensure that the audience can see the right people; but **blocking** also gives you the opportunity to use your positioning to help communicate thoughts, feelings and atmosphere. It can be used at any time during the rehearsal period.

Examiners' tip

To portray your role effectively you must know and understand your character, its purpose and its importance. You also need to identify the most important moments in your piece, structure your work clearly and ensure that it is visually attractive. All these rehearsal activities will enhance your presentation skills and enable you to communicate more effectively with your audience.

Rehearsal techniques at a glance

	General help	Help with character	Help with movement	Help with blocking
Off-text Improvisation	■	■	■	
On-text Improvisation	■	■	■	■
Character modelling	■	■	■	
Character objectives	■	■	■	■
Hot-seating	■	■		
Emotional memory	■	■	■	■
Internal dramatic dialogue	■	■	■	■
Tableau	■	■		■
Thought-tracking	■	■		■
Mime	■	■	■	■
Units	■	■	■	■
Blocking	■		■	■

A3 Personal performance techniques

Using this section of the book

These performance techniques are all ones which make up a performance, and therefore are all ones which will be assessed in your final presentation of work. It is a good idea to experiment and try a number of ways of doing things, as sometimes your first idea might not be the best idea.

Under each of the techniques listed below you will find activities to try. These are identifying specific techniques and asking you to focus on them, so that you understand their individual contribution to what you are doing. In reality, they are, of course, interlinked, so that the use of several techniques at the same time ensures the overall picture. By doing the activities you will improve each of your performance techniques, and be able to select the most relevant ones for the mini-projects (pages 63–122), and later for actual assessment.

Some of the activities in this section are based on *The Audition*, printed below.

The Audition by R. D. Price

Location:	A rehearsal room. An empty space.
Characters:	ACTOR: used to be a 'name', but since working on a soap he/she has found it difficult to get work and leave the soap character behind. Charming and eager to please.
	DIRECTOR: dislikes auditioning. He/she is seeing this actor against their better judgement, but has been talked into it as a favour for a friend. Weary and cynical.

The ACTOR walks into the empty space, obviously a little nervous and worried that there appears to be no-one to meet him/her. They look around. When the ACTOR has their back to the door the DIRECTOR enters and takes the opportunity to 'size up' the ACTOR. The DIRECTOR coughs to attract attention, and the ACTOR spins round.

	ACTOR	Hi, I'm Sam.
	DIRECTOR	I know. Nice to meet you.
	ACTOR	Is there only me here today?
	DIRECTOR	Yup, just you.
5	ACTOR	Where shall I put my stuff?
	DIRECTOR	Somewhere over there.
	ACTOR	Well . . .
	DIRECTOR	You do know the part is not that big?
	ACTOR	No such thing as a small part: only a small actor.
10	DIRECTOR	Quite.
	ACTOR	So, what do you want me to do?
	DIRECTOR	Right, well . . . The character has to wander into the Casualty Department at the beginning; and looking vulnerable, sit down, nursing what appears to be an injured hand.
15	ACTOR	Right. Where is the door?
	DIRECTOR	Wherever you want it. Oh, say here.
	ACTOR	Okay. Just give me a minute.

	DIRECTOR	Anything wrong?
	ACTOR	I'm just having trouble with 'vulnerable'.
20	DIRECTOR	Take your time.
	ACTOR	Look, I'm sorry. This is a bad idea. I'm wasting your time.
	DIRECTOR	Let me be the judge of that.
	ACTOR	I'm wrong for this. You have been very kind. Bye. (*Gathers his/her belongings and leaves.*)
25	DIRECTOR	Oh, how the mighty have fallen. Mmm, time for lunch. (*Leaves.*)

The techniques are listed in three parts: to do with **1** Body and movement; **2** Voice; and **3** General. While all of these techniques are important, they may not all be relevant to every piece of work. You need to become familiar with all of them, so that you can concentrate on the ones you need for any particular task.

1 Body and movement

Posture

This is how you stand or hold your body.

A defensive posture with a gesture asking for help

Posture can reflect the type of person you are: e.g. a strict person may stand in a very stiff and upright manner.
Posture can also change because of the situation or the character's feelings, e.g. a naughty child might stand in a slouched way with head down in shame. You will need to think about the type of person you are playing, the situation that they are in, and how the character feels at different points in the performance. In Dance/Drama and in certain styles/genres, **posture** needs to be exaggerated slightly in order to communicate character, feelings and thoughts.

A3.1 activities

1 Choose a character from *The Audition*. Pick three key points in the story and experiment to see how the character's posture would change from one key point to the next.

2 With a group of three others, produce a tableau where your posture reflects the types of people you are. Try changing your posture to show how you feel.

Movement

This is simply how your character moves around the performance space, and how the character's **movement** may change because of what they are doing or the location they are in.

When deciding on your **movement** you need to work with the whole body, and with attention to detail. Experiment with questions such as: does my character move quickly and with a short stride? Does my character wander around the space or move with purpose? What about if I sit down? At what points should my character stay still? The questions you need to ask will be based on your character and what you have to do in your performance piece. In Dance/Drama, **movement** obviously has a more specialised purpose. You are trying to convey a general feeling of **movement** or emotion, rather than trying to show exact, detailed **movements** so that, in general terms, **movement** and gesture tend to be far larger than in other Drama.

A3.2 activities

1 Move around a space, changing your movement according to different locations. You can include such places as a dense crowd of people, the Arctic in a blizzard, the jungle or a scary dark alleyway at night. Try moving at different speeds, in different directions and with different body positions.

2 Working with a partner, watch each other to see if you can guess what mood or emotion the other is communicating by the way in which they move around the space. You could, for example, include the following feelings that can be shown through movement alone: fear, anger, confusion, boredom, panic, shock, sadness.

Gesture

This is a symbolic movement or action that has a particular meaning.

A **gesture** is used to tell someone something in a quick, simple and easily recognised way: e.g. 'Stop!' by raising a hand, palm forwards, in front of you; 'Come here' by beckoning with your first finger. Often people acting do not know what to do with their hands; but by using gesture you will communicate more effectively, and your performance will be less 'stiff'. You can **gesture**, however, with more than just hands: e.g. opening your arms wide in welcome; shrugging your shoulders to show you don't care; raising an eyebrow to indicate a question. This is particularly important in Dance/Drama, where **gesture** becomes an essential way of conveying conversation, relationships and feelings. Transferring hand **gestures** to other parts of the body is often used in Dance/Drama, e.g. a lifted right leg and foot emphasises the lifted arm and hand **gesture** of 'Stop!'

A3.3 activities

1 With a partner, stand across the room from each other. Try to send a message to each other through gesture alone. Don't mouth the words but trust signals that we all understand. Resist the urge to use gestures that are rude and which may offend!

2 Build up a 'vocabulary' of gestures. What gestures can you make that do not use hands? List as many as possible.

Facial expression

This is just what it says – the expression on your face!

Examples of three powerful facial expressions. What do they communicate to you?

When we look at someone we normally look them in the face. If we want to know how someone feels we look at their face. The face is a vital communicating tool for the performer. As part of your own character you will have a number of **facial expressions** that you use regularly. At first, it will feel strange to be twisting your face into expressions which reflect the character you are playing but it is a performance element that you must include.

A3.4 activities

1 Imagine that you are walking around an art gallery. Try to express how you feel about different pictures through your face. You might see a picture that you think is shocking, or a piece of very abstract art.

2 Imagine that you are opening your birthday presents. There will be presents that you are delighted with and others which do not please you so much. Experiment and try to find a number of different reactions that can be shown through facial expression.

Circles of attention/focus

This is where you, the performer, focus your eyes: and in so doing draw the audience's attention to the same place.

As was mentioned under facial expression, the audience looks at the performer's face. It is therefore very important to think about where on the stage your character should be looking. Don't look past someone you are talking to, unless you want to communicate that you are not interested in what they are saying or that you are being deliberately rude. If your **focus** shifts, the audience should follow or understand your change of attention. On the other hand, a lack of focus in your **circle of attention**, or the shift to an inappropriate circle, can often indicate your loss of concentration.

Notice the different focuses of attention within this group

A3.5 activities

1 As a solo activity, imagine that you are a busy chef cooking to a deadline. You have numerous pots on the cookers and an imaginary staff to keep an eye on. Communicate how much you have to be aware of through the changes in your circles of attention.

2 With a partner, improvise a scene in which two friends have fallen out. Friend A is guilty of being disloyal and is ashamed, while Friend B is determined to get A to be honest about what he/she has done. Concentrate on how circles of attention will communicate the situation and feelings of both characters.

2 Voice

Tone

Tone is the mood or feeling that we apply to the way we speak the dialogue.

For example, when you have not given in your homework, the teacher will speak in an angry **tone**; or you recognise a friend's sarcasm through the **tone** of their voice. It gives the actor a method of communicating feeling or intention, and it should change throughout the performance. As we speak, our voices go up and down, giving greater meaning and interest to what we say. This variation is known as **intonation**.

A3.6 activities

1 With a partner, perform an improvisation where a customer is returning a faulty purchase. The sales assistant cannot give the refund the customer demands. Try this improvisation using combinations of the following choices of tone: patronising, sarcastic, angry, patient, nervous, sly.

2 Look again at *The Audition* script. Choose a suitable tone for both the actor and the director. Make decisions about where there could be changes in the tone.

Pitch

Pitch is the level of sound at which we speak.

Some people have a high natural **pitch** to their voice or speak in a high **pitch** when they are nervous. A low **pitch** may be used for an older character or when someone is being quietly angry.

A3.7 activities

1 With a partner, create an improvisation in which one character is being questioned by a police officer about something they did not do. Focus on the pitch of both characters, to show the nervousness of the accused and the suspicion of the police officer. Try the scene again, but use pitch to show the accused's indignation and the officer's determination to find out the truth.

2 Once again look at *The Audition* script, and this time play the actor as a child or someone quite young, and the director as elderly and tired. How would pitch help to communicate their age as well as their feelings?

Volume

This is simply how loudly or quietly the dialogue is spoken.

When considering the character and your use of voice, **volume** is a vital consideration. As well as using it to make sure that you can be heard, you can also use it to show your feelings or the situation you are in. For example, when angry you can choose between speaking with a loud, dominating voice, or in a quiet way to communicate menace. If your scene takes place in a busy street or in a noisy factory then a loud **volume** may be appropriate. If the **volume** of your voice sounds alright to you, it probably means that you are not speaking loudly enough, and only you and those near you can actually hear you. An audience only gets one chance to hear what you say; if they miss it, they cannot ask you to repeat it, and they may lose essential dialogue.

A3.8 activities

1 With a partner, perform an improvisation that takes place on a building site between a builder, who is getting something wrong, and the architect, who is trying to explain how it should have been done without shaming the builder in front of his employees. As your scene moves through the space, try to reflect the external noise and the situation by the volume both characters use.

2 In a group of five or six, create an improvisation located in a junior school playground at playtime. One of the group is a teacher, another a 'telltale', one a lonely new child, whilst the others are playing a noisy game of 'tag'. Can you achieve a variety of volume levels in this performance, and adjust them at points so that the audience can hear what is important?

Accent

This is the way in which a person speaks with the characteristics of their particular class, region or nationality.

Accents can be very useful in adding variety to a performance, or for emphasising the specific place from which the characters come. For many students, talking with a different **accent** is a difficult thing to do, but it may well be essential in some presentations. If you need an unfamiliar **accent**, you must listen to someone who has the one you require, and constant practice is the only way to ensure success. When you do use one, make sure you don't drop it or change it to another one during the performance; and realise that you need to speak slightly more slowly and clearly than usual to make sure that words are heard and understood – an audience takes longer to adjust to your voice.

A3.9 activities

1 Listen (without watching!) to an episode of a television programme where accents are used. Try to use the same one, without slipping into something else.

2 Take well-known regional phrases and use these as a basis for your research and experimentation with your chosen accent.

3 Look again at *The Audition* script. Would the use of accents improve the characterisation? Try as many different accents as you can for each character. Do some work better than others?

3 General

Levels

This is when you use different heights for your positioning, movements or set to add extra meaning or visual interest.

In this accident scene, how many different levels are created by the performers? Notice how it creates visual interest

You may decide, for example, that a moment in your scene would look more interesting with A on the floor, B on a chair, C leaning against a table, and D on a ladder. Or that your own movement would look better if you did different actions at different **levels**: so you might pick up the shopping bags from the floor, carry them to the table, and then put everything away in cupboards at different heights. Or your stage furniture could add interest and help to emphasise the relative importance of people or things. So in your courtroom, your magistrates could be higher than your accused, who would be higher than the solicitors. In Dance/Drama, the use of different **levels** of movement is essential to the interest. Remember, though, that whatever you decide must look natural to the scene you are presenting – otherwise your use of **levels** will appear awkward and artificial: instead of adding visual interest, it will add visual discomfort.

A3.10 activities

1 In a solo mime, you get up late on a weekday morning. Think consciously about including actions which use different levels. Try to feel how it improves the visual interest at the same time as emphasising the panic and hurry.

2 Work in a group of five, where you have at least one parent, one teenager and one police officer. The scene is a typical evening at home, interrupted by the arrival of the police officer(s): but in each unit of the scene, a different person dominates what is happening. Use different levels to emphasise these changes in domination.

Mannerism

A **mannerism** is a particular movement or speech pattern that a person will use without thinking, and it does not have a specific meaning.

Mannerism is a good physical way to reflect character and is good detail in a performance. We all have our own **mannerisms**, e.g. twisting our hair or biting our nails when nervous. We also have vocal **mannerisms** that can be used in performance. Do you know someone who always adds unnecessary words to the end or beginning of their sentences? Common examples are the words 'okay' or 'mate' or 'you know?'.

A3.11 activities

1 Look around your Drama class or at your friends at break time. Make a list of their mannerisms. Why do you think they use these mannerisms? What are your own mannerisms? You may have to ask someone who knows you well.

2 Look again at *The Audition* script. Would particular mannerisms help to give the characters extra interest or make them more believable? Try out several possible mannerisms of both voice and movement, and try to find one which suits the role you are playing.

Strength/tension

This is the level of power in your movement or atmosphere.

Your muscle power and **tension** will be very different for different **strengths** of movement: e.g. shifting a heavy piano will be totally different from catching a butterfly or kicking a football. Equally, characters show different levels of muscle **strength** and **tension** in different situations: the muscles of someone lying on the beach enjoying the sun will be far less tense than those of someone getting ready for a fight. This will also affect the atmosphere: if everyone is relaxed the atmosphere will be happy and calm, but if everyone is tense then the atmosphere will also be tense. You must think carefully about the **strength/tension** of your body as it communicates a great deal of thought, feeling and atmosphere.

A3.12 activities

1 Repeat the group scene which you did for **levels** (A3.10.2), but this time concentrate, too, on the strength/tension of your movements. Through this tension show how each person is feeling, and how this changes at different times in the scene.

2 Work in threes, on a situation with two parents and a teenager who comes home late. Use the strength/tension of your posture and movements to show the build-up of worry; and the eventual release of tension when the son/daughter arrives home safe.

Pace

This is simply the speed which you use for movement, speech or action.

This is another very important performance element: and you must achieve a variety of **pace** in your movement and in the delivery of your dialogue. If you are in a hurry you will move quickly and speak quickly. If you are bored you may move slowly and speak slowly. You need to identify where you can apply changes of **pace** to your voice and movement; such changes are particularly important in building up any emotion or action. In Dance/Drama, this will be reflected in the accompaniment, if music or other sound is being used.

In speech, if the **pace** of your words sounds right to you, it probably means that you are speaking too fast for the audience and only the actors will pick up the words. The audience only gets one chance to hear you, and if you speak too quickly, they cannot ask you to repeat what they have missed.

A3.13 activities

1 With a partner improvise a scene in which one character is nervously searching for something they have lost while the other character knows where the item is but is not saying. At what pace do you think each of the characters should move and speak? Can you build into your improvisation a point at which the pace changes?

2 Look again at *The Audition* script. Identify where changes of pace for different characters would help to emphasise their characters or how they are feeling; and where changes in the pace of the script are needed to create atmosphere or interest.

Pause

This is a temporary stop in speech or action, a moment of silence or stillness.

When we speak normally, we do not continue at the same pace without drawing breath. **Pause** in both speech and movement can be used in a performance to achieve a number of effects: e.g. to show that you are unsure about something or to show what you are thinking; to draw attention to something that is happening; or to give importance to something that is said or going to be said. It can reflect character, as with a timid person who may **pause** often in his/her speech and movement. Good use of **pause** can be very effective in emphasising emotion, action or anticipation, especially in Dance/Drama.

A3.14 activities

1 In a pair improvisation, A is spending birthday money on new clothes and does not have a great deal of confidence. B thinks A has dreadful taste and chooses the strangest things. How could both these characters use pause to communicate their feelings? Experiment to see if you can create comedy in this scene through your use of pause.

2 In a group of three, improvise a situation where A feels under threat from B, while C becomes the one to dispel the threat and to bring back a sense of calm and reassurance. Can you use pause at key moments to help the build-up of threat, action and emotion, and the release of tension?

3 Look again at *The Audition* script. Where could you use pause to say more about the characters, or to make the audience react to the actor? Try the scene again using your decisions.

Rhythm

This is the regular pattern of movement to a heard or felt beat: and the rhythmical pattern of speech.

For example, in speech, an argument will have a faster, more persistent **rhythm** than a friendly chat on the park bench; in movement, a soldier marching will move to a very definite beat or **rhythm**; someone chopping wood will get the greatest effect by moving the axe rhythmically; and a child skipping will turn the rope rhythmically. The good dancer will feel **rhythm** to such an extent that it becomes an automatic part of the whole movement. In all Drama, it will affect other techniques such as pace, flow, and strength/tension.

A3.15 activities

1 Working with a partner, and to the regular but steadily getting faster beat of a drum, show the build-up to an argument or fight from the first moment of aggression right through to the climax. Notice how the rhythmical pace actually helps to increase tension.

2 With your partner, imagine that you are in a rowing boat: you are sitting next to each other, each having one oar. Get into a rhythm where you are both rowing together, and then change the pace of the rhythm,

experimenting with speeding up and slowing down. Notice how the pace affects the atmosphere: rowing slowly in perfect rhythm can be very peaceful and calming; getting faster suggests more of a competitive spirit; while if you get too fast it will make the action comic.

3 In a group of four or five, imagine that you are working on a conveyor belt, sticking parts of dolls together. Construct your dialogue to fit the physical rhythm of your actions.

Flow

This is the way in which a scene or action moves and develops into the next.

The **flow** of movement may be smooth as with a swimmer; or it may be uneven or interrupted as in panic. The story itself may **flow** easily through a beginning, middle and end; or it may have several interruptions as mishaps, misunderstandings, twists or new introductions occur. However, if the interruptions are unintended as, for example, with long scene changes, unnecessary announcements, or slow costume changes, the **flow** of the whole piece is spoilt, and the interest is lost. In Dance/Drama, **flow** is extremely important both visually and emotionally. If it is smooth, it communicates a sense of well-being and calm; if it is irregular it suggests tension, aggression and conflict.

A3.16 activities

1 You and a friend are relaxing on the beach. You eventually fall asleep. In the dream which follows, you imagine that you are in various peaceful, relaxed situations, all of which change and flow into one another perfectly smoothly. You might dream that you are on a flying carpet floating above the beach – then a bird using the thermals to glide across the sky – then a flower waving gently in the breeze – and so on until you suddenly wake. Try to make sure that there are no pauses or sudden changes of pace until you wake at the end. Notice how the gentle, smooth flow of one thing into another helps to create the feeling of calm.

2 Your group of three or four is having its first experience of white-water rafting, and you are being taken on a river which has a variety of experiences and speeds. Try to show when the raft is on reasonably calm, even if fast-flowing, water; when it is racing, bumping or swirling through the rapids; and when it has to take a sudden diversion to miss a huge rock in the way. Make sure that you have variety, with stretches of calm water between the more exciting stretches, and that each flows into the next without pause. Notice, however, how the interruptions to the stretches of calm water aid the feeling of fear and excitement.

A

For the future

Remember that all of these techniques are suitable for assessment, and, as long as they are relevant to your piece of work, the more skills you show, the higher your marks. So keep coming back to this section to remind yourself of techniques which you should consider each time you work for a performance.

Examiners' tip

To become a successful actor, you must be able to use voice, movement and other personal performance techniques in an appropriate and precise manner. Remember that all these different skills combine to reflect the fullest presentation of your character. Investigating the close relationship between them and recognising the most relevant ones for any particular role will result in a more appropriate and confident performance.

Personal performance techniques at a glance

	General skill	Skill in character	Skill in movement	Skill in blocking
Posture	▪	▪	▪	
Movement	▪	▪	▪	▪
Gesture	▪	▪	▪	
Facial expression	▪	▪		
Circles of attention/focus	▪			
Tone	▪	▪		
Pitch	▪	▪		
Volume	▪	▪		
Accent	▪	▪		
Levels	▪			▪
Mannerism	▪	▪		
Strength/tension	▪	▪	▪	
Pace	▪	▪	▪	▪
Pause	▪	▪	▪	
Rhythm	▪		▪	▪
Flow	▪		▪	▪

A4 Group performance techniques

Using this section of the book

These group techniques will give you foundation ideas for successful presentations. Obviously you will not wish to use them all every time, but they all have particular attractions for particular styles or issues or audiences, and should, therefore, be carefully considered. It is always worthwhile to experiment with some of these ideas in the early stages of getting started and developing the work, so that you can find which ones suit your purpose best. By using a variety of these group techniques, your group will increase the interest in the presentation.

Under each of the techniques listed below you will find activities to try. By doing these activities your group will improve their performance skills and you will find it easier to select the most relevant ones for the mini-projects (pages 63–122) and later for your actual assessment. Most of the activities are based on the script of *The Ruined Abbey* by Joy Morton, and the scenario for an improvisation of *The School Staff-Room*. The techniques are listed in alphabetical order.

The Ruined Abbey by Joy Morton

The stage is set as in the ruins of a medieval abbey, with visitor signs marking 'The Cloisters', 'To the Abbey Church', 'To the Dortoir', etc.

Brother PETER, *not immediately obvious as a monk, is sitting apparently asleep on one of the window seats.* MUM *and* DAD *enter, walking in unison, wearing hiking boots, carrying rucksacks, etc. They slow to a halt.*

	DAD	C'mon Son, don't lag behind. You should be fit enough to keep up with us!
	PETE	(*appearing unwillingly*) I'm coming. But I just don't see what the hurry's for. You've only dragged me along to see some old ruin!
	MUM	Well, it makes a change from looking at us!
5	PETE	Oh, ha, ha! You know I didn't want to come.
	MUM	Yes, we know. But here we are – and you may as well make the best of it.
	DAD	And what's more, we would quite like to enjoy your company!
	MUM	Let's pause for a moment. Look there's a seat – just as it's been for centuries. (*sitting down*) These may be ruins, but with a little bit of imagination you can see
10		just what they were like when it was a working abbey.
	DAD	Yes, Son. Sit down. Look at the ruins – at the walls, the windows, the stones. Sit quietly . . . soak up the atmosphere . . . feel the peace . . . and begin to understand.

Pause. A moment of total silence, whilst they all look around them.

	PETER	(*sitting up and talking directly to* PETE) He's right, you know. It was the peace which attracted us here. The feeling that God exists in this magnificent setting.
15	PETE	I'm sorry, Sir, I didn't notice you there. (*approaching him*) Who are you?
	PETER	Me? I'm Brother Peter.
	PETE	But that's my name, too. How strange! May I join you?
	PETER	Of course. Pleased to meet you, Peter. I can tell you – I've enjoyed the peace here for many a year; and now I look forward to dying here, too.
20	PETE	Dying? Why talk about death?

	PETER	Death comes to us all, you know! You are too young to think much about it – but I'm close to it now. I've had a wonderful life here. I have no regrets.
	PETE	What do you do here?
25	PETER	Me? I just try to live humbly and give help where I can. I no longer have a specific task – my days for that are over. I used to be the Hospitaller – responsible for all the guests. I loved it. But the task is one for a younger, more energetic man. Sometimes there might be more than twenty pilgrims, including the women and children, who were looking for sanctuary with us. I loved it.

Enter two monks carrying a trunk.

	PETE	Who are these? What are they doing?
30	PETER	(*introducing them*) Brother John. Brother Amos. They are involved in a sad task.
	PETE	Brothers, good afternoon. May I ask what you have in the trunk?
	JOHN	You may. Some of the Abbey treasures.
	AMOS	We're on our way to Littlechurch with them.
	PETE	Treasures? What treasures?
35	AMOS	Gold and silver . . . and pictures . . . and some of our holy relics. We're taking them to friends for safe keeping.
	PETE	But why?
	JOHN	You haven't heard? Thomas Cromwell has ordered that all the monasteries be stripped of their wealth – and the abbey buildings destroyed.
40	PETE	But that's senseless! Why destroy such lovely buildings? And what about the monks? What'll happen to you? Aren't you afraid?
	MONKS	(*together*) Afraid? No.
	JOHN	We put our trust in God. What He wills be done.
	PETER	Amen. We wait. But that doesn't mean we're idle.
45	AMOS	We have been moving the treasures for several days now, hiding them away.

Monastic singing is heard in the background.

	JOHN	We must get on now: we don't have much time.
	J AND A	God be with you, young man. God be with you, Brother.
	PETE	Goodbye, Brothers.
	PETER	(*at the same time*) God be with you, Brothers.
50	PETE	But that's terrible! It shouldn't be allowed. It's not right.
	PETER	Right? What's right? Who are we to judge?
	PETE	Listen. The singing's getting louder.
	PETER	It's almost time for Mass, and some of my brothers are preparing in church.
	PETE	But it's lovely. I never realised singing could be so peaceful – and in the midst of such a threat to your lives.
55		
	PETER	This is a troubled world, but we try to be at peace with God. But enough of talking. The singing reminds me that it is time to move on. I must prepare. And you – you must return to your parents, my namesake.
	PETE	My parents? Oh yes – I'd forgotten about them! (*Looks at them.*)
60	PETER	(*to the audience*) You know, it's amazing what happens when you give an atmosphere the chance. When you empty your minds of all the everyday things. The very stones of a building, even the valleys and hills and rivers around you, retain their personal histories. They can transmit their stored memories to any who are prepared to sit and listen. Pete's just an ordinary teenager – but look what happened for him! (*Exits towards the church.*)
65		
	MUM	(*getting up*) Come on, Pete – we've rested here long enough. We ought to look at the abbey church . . .

| DAD | (*also beginning to move*) C'mon, young Pete. Don't just sit there – as if you've seen a ghost! It's time to move on! |
| 70 PETE | That's strange – that's just what he said, 'It's time to move on . . .' (*Looks at the spot where* PETER *had been sitting; then at his father. Gets up slowly as the lights fade.*) |

General scenario for *The School Staff-Room,* an improvisation

A short introductory scene sets the location in a comprehensive school. This introduction ends with a bell ringing for the beginning of break, and it leads into the main scene which is in the staff-room. Soon teachers are rushing in for their morning coffee, photocopying, chat, etc. A particular pupil, Sam Smith, is mentioned and straightaway three or four teachers all have stories to tell of Sam's latest exploits. Eventually 'outdoing' the others, Chris Jones tells what happened in this morning's Drama lesson just before break. Other staff listen, question, comment, etc., but at last separate to get on with the urgent things which need doing before the next lesson. Time has gone, the bell goes, and they rush or drift off.

Banners (or Placards)

These are simply written notices which signpost particular points which you want emphasised.

For example, in presenting a silent film, you might want **banners** which tell the audience something extra, such as 'Bang! Crash! Wallop!' or 'Leave me alone!'; you might want to instruct the audience to 'Clap' or 'Boo'. In a symbolic presentation you might want to make sure that roles are clearly understood, so the actors might wear **banners** around their necks or on their costumes saying 'Teenager' or 'Lonely'. In a pantomime, you might want to write out the words of a song the audience will sing.

A4.1 activities

1 Look at the script of *The Ruined Abbey*. Notice the use of banners in the setting. What was the playwright wanting to achieve by using these banners?

2 Look at the scenario of *The School Staff-Room*. It might be possible to use banners, e.g. in the introduction, or for the staff telling the stories about Sam. Where might you use this technique to improve the effectiveness of the scene? What would they say?

Chorus

This is simply where two or more members of the group move or speak at the same time.

Originally, the role of the **chorus** was to comment on the action, to introduce characters and events, to report on key events which happened offstage, and to warn of the consequences of various actions. If you are studying a Greek play, for example, you will find this traditional role. But nowadays the use of **chorus** has widened considerably to include any group movement or speech. You might wish to emphasise the importance of a key moment: e.g. when the characters hear footsteps outside the door, they might all look towards it at the same time; or, when a question is asked, everyone might speak together. You may want simply to emphasise the importance of the group: e.g. a group of bullies advancing on a victim; or the sound of a group of people, e.g. at a party. In Dance/Drama, much of the group movement may be **chorus** work, and may be more closely synchronised than in other types of Drama.

A4.2 activities

1 Look at the script of *The Ruined Abbey*. Where is chorus used? Why? Might you use it anywhere else? What would you hope to achieve?

2 Look at the scenario of *The School Staff-Room*. It might be possible to use chorus, e.g. to set the scene of a noisy staff-room. Where might you use this technique to improve the effectiveness of the scene? Why? Try out your ideas. Were they successful?

Counterpoint

This is when you balance two or more actions or speeches against each other.

You might have two characters **counterpointing** each other by speaking their different thoughts at the same time – either in unison or taking turns to speak a phrase or two. You might have one character speaking and **counterpointing** another who is miming/dancing. Or you might have three characters, each miming/dancing simultaneously, **counterpointing** the others, each in his/her own spotlight.

A4.3 activities

1 Look at the script of *The Ruined Abbey*. Where is counterpoint used? Why? Might you use it anywhere else? What would you hope to achieve?

2 Look at the scenario of *The School Staff-Room*. It might be possible to use counterpoint, e.g. when three teachers are all telling their stories of Sam. Where might you use this technique to improve the effectiveness of the scene? Why? What would you hope to achieve? Try out your ideas. Were they successful?

Flashback/forward

This is when, during the action of a piece, you suddenly move backwards or forwards in time to see the same characters in a different situation.

You might be looking at a photograph album, and you use **flashbacks** to show what had led up to each of the photos that have been kept. You might be showing how the situation in Northern Ireland has built up over the generations, by using **flashbacks** to significant moments in Irish history, and a **flashforward** to see what might be happening in the future. They can be particularly useful for the audience, to fill in past detail about characters or events which are especially relevant. However, in mime or in Dance/Drama **flashbacks** can be confusing, so are not usually advisable.

A4.4 activities

1 Look at the script of *The Ruined Abbey*. Where is flashback used? Why? What has the playwright achieved by using it? Where do you come out of the flashback?

2 Look at the scenario of *The School Staff-Room*. It might be possible to use flashback, e.g. to show what actually happened with Sam during various lessons. Where might you use this technique to improve the effectiveness of the scene? Why? What would you hope to achieve? Try out your ideas. Were they successful?

Monologue/solo

This simply means 'a solo speech', and is when one character speaks at length, often directly to the audience and often showing particular emotion or feeling.

Monologue is often used in combination with tableaux, because it allows characters to tell the audience how they feel about a situation or other character, whilst the rest of the group is 'frozen'. **Monologue** is used, too, to link different scenes, not so much by narrating what happens (see Narration), but by telling the audience about the importance or feeling in the two scenes. Obviously, as this is a speech technique, you will not have a **monologue** in mime or Dance/Drama, although you may well have a piece of solo performance.

A4.5 activities

1 Look at the script of *The Ruined Abbey*. Where is monologue used? Why? What has the playwright achieved?

2 Look at the scenario of *The School Staff-Room*. It might be possible to use monologue, e.g. for the Headteacher explaining his hopes for the school. Where might you use this technique to improve the effectiveness of the scene? Why? What would you hope to achieve? Try out your ideas. Were they successful?

Narration

This is when one actor takes on the role of storyteller. They speak directly to the audience as they tell the story.

Many primary schools use a **narrator** to link the scenes in their Christmas shows, and you are probably familiar with **narration** in this context. However, you can use **narration** in any situation where you need to let the audience know more than you are showing them; e.g. events which have happened offstage, the background to characters and their feelings towards each other. The **narration** may be given at the same time as the action, or it may link different scenes.

A4.6 activities

1 In role as an Infant teacher, retell a well-known fairy story to a group of small children. Use as much variety in your voice as you can; and try to get them actually to join in at times.

2 Look at the scenario of *The School Staff-Room*. It might be possible to use narration, e.g. to bring your audience up to date with what then happened to Sam. Where might you use this technique to improve the effectiveness of the scene? Why? What would you hope to achieve? Try out your ideas. Were they successful?

Physical theatre

This is when members of the group act out a role which is non-human or non-naturalistic.

Physical theatre can be used when you want to add understanding or humour, so the whole group becomes the different parts of a machine of some sort, e.g. clock, washing machine, computer; or the group becomes parts of a set, e.g. a cottage or a forest; or, you act out a fantasy situation, e.g. toys coming to life, robots, animals, growing plants. It can be extremely effective when the change between reality and **physical theatre** flows smoothly from one to the other; and when the audience can totally accept the acting of the non-human role.

A4.7 activities

1 A group of four or five friends gather to watch a video: as they put the video in, they become the VCR, and when they stop the video, they return to being the friends. Try to get as smooth a change from one to the other as possible, making sure that your movements and voices change completely between the two roles.

2 Look at the scenario of *The School Staff-Room*. It might be possible to use physical theatre, e.g. to show a coffee machine or photocopier in the staff-room. Where might you use this technique to improve the effectiveness of the scene? Why? What would you hope to achieve? Try out your ideas. Were they successful?

Repetition and echo

This is simply when you repeat words, phrases or actions deliberately.

One speaker may repeat what they have said; or different speakers may repeat after the first one; or they may **echo** by saying the last words slightly overlapping with the first speaker. The same technique can also be used with movement. You might use **repetition** to make sure that your audience have understood something, or to emphasise the importance of key words, key moments or even the appearance of a key character: so that by using **repetition** particular attention is drawn to that word, moment or character. You might use **repetition** or **echo** in your characterisation, e.g. a hesitant character might repeat what someone else has just said, or a henpecked husband might **echo** the last words his wife says.

A4.8 activities

1 Look at the script of *The Ruined Abbey*. Where might repetition or echo be used by the actors? What would you hope to achieve?

2 Look at the scenario of *The School Staff-Room*. It might be possible to use repetition or echo, e.g. when staff ask questions about or comment on the stories. Where might you use this technique to improve the effectiveness of the scene? Why? What would you hope to achieve? Try out your ideas. Were they successful?

Slow motion

This is when you deliberately slow the action down as if you were slowing a film, so that every movement is performed at a very slow pace.

Slow motion may be used to improve the understanding of an action which might be too quick to be seen properly, e.g. the actual stabbing in a murder, or the putting of a drug in a drink at a pub. The technique may also be used to ensure the safety of the actors, e.g. during a fight or when chasing a thief on and off the stage. **Slow motion** often has the effect of adding humour, so can be used deliberately in moments of comedy or farce. In Dance it can also add to the beauty and power of a movement or sequence of movements.

A4.9 activities

1   Look at the script of *The Ruined Abbey*. Where might slow motion be used? What would you hope to achieve?

2   Look at the scenario of *The School Staff-Room*. It might be possible to use slow motion, e.g. during the Drama lesson to show a particular key moment more clearly. Where might you use this technique to improve the effectiveness of the scene? Why? What would you hope to achieve? Try out your ideas. Were they successful?

Synchronised movement/unison

This is when two or more of the group do chorus movements exactly in time with each other.

Synchronised movement can be used to add humour to an action, e.g. when three people sit down, cross their legs, take out their sandwiches, etc, all at the same time. It may actually be the reality of a situation, e.g. with soldiers marching or in a mirror image. It may give the effect of group unity, especially in Dance/Drama. In fact, **synchronised movement** is frequent in Dance/Drama anyway, just by the very nature of Dance.

On a girls' night out, checking the make-up

A4.10 activities

1 Look at the script of *The Ruined Abbey*. Where might synchronised movement be used? What would you hope to achieve?

2 Look at the scenario of *The School Staff-Room*. It might be possible to use synchronised movement, e.g. as the teachers drink their coffee. Where might you use this technique to improve the effectiveness of the scene? Why? What would you hope to achieve? Try out your ideas. Were they successful?

Note

The work you have done in this section will be explored further in mini-project 3 (pages 73–6), where you can develop *The Ruined Abbey* or *The School Staff-Room* for performance.

Examiners' tip

These techniques will be invaluable for you in selecting the type of performance you wish to prepare: they can make the presentation memorable, interesting and highly effective; and they will add purpose and clarity to your performance. However, take care that you do not include them just to show that you know them! They must be appropriate to the particular task if they are to improve, rather than confuse, the communication.

Group performance techniques at a glance

	General skill	Skill in character	Skill in movement	Skill in blocking
Banners	■			
Chorus	■	■	■	■
Counterpoint	■			
Flashback/forward	■	■	■	
Monologue/solo	■	■		■
Narration	■			■
Physical theatre	■	■	■	■
Repetition and echo	■		■	■
Slow motion	■		■	■
Synchronised movement	■		■	■

A5 Techniques for styles/genres/types

Using this section of the book

Style and genre are more or less interchangeable, and mean the distinctive way or manner in which the play is written or improvised. In Dance, the word used is type.

This section will help you to understand what each **style/genre** (**type** in Dance) means. It will give you pointers of what each involves in terms of acting and design skills and techniques, and guidance on how to achieve the audience response that you want.

Under each heading below you will find a simple description of the style or genre, followed by the essential 'ingredients' and acting skills involved. There is also basic guidance for technical designers. If you know, or look up, the good examples given from theatre, literature, television or film, these will help to reinforce your understanding. They will also provide you with possible comparisons for your written coursework.

The styles are grouped so that you can understand the differences more clearly, and they are followed by some activities to help you to develop the right techniques – some focusing on performance, and some on technical aspects. All of them need a short period of preparation and rehearsal before presenting them to a small audience. As you experiment with different styles, don't worry too much about interesting content: concentrate on getting the right response from your audience. If you don't get it, then try to discover why. You must have been doing something in the wrong way, and therefore giving out the wrong signals. You now have to learn to give out the right signals!

Straight/Serious

Straight or **Serious** Drama is realistic drama where laughter is not intended.

It often deals with serious issues connected with everyday life, and is intended to highlight a particular situation or character; and for this reason, it is often useful for teaching or informing. To be successful, actors must play characters and situations as naturally as possible, although they must avoid the trap of trying to look and sound very serious, as this can often cause unwanted laughter! Realistic emotion is also an essential part of **Straight** Drama, and actors must be able to communicate feelings and thoughts, and to create atmosphere and anticipation.

On the **technical** side, designs should be realistic, so that nothing distracts from the issue, characters or situation.

Good examples include
Talking Heads by Alan Bennett
A Taste of Honey by Shelagh Delaney
The Winslow Boy by Terence Rattigan

Tragedy

Tragedy occurs when order breaks down into confusion or chaos in the real, everyday world, so there are victims and often deaths.

Basically this is an example of Straight/Serious Drama which just goes further into exploring the worst possibilities of a situation. A straight play might deal with the difficulties of young lovers who come from warring families; in a **Tragedy** the lovers' deaths will be the inevitable consequence of their situation, the only possible ending. To be successful, an actor must fulfil all the skills necessary for straight acting, but must also be able to handle emotions involved in situations such as madness, disability and death.

On the **technical** side, remember that this is basically Straight/Serious Drama, so the same things apply. It may be that designs will be 'darker' in **Tragedy**, but you probably do not want to depress your audience by being uniformly dark. Neither do you want the lighting to be so dark that the audience cannot see the actors!

Good examples include   *Oedipus Rex* by Sophocles

Plays of *The Diary of Anne Frank* (various adaptations)

Pack of Lies by Hugh Whitemore

A5.1   activities

1   Prepare a short **Straight** scene between an adult and a teenager. Remember that you do not want your audience to laugh, therefore you must identify and cut out anything which makes you and your partner smile, giggle or laugh whilst you are rehearsing.

2   Now repeat or extend the scene but this time as **Tragedy**. Remember you may need to build up to the tragic moment, or even to stop just as the tragedy occurs. Can you communicate emotion?

3   Now show one to your audience without telling them which style you have chosen. Do you manage without getting any laughs? If so, how? If not, why not? Do you manage to communicate any emotion? Do they recognise which style you have shown?

Comedy

Comedy is intended to make the audience laugh, and yet, in general, to make them accept and believe what is happening.

The right audience will laugh readily at amusing characters and the way they behave and speak; amusing situations and how these affect the characters; and amusing dialogue, including jokes, double meanings, irony, puns and misunderstandings. It is very difficult to make every member of the audience laugh at the same things, and every audience respond as you want. To be successful, you need to overplay your characters and scenes slightly, so that the audience can immediately see that you are not taking things too seriously. It usually takes an audience a few minutes to 'warm up', so that the smiles become giggles and then outright laughs, and they need frequent rests from constant laughter, otherwise they get tired and the laughter dies.

On the **technical** side, **Comedy** allows for realistic design and a happy atmosphere.

Good examples include   *She Stoops to Conquer* by Oliver Goldsmith

The Importance of Being Earnest by Oscar Wilde

Relatively Speaking by Alan Ayckbourn

Farce

Farce is a style of exaggerated Comedy. It is intended to make the audience laugh, but it goes 'over the top' and beyond belief.

Much of what is said about Comedy is just as relevant to **Farce**. The main difference is that you must overplay significantly and become 'larger than life'. Even names may be ridiculous or with double meanings, the characters and their dialogue may be totally laughable. Situations which may be quite chaotic, and getting worse, will suddenly become totally sorted out – the coincidence often causing the 'last laugh'.

On the **technical** side, **Farce** allows for much more exaggerated and/or symbolic designs, although realism is also acceptable, especially if you are wanting to suggest that these unbelievable happenings could actually occur in everyday life.

Good examples include   *No Sex, Please, We're British* by Marriott and Foot
School for Scandal by R. B. Sheridan
Gosforth's Fete by Alan Ayckbourn

A5.2   activities

1 Prepare a short **Comedy** scene which takes place at school: remember that although you want your audience to laugh, you also want them to believe what is happening, so take care not to go over the top.

2 Now repeat the same scene as a **Farce**. This time you want your audience to laugh, but you do not expect them to believe it, because you do go over the top. However, if you go too far and make it stupid, the laughter will die, so you have to find the right limits!

3 Now show one to your audience without telling them which style you are choosing. Do they laugh? If so, why? If not, why not? Was it believable or not?

Pantomime

Pantomime demands audience participation, by shouting out, singing, doing actions, and providing volunteers to help the actors out.

To be successful with **Pantomime**, you must be able to control your audience: you must be able to use the right conventional words to get the right response, e.g. 'Where is he?' should bring the automatic answer of 'He's behind you!' You must be able to instruct the audience clearly in the singing, actions and volunteering, so that they know exactly what to do, and you must be happy to talk directly to the audience. The central characters are conventional stereotypes: a beautiful heroine who eventually marries the handsome prince, traditionally also played by a girl; the farcical 'Dame' played by a man, e.g. the Ugly Sisters; a wicked character, e.g. The Wicked Stepmother, although these must be made less frightening by getting the audience to boo and hiss or to 'tell on them'; a goodie such as the Fairy Godmother; and often the faithful 'servant' such as Buttons. Traditionally, **Pantomimes** have been based on fairy tales or other nursery stories, and are therefore suitable for young children; and they have a mixture of styles such as Straight, Comedy and Farce, but all with an overall atmosphere of fantasy, excitement and razzmatazz! In fact, almost any topic can be used as the theme for **Pantomime**, and it is a particularly good way of teaching small children.

On the **technical** side, **Pantomime** mixes realism with fantasy, so designers must look carefully at the particular character or situation. As with the Musical (see page 42), the visual impact is also important, so some designs can be stunning. However, there are also certain conventions with traditional **Pantomime**, such as the use of backdrops and cut-outs for scenery, the use of red and green lights for the genies, or instant changes of costume, and you will need to do some extra research to ensure that you include what is expected.

Good examples include   *Cinderella*
Snow White and the Seven Dwarfs
Aladdin

Melodrama

A **Melodrama** is a stereotyped, romantic and sensational play, with a particular emphasis on excessive emotion, and on audience participation.

To be successful with **Melodrama**, you must be able to over-exaggerate any action, movement, or words which convey feeling: e.g. a hand, palm outwards, to the brow, at the same time as a loud indrawn breath, to suggest faintness. You must accept the essential conventions attached to both the characters and their movements: the beautiful heroine, handsome hero, dastardly villain, horrific happening, a hidden but suggested final kiss between the happy couple. **Melodrama** also demands audience participation, but in different ways from Pantomime. With **Melodrama**, your audience should boo and hiss the villain, sigh with the romantic couple, shout encouragement in a fight, cheer when the hero wins, all without being told: they should recognise the signals. But that will only happen if you give out the right signals – whether by action, voice, movement, look, or simply by the way you enter! The Western is often a variety of **Melodrama**, set in the 'Wild West' of America in the days of the early settlers: although the stock characters and settings are different from traditional ones!

On the **technical** side, there are many conventions, in particular for costume, make-up and lighting, and you will need to do some extra research to make sure that you have what is expected. In areas where you can be more imaginative, colour plays an important part in **Melodrama**, although this may be used symbolically as well as realistically. Sound and lighting can be used to emphasise the mood and atmosphere. With a Western you must obviously ensure that you achieve the right impression of the historical time and place.

Good examples include many of the old silent movies
Maria Marten/Murder in the Red Barn by Constance Cox
medieval Mummers' plays

A5.3 activities

1   Prepare a short scene about *Eviction by a Wicked Landlord* in the style of a **Pantomime**. Make sure that you include opportunities for the audience to call out in the right way at the right moment, to join you in a simple song, to do some simple actions at the same time as you, and to volunteer to help you do something. Make sure that you give them adequate instructions and praise!

2   Now repeat the same scene as a **Melodrama**. Again you want the audience to join in; this time they should boo and cheer, sigh and clap, without being told directly.

3   Now show one to your audience without telling them which. Can you succeed in making them participate in all the essential ways? And when you want them to? If so, how? If not, why not?

Interactive Drama

Interactive Drama is when the play demands a two-way communication with the audience.

This may be in the form of direct question and answer, or may be using the audience in such a way that they become almost part of the cast. To be successful with **Interactive Drama**, you must be at ease with talking directly to the audience, be quick-thinking in order to respond suitably in role to the replies, and be able to adapt the action in response to what the audience does or says. It is therefore extremely demanding, but it can obviously be a useful way of teaching through Drama. You may use any of the main styles/genres or a mixture of them.

On the **technical** side, designs will partly depend on which of the main styles/genres are being used, but they are often fairly basic, so as to direct audience attention onto the actors and the interaction.

Promenade Drama

Promenade Drama is a form of Interactive Drama where the audience actually moves around from place to place with the actors, and under the direction of the actors.

It can be done in a variety of other styles/genres but, to be successful, you must be able to fulfil all the needs of Interactive Drama. In addition, you must be able to communicate very clearly to the audience when and where they move, and whether they are expected to do anything other than watch once they get there! The obvious disadvantage of **Promenade** plays is that they take up a lot of space: the main advantage is that different sets can be prepared and used without using scene changes, allowing the action to be continuous.

On the **technical** side, designs obviously depend partly on which main style/genre is chosen, but detail can be far greater than at other times. The audience tend to be much closer to the actors and the set, so they will notice small details, and without scene changes, sets can be far more elaborate – or even in different rooms. After all, there is no point in moving your audience around if they are simply going to look at another part of a blank stage!
The demands of lighting a **Promenade** performance obviously mean that resources will be stretched to their limits as you must be able to light every area adequately.

Good examples include   medieval Mystery plays
The Roses of Eyam by Don Taylor
Lark Rise to Candleford adapted by the Royal National Theatre

Commedia dell'arte

Commedia dell'arte is where actors work to a general outline/scenario and improvise spontaneously in response to their audience.

Commedia dell'arte originally came from Italy, and is the forerunner of both Pantomime and Punch and Judy. Much of it quickly becomes Farce. It has a set of stock characters, including the beautiful heroine, the handsome hero, the wicked unpopular rich man, the brainy servant and the idiot master. To be successful with **Commedia** you must understand the skills of Farce; be able to think quickly and improvise spontaneously; and be able to talk quite happily directly to the audience, including 'working' them until you get the response you want. The brainy servant, in particular, talks to the audience, even asking for suggestions and commenting on advice. **Commedia** is traditionally a masked performance.

On the **technical** side, **Commedia** must follow stock expectations in the ways of costume, make-up and props, while set and lighting are usually very basic. Research is essential!

Good examples include   *A Funny Thing Happened on the Way to the Forum* by Stephen Sondheim (and its TV offshoot *Up Pompeii*)
A Servant of Two Masters by Goldoni

A5.4 activities

1 Prepare a short monologue suitable for **Interactive Drama**. You are a shop assistant, and you have got to tell a group of students, coming on work experience, what the job entails, and what the manager expects of them. You want them to ask you questions and make suitable comments so that they can learn what they need to do; and this means that you have to have the right answers!

2 Repeat your monologue, but this time imagine that you are actually taking the students around your place of work: so that as you talk to them you move them in a **Promenade** performance around the different places. This time, you don't want any questions until the end of the tour.

3 Now repeat the monologue in **Commedia dell'arte**, where you tell them what they can really expect and what really goes on with the 'stupid' manager, and the various 'stock' customers. You must encourage the audience to make suggestions and comments.

4 Now show one to your audience, without telling them which. Do you get the response you wanted? If so, how? If not, why not?

Mime

Mime is acting and communicating without the use of speech, although it does not necessarily have to be silent. The use of sounds can be very helpful.

Stylised **Mime** such as that of Marcel Marceau is very specialised, and needs to be taught to you by a specialist in this art form. But ordinary **Mime** is a skill well worth developing, as it helps your performance in so many ways. To be successful, you have to communicate your meaning clearly through body movement, gesture and facial expression, all of which need to be exaggerated slightly in order to be seen and understood; and you need to position your actions so that the audience misses nothing essential. Many other styles/genres can be acted through **Mime**, although it is often difficult for an audience to understand Fantasy. Sound is allowed and may help both the understanding and the atmosphere, e.g. sighs, splashing water, music. Good **Mime** can draw from the audience the same depth of response as plays using speech.

On the **technical** side, **Mime** has certain conventions which are based on the need for the audience to concentrate all their energies on the **Mime** itself and not to be distracted. So costume is usually black, allowing the portrayal of any character(s), although the actors may wear single, stereotypical items to symbolise their roles, e.g. a bowler hat suggests a city gent, and a shawl suggests an old lady. Similarly the stage is usually bare, with only essential furniture, e.g. a couple of chairs to suggest a car, or a table to suggest an office. Lighting will be used to help focus attention on the relevant action or detail. On the other hand, sound can be extremely helpful, and may be used continuously through the piece to help emphasise the mood, location or action.

Good examples include   old silent movies
Marcel Marceau

Musical

A **Musical** is a play where music, song and dance are as essential as ordinary speech and movement.

To be successful in a **Musical**, you must be able to sing and dance at least as well as you can act, as you tell your story through a mixture of all three. You must be able to accept the conventions of song and dance: self-consciousness can look dreadful! The **Musical** suits itself to all sorts of other styles/genres, and to a wide variety of topics, as Andrew Lloyd-Webber has shown.

On the **technical** side, designs are often very elaborate, although they may be realistic, symbolic or impressionistic. Whatever you choose, the visual impact is almost as important as the acting, so you can go for really stunning designs. However, recognise that the more stunning they are, the more expensive they will probably be!

Good examples include   Andrew Lloyd-Webber musicals
Oliver! by Lionel Bart
Grease by Jim Jacobs and Warren Casey

A5.5 activities

1 Prepare a short scene in **Mime** of a young couple at the seaside. Remember that you cannot speak, although you can use sounds; and the audience must see everything clearly.

2 Now show it to your audience. Do they understand all that you are doing? If so, why? If not, why not? Did they respond as you wanted them to? If so, why? If not, why not?

3 Now repeat the same scene adding music, song and dance, as with a **Musical**. For the purpose of this activity, the music, song and dance do not have to be very complicated, but make sure that you give yourself totally to it.

4 Now show it to your audience. Do they enjoy the addition of music, song and dance? If so, why? If not, why not? Did they respond as you wanted them to? If so, why? If not, why not?

Fantasy Drama

Fantasy Drama uses imaginary characters and/or situations, which allows non-humans to come to life and humans to appear in places which can only be imagined.

A good **Fantasy** is quite likely to mix a number of different styles/genres such as Straight, Farce, and Pantomime. To do it well, you have to accept some unusual roles, e.g. snails, garden gnomes, teapots, baked beans, devils – in fact, anything which is not human. It may even be a made-up word that tells you who you are: a tooloomooloo or a calapacas. Similarly, your characters can be in Heaven, on Mars, or in a hole in the wall; or they may be in Messitory or Fantasia. **Fantasy** gives wonderful opportunities for using imagination to the full: and can be extremely fulfilling when everyone gets 'lost' in the imagined world.

On the **technical** side, designers can really use their imaginations – although they cannot be so 'way out' that the audience does not understand! Some designs will obviously need to be as realistic as possible, whilst others may be very abstract or impressionistic. **Fantasy** is often a reason for using stronger colours than in most drama; while lighting and sound are a great help in creating atmosphere and mood.

Good examples include   *Alice in Wonderland* by Lewis Carroll (various adaptations)
Peter Pan by J. M. Barrie
The Hobbit by J. R. R. Tolkien (novel)

Sci-fi

Sci-fi is a particular kind of Fantasy Drama, based on scientific reality, but extended into the realms of the imagination for the answer to: what might happen next?

To be successful, you must be able to fulfil all the needs of Fantasy, and possibly those of Horror as well (see below). You must also be able to understand something of the scientific reality on which the play is based, e.g. cloning or transport. You must have the imagination to see where such inventions might lead: e.g. the time when humans are cloned to order; the personal vehicle which will take people from place to place by a word of command. You must be able to see both good and bad potential for the future.

On the **technical** side, **Sci-fi** mixes realism with fantasy, so designers must take both aspects into consideration. The opening scenes will usually be realistic, and may be fairly detailed. The future may be much more abstract, symbolic or impressionistic: and it allows you to use as much imagination as the actors – provided your ideas help the objectives.

Good examples include   *The War of the Worlds* by H. G. Wells (novel and film)
Frankenstein by Mary Shelley (novel and film)
The Day of the Triffids by John Wyndham (novel and film)

Horror

This is simply intended to horrify the audience.

Horror plays have horrifying, gruesome or violent themes, situations and/or characters; although these are often mixed with everyday situations and characters to make the whole scenario appear more believable. The horrific situation/character usually has to be overplayed, as does the emotion, and it is often a mixture of various other styles/genres with a strong leaning towards Fantasy and Melodrama. Despite the fact that it is intended to horrify, the audience will often laugh at the **Horror** – to release the tension and dispel the fear.

On the **technical** side, **Horror** offers the opportunity to mix realistic, symbolic and horrific designs, although even the horrific must have an element of reality – otherwise the audience will not be horrified! Designs will emphasise the threatening, 'dark' atmosphere.

Good examples include   *Tamburlaine the Great* by Christopher Marlowe
The Woman in Black by Susan Hill, adapted by Stephen Mallatrat
Silence of the Lambs by Thomas Harris (novel and film)

A5.6   activities

1   You are part of the design team for a play on *Space Travel*. Draw some preliminary sketches or list your ideas for your designs for a **Fantasy** production on this theme. Remember that the audience must recognise the fantasy, but if you go too 'way out' they may not understand your ideas.

2   Now draw some preliminary sketches or list your possible ideas for a **Sci-fi** production on *Space Travel*. Remember that the audience must be able to recognise the reality from which the fantasy has come.

3   Now draw some preliminary sketches or list your possible ideas for a **Horror** production on *Space Travel*.

4   Choose the design you think is best, and show it to your audience without telling them which of the three genres you have chosen. Can they guess correctly? If so, how have you succeeded? If not, why not?

Historical Drama or Period Drama

Historical or **Period Drama** refers to plays set in a particular historical period. They may have been written in the past; or may be modern plays set in the past.

These may be of any style, depending on their purpose. For example; Elizabethan Tragedy, Restoration Comedy of Manners, or an Interactive lesson about Queen Victoria. The main problem is understanding the historical period in which the play is written or set, and this includes not only aspects such as costume and props, but also the way in which people spoke and behaved – this may need a great deal of research to succeed.

On the **technical** side, **Historical Drama** gives a wonderful opportunity for more detailed designs, and for something different and often very dramatic. Plenty of research needed!

Good examples include   television Costume Dramas
An Inspector Calls by J. B. Priestley (Straight)
Murder in the Cathedral by T. S. Eliot (poetic)

Whodunnit

A **Whodunnit** is basically a detective story, where a crime is committed and solved.

A **Whodunnit** is often acted as a Straight play, but it lends itself to most other styles/genres. The crime may be of any severity, although in most straight **Whodunnits** it tends to be murder; while in Farce, it tends to be frivolous, such as the theft of 5p. The skills needed will depend on the style/genre you decide to use, but if you are improvising your **Whodunnit** you will need to construct the piece very carefully. You must ensure that the audience is given enough hints to feel that they can solve the mystery, without it being so obvious that they have no interest. You must also ensure that the play develops steadily, with something new (sometimes irrelevant) being discovered in each unit of the piece.

On the **technical** side, it will partly depend on the main style/genre you decide to use, but it will often need to be fairly realistic and detailed, and should give clues to help the audience.

Good examples include   most Agatha Christie books/plays (Straight)
Brother Cadfael books by Ellis Peters (Historical – novel and TV)
Cluedo (Interactive)

A5.7 activities

1   You are part of the design team for a performance of a **Historical play** set during World War II. Draw some preliminary sketches or list possible ideas for your designs.

2   Now imagine that you are designing for a **Whodunnit** set during World War II, in the same location you used for the first part of

this activity. Draw some preliminary sketches or list possible ideas for your designs.

3   Now choose the design you think is best and show it to your audience without telling them which genre you have chosen. Can they guess correctly? If so, how have you succeeded? If not, why not?

Examiners' tip

Experimenting with as many different styles/genres/types as possible will help both your written Coursework response and your choices for practical work. But remember: you must understand the special skills necessary if you are to be successful.

A6 Technical techniques

Using this section of the book

If you have chosen a technical skill for your coursework, this section will advise you on some of the general techniques that you will be expected to use or consider. Some of these are required for all of the technical options: whilst others will be specific to your chosen skill. You can find out more about these in Section C (pages 153–98). Take the opportunity to try out your chosen skill by working on one of the suggestions in the mini-projects (pages 86–122).

Under each of the headings below you will find a description of the technique and how it may be relevant to your presentation. There are also activities for you to try before applying the techniques to the mini-projects, and later to your assessed pieces of coursework. Some of the activities in this section are based on *The Accused*, printed below.

The Accused by R. D. Price

Context: The interview of a suspect for a crime. The suspect has been arrested following a firebomb being put through the letterbox of an Asian family. He/she was seen by several witnesses.

The DETECTIVE is a calm and weary character. Very patient, but one feels that the patience is wearing a little thin.
The ACCUSED is almost a stereotypical skinhead/fascist. This character is aggressive and responds like a caged animal.

The scene opens with only the ACCUSED *in the room, who establishes something of his/her character and the atmosphere through an opening solo sequence. After a while, the* DETECTIVE *enters and pulls up a chair. There is a long and uncomfortable pause while the two characters stare at each other.*

	DETECTIVE	Well?
	ACCUSED	What?
	DETECTIVE	Are you going to talk to me?
	ACCUSED	About what?
5	DETECTIVE	Give it a rest. I want to get home.
	ACCUSED	Back to your pig sty.
	DETECTIVE	Nice.
	ACCUSED	What?
	DETECTIVE	Your manners. Make a nice impression on the judge.
10	ACCUSED	Magistrate.
	DETECTIVE	Oh no. Got it wrong there. Judge. This one's a Crown Court job.
	ACCUSED	Why? Who's killed who, then?
	DETECTIVE	That's why we're talking.
	ACCUSED	Get stuffed!
15	DETECTIVE	Calm down. Don't get yourself into more trouble. Sit down.
	ACCUSED	I don't take orders from anyone.
	DETECTIVE	Sit down.
	ACCUSED	Don't you come near me. I'm giving you a warning.
	DETECTIVE	I said for you to calm down and sit down.
20	ACCUSED	You're not getting me for this.
	DETECTIVE	For what?

	ACCUSED	I'm not going down. I'm not going down for this.
	DETECTIVE	For what?
	ACCUSED	No one was in.
25	DETECTIVE	Why? Did you check?
	ACCUSED	No . . . you don't trick me. I'm too clever for you.
	DETECTIVE	Yes, very clever. Well, I've enough to go on for now. Try to leave some of the room in one piece. (*He exits.*)

ACCUSED goes berserk as the lights fade.

Research

This is finding information from a number of sources, to help both your understanding and the development of your piece of work.

Research is an essential part of any technical work. Obviously, the chosen piece will lead to major **research** into the theme, historical period and background. This could be of great help to your group, and could influence the development of their work. If you are doing a play script you could **research** the playwright, or past professional productions of the play. You may need to **research** materials and equipment that are available for you to use; as well as materials and equipment that in an ideal situation you would have liked to use. Your **research** may include the work of professional designers for the theatre, and the methods that they use. You could show how they influenced your ideas or working methods.

Information can come from many places including the Internet, CD Roms, newspapers and magazines, the school and local libraries, historical sources, theatres, or questionnaires which you create yourself.

A6.1 activities

1 Research the history of your chosen design area, e.g. if you are looking at presenting stage make-up you could look at how stage make-up used to have a lead base. For set design you could explore how at one time all scenery was painted on a backcloth.

2 Research how a professional working in your area would approach a performance. You could look at how a stage manager prepares a prompt copy or the equipment a theatre sound engineer can use.

3 Read *The Accused*. You might need to research police interviews; interview rooms; how other writers portray the police interview; possible styles of presentation. Make notes of where you might look for the necessary information.

4 Choose one of the other scripts in this book, and make a list of possible areas for research.

The performance space

This is the space or area where the performance will take place.

It may be a proscenium stage, a studio, a classroom, or even outside. You must be thoroughly aware of the space that you are going to be working in, and how the group will use the space. They may decide to perform 'in the round': this kind of decision has a serious impact on set design and lighting. You need to know the position of the audience – knowing how close the audience is will determine how detailed a costume may have to be or how subtle a stage make-up.

A6.2 activities

1 Create **ground plans** of the performance space available for your group to use. Take accurate measurements. Locate on your ground plan the position of the audience. Make copies, as these may well be useful to you later and save you time.

2 If you are doing **set design**, use the ground plans to identify the 'sight lines'. Where could you place objects or actors so that the action of the play can be clearly seen at all times?

3 If you are producing a **make-up** try some shadowing lines or folds and wrinkles and see how they appear on stage in relation to the position of the audience.

4 If you are doing **lighting**, experiment with some lanterns to see how you could light the action on stage without lighting the audience!

5 If you are producing **properties** for a performance see how far the audience has to be from a constructed object for it to look realistic.

6 If you are performing with **puppets** you might not want your operational techniques to be visible to the audience. How far away would the audience have to be?

7 If you are doing **sound**, check the volume levels of various common sounds and music for various parts of your auditorium. You want your sounds to be heard comfortably – neither too loud nor too soft.

8 If you are dealing with **costume** or **masks**, detail will be affected by how close the audience is. Look at the effect on some available costumes or masks as you move further away from them. How much realistic detail will you need to include? How much can be left out because it won't be seen? What needs to be exaggerated to be seen from a distance?

Designer objectives

These are what you, as the designer, want to achieve in communicating to the audience.

You must decide what you want to achieve as a designer. You must identify your aims for each element of your design, and record your **objectives** in your notes. Everything you do should add to the audience's understanding: as a set designer your **objective** might be to communicate the poverty of a household; as a lighting designer to create a sinister and scary atmosphere; as a costume designer to show the wealth and status of a character.

A6.3 activities

1 What might your design objective be for a performance of *The Accused*? How might you communicate each objective through your designs?

2 Choose one of the other scripts in this book, and identify two or three possible objectives. Try to decide how you might communicate these objectives through different designs.

Plans and diagrams

These include all the drawings you make.

Whatever technical skill you choose, clear **plans** and **diagrams** are important in communicating your ideas and in keeping a record of any developments, although each of the technical skills will have different requirements. You don't have to be a brilliant artist, and your **plans** need not be very complex, but they should communicate clearly how you have developed your ideas, and what the finished effect or product should look like. Final **plans** and **diagrams** should be to scale.

A6.4 activities

1 For **lighting** you could create a plan of the lighting grid and the location of all plug sockets. This will help you to decide where to hang lanterns.

2 For stage **make-up** you could produce a diagram of the face of a doll.

3 For **sound** you could produce a labelled diagram of the sound-mixing desk.

4 For **stage management** you could produce a plan of the performance area for *The Accused*. You could indicate the location of any entrances and exits, the location of properties backstage and onstage, and of the position of any technical equipment and staff.

5 For **set** design you could create a ground plan of the set for *The Accused*.

6 Choose one of the other scripts in this book, and make two diagrams of possible initial ideas for your area of design.

Equipment

This will include any apparatus and machines which you need.

Equipment, often electrical, is needed if you are to fulfil the requirements of your chosen technical skill. It is important that you become familiar with the resources available to you, and learn how to operate the **equipment** with skill and care. Before using any **equipment** you must be aware of the relevant health and safety rules – whether you are using a glue-gun, stage make-up, or rigging a lantern. Even when you are fully aware of how to work safely, your teacher must authorise and supervise your work. Be considerate – you are not the only person in the class; you may have to be patient and wait for the teacher to give you their attention and supervision. Remember that most of the **equipment** that you will be using is potentially dangerous and very expensive, and no Drama department can afford for you to damage or waste the resources.

Once you have made firm decisions about your work you need to discuss your ideas with your teacher to arrange how various materials will be provided for you. One of you may have to ask other departments to loan **equipment** or provide materials, or your teacher may have to order the purchase of materials, which could affect the time management of your project.

A6.5 activities

1 For stage **make-up**, draw up a list of all the make-up and equipment available to you. Experiment with different types of make-up brushes and sponges to see what effect each can create. Using the back of your hand, try blending different colours to create a bruise effect.

2 For stage **lighting**, create a list of all the different types of lanterns that you have available to use. Find out what different qualities each has. How bright is each? What area will each cover? What accessories, such as 'barn doors', can you fit to each type of lantern? Does your department have 'gobos'? What else is there?

3 Choose one of the scripts in this book, and examine it for indications of any equipment which you might need to fulfil your area of design.

Textual or performance demands

These include any **demands** which the performance itself makes on the performers and designers.

For example, if you are designing the set you need to know how many doors are required; for designing a costume you need to know whether characters have to be in uniform; for designing properties, you need to know how the actors will use them and the **demands** made on the object. If your group is performing a script, you must read the script and look for every **demand** the script makes that applies to your area of responsibility. If your group is improvising, it is vital that you listen to how their ideas are developing and be aware of any decisions or changes that may affect what you are doing. If your group is dancing, you need to be aware of their need for movement and use of space. With your growing knowledge and understanding of your chosen area, you will have an important and helpful role to play within a group, as you will be able to say what is possible and what cannot be created.

A6.6   activities

1   Examine the script of *The Accused* for any demands for your area of expertise which the script makes.

2   Choose any of the other scripts in this book and examine them for the textual demands as they apply to your area of design.

Preparing a cue-sheet

A **cue-sheet** tells the operator or the stage manager when something has to happen, such as a sound effect or a lighting change.

A cue may be a line of dialogue in the play or an action on stage, or it might be linked to another technical area, such as a sound effect or a lighting change. These can only be prepared towards the end of the rehearsal process when plans and timings have been agreed. A good **cue-sheet** should allow the operator to be prepared for what is to come: e.g. a lighting **cue-sheet** will allow the operator to pre-set the next lighting state ready for the next cue. As a guide to how detailed a **cue-sheet** should be, imagine that the equipment is to be operated by someone who has no knowledge of the piece being performed: a good **cue-sheet** should allow them to manage without mishap. You may wish to use the sample **cue-sheets** in Appendices 7 and 8, or you may prefer to create your own to relate specifically to your performance space and equipment. Lighting, sound and stage management all need clear, accurate **cue-sheets**.

A6.7   activities

1   For a **stage manager** list all the possible points of change within a performance of *The Accused*. Make a note of entrances and exits, and points when the lighting or sound might change.

2   Create a **lighting** cue-sheet for a performance of any of the scripts contained in this book. Identify where any alterations in the lighting would occur; and how they would affect the lighting of the actors on stage.

3   Create a **sound** cue-sheet for a performance of any of the scripts contained in this book. Identify any points where sound would be needed; how long for; and what its effect should be.

Technical interdependence

In all the technical skills you should be aware of the effects that the other technical aspects have on your ideas. You will need to show that you are aware of other relevant areas and show, in your notes and written coursework, how they have affected your ideas. As you are working on a real performance, you will need to know of any decisions the group has made about other technical areas. For instance, as a costume designer you will want the lighting to complement your fabrics and your colours, and to see that colours will not clash with, or be lost against, the set.

Examiners' tip

> Spend time preparing thoroughly. Thorough research and understanding of the task are essential for successful and effective technical work. Make sure that you have access to all necessary equipment and materials, and that you liaise considerately with all the others in your group. This section should be invaluable in getting you pointed in the right direction!

A7 Written techniques

Using this section of the book

The written parts of the AQA exam reflect on the work you have done:

- in your practical coursework (performance and/or technical tasks)
- in your study of various texts/scripts
- as an audience to a presentation.

You need to develop the following techniques as far as possible in order to get the best marks of which you are capable on the written parts of the exam:

- a written response to your coursework (10% of your final mark)
- a written paper as a final exam (40% of your final mark).

Details for each of these will be found in the later sections of the book. But, obviously, the better marks that you can get for the written parts of the exam, the better your overall grade will be: so it is well worth improving your written skills!

This section will outline various techniques that will help you to create a worthwhile, effective piece of writing for Drama. Under each heading below there are reminders about skills, and various activities to help you improve the techniques necessary. In order to help you to build up these skills, all work in this section is based on the extract from *Find Me*, printed below.

Extract from *Find Me* by Olwen Wymark

Find Me in rehearsal, showing a moment of tension. Note: posture, gesture, body and facial expression.

NARRATOR   In November 1975, at the age of twenty, Verity Taylor was charged by the Police with damaging a chair by fire . . . in a locked ward of a mental hospital where she was a patient. She was remanded in custody . . . was subsequently tried . . . and in February 1976 an order was made for her admission to a maximum security hospital. . . . She was admitted to Broadmoor, from where she may not be discharged or transferred elsewhere without the permission of the Home Secretary.

The lights fade, and then come up again on EDWARD, VERITY'S *father.*

EDWARD She usually plays alone. She doesn't seem to get on a wavelength with other children somehow. We've noticed that she veers between being a little too – er – high-spirited or closed up in a funny way. You get children like that, don't you, who are just solitary by nature. She always seems so much happier playing in her own little private world.

Lights come up on VERITY.

When she was very small she used to play for hours on end with a village she built out of blocks.

VERITY (*building her village, very concentrated*) There's the school – and the church – and here's all the houses – and here's the park – and this is the castle. (*She sits back on her heels and looks at it.*) It's my village. It's tiny tiny tiny, and it's all mine. I'm big and I look after all the people. (*She stretches her arms out over the village. Crooning.*) I'll take care of you. I'll take care of you. (*She starts building again.*) I'll make a lovely big swimming-pool – and here's where the horses live. There's a hundred horses and if they want to they can gallop through the whole village. Gallop gallop gallop down the streets, and jump over the hedges and in the gardens and . . .

EDWARD enters.

EDWARD Hello, Verity. What's that you're making?

VERITY *is immediately silent and stiff.*

VERITY (*sharply*) Be careful. You'll step on it.
EDWARD I won't. I won't. I'll be careful. What is it?
VERITY (*still warily*) It's my village.
EDWARD Oh, it's very nice. Clever girl.
VERITY This is my castle. (*She looks at him sideways.*) I'm inside it.
EDWARD Are you?
VERITY Yes. And nobody else can get in.
EDWARD Well well!
VERITY It's all locked up and safe and they can't get in.

JEAN, VERITY'S *mother, comes in.*

JEAN Hello, darling. You're back. (*She moves to* EDWARD.)
VERITY Look out!
JEAN What?
VERITY You're knocking it over!
JEAN (*good-naturedly*) Well honestly, Verity, you've taken up nearly the whole floor. Look, you'll have to move it now anyway. We're going to have tea in here. (*She stoops to pick up a block.*)
VERITY (*fiercely*) Don't touch that!
EDWARD (*with a warning look to* JEAN) We won't touch any of it, Verity. You put it away yourself.
VERITY I don't want to put it away. I want to play with it.
JEAN You can play with it later.
VERITY I don't want later. I want now!
JEAN We're going to have tea.
VERITY I don't care! Now now now! I want my village now!

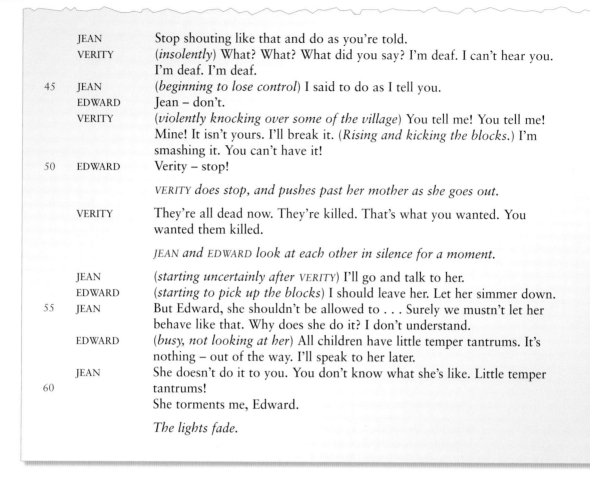

	JEAN	Stop shouting like that and do as you're told.
	VERITY	(*insolently*) What? What? What did you say? I'm deaf. I can't hear you. I'm deaf. I'm deaf.
45	JEAN	(*beginning to lose control*) I said to do as I tell you.
	EDWARD	Jean – don't.
	VERITY	(*violently knocking over some of the village*) You tell me! You tell me! Mine! It isn't yours. I'll break it. (*Rising and kicking the blocks.*) I'm smashing it. You can't have it!
50	EDWARD	Verity – stop!

VERITY does stop, and pushes past her mother as she goes out.

| | VERITY | They're all dead now. They're killed. That's what you wanted. You wanted them killed. |

JEAN and EDWARD look at each other in silence for a moment.

	JEAN	(*starting uncertainly after VERITY*) I'll go and talk to her.
	EDWARD	(*starting to pick up the blocks*) I should leave her. Let her simmer down.
55	JEAN	But Edward, she shouldn't be allowed to . . . Surely we mustn't let her behave like that. Why does she do it? I don't understand.
	EDWARD	(*busy, not looking at her*) All children have little temper tantrums. It's nothing – out of the way. I'll speak to her later.
60	JEAN	She doesn't do it to you. You don't know what she's like. Little temper tantrums! She torments me, Edward.

The lights fade.

Note-taking

This is one of the two most important skills which you need to master if you are to produce good, focused, relevant written work. (The other is essay writing, pages 57–61.) Good notes should help you to:

- record what you have done, and so act as reminders
- provide a framework for your thoughts and writing
- make clear in your own mind the importance of different ideas and thoughts
- focus your mind on different needs and targets
- recognise what is relevant, and so act as pointers
- understand how your technical/design skills fit in with other design skills.

Headings

These consist of just one or two **key words** which show what the whole section is about.

Good notes will be well organised under short **headings**: e.g. Stimulus, Style, Historical background, Research. These should give you the framework which you need for later essays, as they often represent the themes of complete paragraphs.

A7.1 activity

You are playing either Verity or Edward in this extract from *Find Me*. Which of the following headings might be useful as the framework for your notes for this scene?

Background	Key moments	Lighting
First ideas	Difficulties and solutions	Movement
Staging	Costume	Materials
Task	Research	Evaluation
Audience reaction	Objectives/intentions	Voice

Are there any other headings that might be useful? Arrange all the headings you have chosen into the most logical order for your purpose as an actor.

Reminders

These are words or phrases which will later act as memory-joggers.

Good notes will not be in sentence form, but will be short, often only one- or two-word **reminders** of points which you want to remember: e.g. for acting a shy character – *quiet, stammering, head and eyes down, small steps, shoulders hunched*; for designing a costume for Sleepy – *baggy trousers, bright pyjama-like top, wide belt, nightcap*. Good **reminders** will help you to see what is relevant, and to make clear in your own mind the importance of different examples and details.

A7.2 activity

You are designing one of the technical aspects for a performance of this extract from *Find Me*. Under the heading of 'Needs of the actors', which of the following words/phrases might be useful reminders for you?

Verity moves quickly	Narrator's spot
Blocks – Verity	Jean preparing tea
Space to move	Verity's monologue L
Edward comes in from work	Jean and Edward stand together CR

Are there any other words/phrases which might be useful reminders for you? Arrange the ones you have chosen into a logical order for your purpose as the designer for this particular extract.

Reminders may also be about ideas suggested, problems faced and solutions tried. For example, for the balcony scene from *Romeo and Juliet* – ideas: *set in Elizabethan times, or modern times? In Italy or in England?*; problem: *how to create the balcony*; possible solutions: *using rostra (blocks), using the front of the school stage, using the lighting gallery in the studio, using spotlighting*.

Audience reactions

Good notes record key points from the response of your audience.

Your audience does not have to be from a full final performance. An audience might only be one person, such as your teacher or your working partner; it might be another group from your class, or a small group of friends who do not do Drama. **Reactions** can be gathered at any time during the rehearsal period or from the final performance. Do **reactions** change because of earlier comments? You may record useful short quotes of what people actually said; or you may record **reactions** such as laughter (was it intended?) or stillness. For a puppet performance, **reactions** might be: *good facial expression; movement too repetitive; voice suitable for character but not always easy to hear; laughed when the head fell off (not intended!); but also laughed at jokes.*

Pinpointing future needs

Good notes help you to identify things which need to be done at all stages of the rehearsal and presentation.

For example, during a rehearsal period, they might include: *practise costume change, use actual drinks, complete sound recording, adjust hemline on the dress, make mouth-hole larger on the mask.* After a final performance, they might include: *next time – learn my lines sooner, make sure my voice can be heard at all times, write more clearly in the prompt copy, check lighting cues more thoroughly.*

Example of good note-taking

The following extract from a student's notebook (for Properties) shows how good notes can help to create a clear focus:

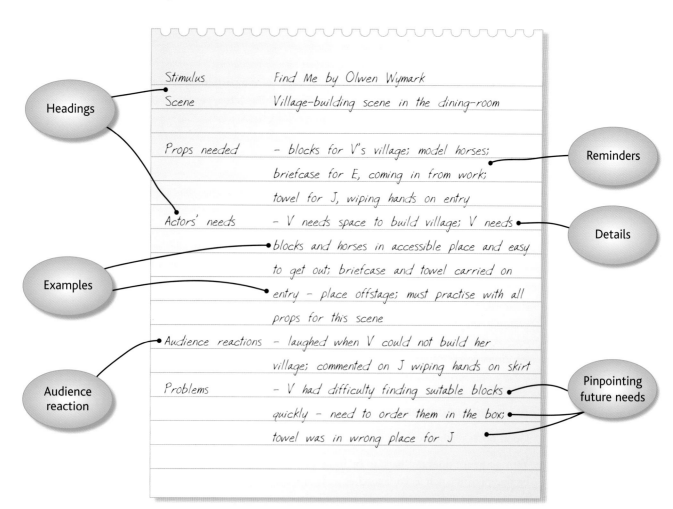

Stimulus	Find Me by Olwen Wymark
Scene	Village-building scene in the dining-room
Props needed	– blocks for V's village; model horses; briefcase for E, coming in from work; towel for J, wiping hands on entry
Actors' needs	– V needs space to build village; V needs blocks and horses in accessible place and easy to get out; briefcase and towel carried on entry – place offstage; must practise with all props for this scene
Audience reactions	– laughed when V could not build her village; commented on J wiping hands on skirt
Problems	– V had difficulty finding suitable blocks quickly – need to order them in the box; towel was in wrong place for J

(Labels around notebook: Headings, Reminders, Details, Examples, Audience reaction, Pinpointing future needs)

Remember that:

- the **headings** will provide the framework
- the **reminders** will give examples and details
- the **audience reactions** indicate your success in communicating
- **pinpointing future needs** shows what you still need to do.

Essay-writing

50% of your total marks may be awarded on your essays, so this is the most important written technique to try to improve. A good Drama essay will not waffle or give unnecessary and irrelevant information, but it will:

- *answer the question asked:* this means that you must read the question carefully in the first place to ensure that you know exactly what it is that is being asked. This also includes writing to the length expected!
- *be written grammatically* in full sentences and suitable paragraphs
- *be clear to the reader*, both in the writing (word-processing?) and in the meaning
- *use specialist Drama terms* correctly (Techniques sections A1–A6). Make sure you spell them correctly!

Where relevant, a good essay will also:

- enable the reader to **imagine the work** which you are describing: e.g. how you achieved an atmosphere of evil, threat and magic in your presentation of a scene with the Three Witches
- show **evidence of your research**: e.g. information about the way that Australian Aborigines live and behave as you prepare to present a piece of work on *Walkabout*; facts about smoking, the subject of a piece of Theatre-in-Education
- show an **understanding** of aspects of a stage performance other than the one you are offering e.g. lighting, movement needs, special effects, masks
- show your knowledge of **other scripts and texts** which can be compared in some way with the one you are discussing: e.g. in writing about how you acted Hansel or Gretel, you might refer to how this might compare with acting Micky or Eddie in *Blood Brothers*, or a young child in an improvisation based on a recent newspaper report; in designing a set for an improvisation on bullying, you might want to refer to how this might compare with one suitable for a Dance/Drama on the same theme
- show that you can identify **your own contribution** to the work in progress, recognising both your strengths and your difficulties
- show that you can **express appropriate opinions** about work done or seen, and back up your opinions with reasons.

Below are some guidelines on the general construction and content of your essays, and how to use the notes you have made.

Framework

This is the organised outline of your essay.

If your notes had the most suitable headings, it is likely that these will give you the topics needed for each paragraph of your essay. Similarly, if you order those headings in a logical way, so that one follows naturally on from another, you will have an obvious order to your essay. Simply add a paragraph at the beginning to explain the context, and complete with a paragraph drawing some conclusions, e.g. what you have learnt from the piece of work, or a comparison with another piece of work you have done.

A7.3 activities

1 Imagine that you have been studying *Find Me*, and you have been asked to write the following essay: *'Discuss, in detail, how you would wish to play either Verity or Edward in this extract. You will need to refer to voice, movement, gesture and facial expression, as well as to how your chosen character responds to others onstage.'*

2 Look at the list of headings you chose for the note-taking activity A7.1. Re-read your question carefully, and decide which of your headings are relevant to this particular essay, and list them in a suitable order. You will find that they have become suitable topic headings for each paragraph of your essay.

Example

You might decide that the most suitable headings are the ones given below. This is not the only way to order your essay, but it is logical and easy to follow, and it keeps you focused on the question asked.

1 Character
2 Actor objectives
3 Voice
4 Movement
5 Gesture
6 Facial expression
7 Response to others on stage

Introduction

The opening paragraph should explain briefly what your essay is about, and so give the reader the right context for the work.

You will often need to say exactly what *task* you were given: e.g. *we have been looking at possible sound for* Find Me *by Olwen Wymark;* or *we have just performed a Dance/Drama on a schizophrenic.* You may need to give a few words of *explanation* or background to make it clear for your reader: e.g. *we wanted to use dramatic sound to reflect Verity's moods; our central character was John, who behaved quite normally at times, whilst at others thought he heard voices telling him what to do.* You may need to give a *detail* which helps to explain your objectives: e.g. *this play was set in 1977, but is just as relevant today;* or *we hoped to produce a powerful Dance/Drama which made the audience question their own reactions to mental illness.*

A7.4 activity

You have been involved in a presentation of *Find Me*, and have now been asked to start your essay on '*Discuss your contribution, in detail*'. Write an opening paragraph of about six lines to introduce your essay. You will need to include information such as the title of the play, the type of performance your group chose, which performance or technical aspect you did, and what overall effect you wanted to create.

Details

These are the small points and clues which are really going to show your understanding, and enable the reader to 'see' what you mean.

A good Drama essay will be full of examples, details, and reasons. If you made good notes during preparation and rehearsal, you should have reminders of lots of examples that you can use. The example below shows you how you can use notes to fill in the detail when you write an essay.

Example

Imagine that you have been asked to write a paragraph or two on how you achieved a suitable voice for your role as Verity or Edward. You might have the following notes on Verity's voice:

mood changes	*varied volume*	*varied pace*	*varied pitch*
rhythmical	*insolent*	*excited*	*singsong*
violent	*sharp*	*angry*	*sulky*

Now, in writing a paragraph or two on the use of voice for Verity (words from the notes have been underlined), you might say:

> It was quite difficult to get Verity's voice right, because she uses so many <u>changes of mood</u>. These have to be shown by frequent <u>changes of pace, pitch and volume</u>; and she often switches very suddenly from one to another. For example, when she is absorbed in her village, I tried to speak with a fairly low pitch, quietly and slowly, almost <u>rhythmically</u>, as she names different buildings, and to draw out the phrases slightly. We are told that she croons one part, and for this I tried to use a much more <u>singsong</u> voice – still <u>rhythmic</u>, but of higher pitch and louder volume. By the time she gets to the end of this monologue, she is racing with the horses, and her voice is becoming faster, louder and more <u>excited</u>. When Edward enters, she first goes silent, and then speaks <u>sharply</u> to him.

Reasons

These are the reasons why you did something, and they underline your understanding of all that you have done.

Good Drama essays will always give reasons for any decisions which have been made. Do not leave the reader wondering why you have used a particular technique, or why you thought that a particular idea was the best. If you find that it is difficult to remember your reasons later, make notes of them as you go.

A7.5 activity

Read the following paragraph from an essay on *Find Me*:

One of the key moments in the village-building scene is when Verity smashes up her village. This is particularly important as it is the first time we have seen her violence in action and the effect it has on her mother. We wanted our audience to be shocked by the incident rather than laugh at Verity's behaviour. In order to get the greatest impact, we had to build up to it as realistically as we could. We also wanted to emphasise the tension by focusing on the contrasting reactions – Verity's built up very quickly, Edward remained calm, and Jean showed her sense of helplessness.

There are four different reasons given in this paragraph to show why the group made certain decisions. Can you find all four?

Wider knowledge and understanding

You are expected in this syllabus to show that you have both a knowledge and an understanding of other plays and texts, of other styles and genres, and of other cultures and times.

You must, therefore, be able to refer to examples of Drama other than the one for which you are writing. Look at the examples below. All of these were written in essays on *Find Me* and they show a little extra knowledge or understanding beyond the one play. In the full essays, these extracts were often followed up with more detail of how the extra knowledge helped in the preparation of the presentation.

Examples

1   I watched a television documentary on personality disorders in children, and it was interesting to see how some of the things which they did were similar to Verity's actions. This helped me to decide on suitable movements and gestures when I acted Verity in our performance.

2   I saw *A Day in the Death of Joe Egg*, which was another play looking at child disability and the effect it has on the family. It helped me to understand further how desperate and helpless the parents would feel.

3   I watched another group performing *Find Me*, but they had exaggerated the voices and actions to such an extent that the audience laughed and joined in what became, at times, almost melodramatic and farcical. These were quite the wrong styles for this play.

4   Before doing this, we had looked at the technical skills needed for good episodic drama, and this helped us to decide on suitable staging, lighting and costume for our production.

5   It is interesting to compare how disability was dealt with in earlier literature: e.g. Caliban in *The Tempest* or Smike in *Nicholas Nickleby*.

6   In the TV serial *Keeping Mum*, the old mother also had times, like Verity, when she appeared to be totally 'normal', while at other times she was obviously unstable.

Grammar

Have you written as correctly as you could?

Good essay-writers will always check their work at the end to make sure that they have not left any careless mistakes which they could have avoided. If you have word-processed your work, then it is sensible to use the spell and grammar check on your computer. Just make sure that it is working to English grammar and spelling rather than American! And remember that it cannot pick up any word which is used in the wrong sense. If you have written it longhand you might be able to ask someone else to help check your accuracy. In any case, you need to read carefully so that you pick up any mistakes you could have avoided.

As far as specific Drama terms are concerned, you can check with the first sections of this book, where different techniques are explained. You can also check names and facts from scripts and texts which you have used.

Extra methods of presenting written coursework

If you find writing essays of 500 words particularly difficult, or if you feel that the essay-form is not the most suitable way of presenting the necessary information on your particular piece of coursework, this syllabus allows you to use other methods in addition, such as:

- recording
- graphics
- mixed words and graphics.

Audio-recording

You may use a tape recorder to present your information. However, if you use this method, do listen to the recording at the end and make sure that you can be heard clearly, and that you make it understandable to someone who has not actually seen your piece of work.

Video-recording

You may record your work on video. If you are presenting a performance option, make sure that you can be seen (including your facial expressions – tie your hair back if necessary!) and heard clearly. If you are presenting a technical option make sure that the camera gives plenty of time to see your artefact in detail, and try to explain clearly each part of the artefact which you want to bring to your audience's attention. The camera may obviously need to zoom in at times to show, for example, facial expression, hand gesture, detail of a prop or make-up.

Graphics

This may include sketches, drawings, photographs, computer-aided designs, plans or models. You will need to take care that these are accompanied by explanatory notes so that your meaning is clear and that you are fulfilling all the examination requirements.

Mixed words and graphics

This might include work presented as wall-display material, or as a detailed programme to accompany a performance, or as a notebook to accompany the stages in presenting a technical design option. It would obviously have the required number of words, but these might be in sections; some of it might even be in note form or as quotes. It would have illustrations, photographs and sketches to help you to communicate your knowledge more clearly.

Examiners' tip

This is a very important section in preparing both for the written response to your Coursework, **and** for the Written Paper. Remember that you need to compare and contrast other texts you have studied with your own practical project, saying how you made use of what you learnt (Part 1 Assessment essay); what you feel should be done (Written Paper Section A); and what you saw (Written Paper Section B). Follow carefully the advice on note-taking and essay-writing, and it will help you to express your ideas clearly. The emphasis on simple, relevant statements with good reasoning and justification will make you very popular with the examiners!

Applying your skills through mini-projects

B1 Mini-projects

Using this section of the book

On the following pages, you will find a number of mini-projects which you can use to practise what you have learnt in Section A of this book. They will help you to use various techniques in a practical situation, and to see how the techniques fit into an actual presentation. If you work through a number of relevant projects, you should find that many of the routines become second nature to you and help you to improve the standard of your presentation.

Some mini-projects can be worked through in a short space of time but others may take four to five hours to complete. However, there is sufficient in them to enable you to work for much longer and to produce a much deeper, more extended piece of work if you wish to try working on something for eight or even ten hours. Obviously, the longer you have, the more preparation, rehearsal and performance techniques you will be able to employ.

So how do you get started on these projects? Below you will find a general guide to the stages that you need to go through whilst you are preparing a piece of work for presentation.

Stages of preparation and rehearsal

1 Look at **resource material** – stimulus, pictures, context, quotes, etc. – and discuss. Also **research** any necessary additional information.

2 Get into pairs or small working groups: **brainstorm** ideas of what you might include.

3 Try **improvising** two or three possible scenes, extracts or movement sequences. Designers: draw first sketches/make first notes of ideas.

4 **Discuss** your success, possible improvements and any possible developments, including group performance techniques (Section A4).

5 **Repeat** the same scenes, adjusting in the light of your discussion; and try other possible scenes, extracts or movement sequences which you might wish to include. Designers: adjust first ideas in the light of the discussion.

6 **Discuss** and **experiment** with rehearsal and personal performance techniques (Sections A2–A4) which improve **characterisation** and group **positioning**. Designers: discuss and draft developing ideas.

7 **Get to know your piece.** Begin to work to a time limit (four to five minutes?), with discussion and analysis of what you are doing, and choosing the best ideas whilst discarding the least suitable. If you are looking at a script, you should be learning your words as you practise: do not see them as an isolated activity, although you may need to put in extra time out of lessons to ensure that you are word perfect. You cannot improve your characterisation or action until you can put your script aside. If you are doing a Dance/Drama, make sure you know your intended movement sequences. Designers: consider other technical aspects.

8 **Experiment** with rehearsal techniques which improve the **emotion** and **atmosphere** of the scene. If you are using music or other sound, make sure that it fits the emotion and atmosphere you want. Designers: experiment with how to achieve the effects you want.

9 Organise essential **technical aspects** – such as costume, props, sound, set and special effects. Designers: make further adjustments as necessary.

10 **Polish** and **refine** until ready for performance. During this time, you may need to return to some of the rehearsal techniques to improve a particular aspect of your presentation. It is helpful to show a small audience the work in progress, and ask for constructive criticism. For example, do they see it as you intend? Do you need to do some things better? Do you need to cut out or add things? If your school or Drama Department has a video, this may be a good time to video what you are doing, so that you can see for yourselves! If you feel you are making no further progress with the scene, then you are probably ready to show it to an audience, but be prepared for the fact that they may still see things you could have done to improve the work!

Mini-project 1   Exporting children

To help you to use various **rehearsal techniques**.

Task

To produce an improvisation which tells the story of two brothers or sisters who were 'exported' to Australia.

Context

During the four decades until 1967 more than 10,000 children were uprooted from children's homes and poor or broken families in the UK, and transported to a new life, sometimes better but often worse, in institutions and farm schools throughout Australia. Some were told that they were going on holiday. The idea was to empty the crowded children's homes in Britain, and populate Australia with a future workforce.

On arrival in Australia, it was common for brothers and sisters to be split up. Some were even exported as babies, and grew up not knowing that they had brothers or sisters. Some children found themselves being used as slave labour in a new life which was brutal, violent and lonely.

Quotes

'I was told I was only going for 6 weeks.' *7-year-old*

'We arrived near Perth, and there were these nuns. I was expecting aunties and uncles. I asked where the aunties and uncles were. No-one replied.'   *10-year-old*

'We were frightened and scared on the ship. We were locked in our cabins, crying that we didn't want to go.'   *8-year-old*

'I never forgave her (mother) for the fact that she signed the papers and gave up responsibility for Sis and me.'   *9-year-old*

You could include:

- their situation at home in Britain
- setting off on their journey
- how they became separated
- life in Australia
- their reunion as adults.

Possible research:

- conditions on transport ships
- child migrants
- their life in Australia since migrating
- causes of overcrowding in children's homes.

Rehearsal techniques to be tried

Character modelling	Objectives	Hot-seating	Mime
Emotional memory	Thought-tracking	Tableau	Units
Internal dramatic dialogue	Improvisation	Blocking	

Focus   To help you to use various rehearsal techniques to help your preparation.

1   **The resource material**

Look carefully at the **photograph**.

- What do the clothes tell us? Costume often tells us something about the character of the person: can you see any characters in these children? Or are they all going to be the same? What brings you to your decision?
- How do you think the children are feeling? Are they all feeling the same? Or can you see different feelings in their body language and facial expressions? Do they seem to know anyone else?
- What are they taking with them? Try to imagine how much they could get into their luggage, and what decisions were made in choosing the things they could take.
- Are there any adults there? What are they doing? What can you tell about their thoughts and feelings?

Look at the **context**.

- What was going to happen to the children? What kind of life would they be expecting? What kind of life might they actually find?
- Why were children 'exported'? Do you think these were good reasons? Was this the best way to meet the two targets given: clearing the children's homes, and populating an empty country? Will your thoughts and feelings have any influence on your objectives/intentions for this piece?

Look at the **quotes**.

- What do these add to your understanding of the scene and characters? How might they help you in your role as one of the children?
- Do they give you any ideas for a scene you might improvise? Might they help you to decide on your actor objectives?

Might some extra **research** help you? Look at the suggestions but be realistic about time.

2   Get into pairs and look at the **you could include** box.

- **Brainstorm** ideas for your characters: how old are you? What is your home situation in England? Why have you been chosen to go to Australia?
- **Brainstorm** ideas for your scene: which parts of the story might be the most powerful? How could you make them effective? What are your objectives going to be? Which scene might help you to achieve your objectives best? How might you start, develop and end the scene?

3   Try quick **improvisations** of one or two possible scenes or extracts.

4   **Discuss** how they went. Did they go well? Or do you need to try a different scene? What would be good to leave in? What didn't work very well? What might be added to make them more effective? Were you managing to communicate emotion? Discuss possible personal performance techniques (Sections A3 and A4) which might help.

5   **Repeat** the same scenes and make suitable adjustments to them, in the light of your discussion. Try out any others which you think might be better.

6   **Discuss** how they went this time, and think about your own performance in greater detail. How will you develop your performance techniques to suit this role? This is the time to *experiment* with different ideas and techniques. Look at the **rehearsal techniques** which will help you to portray and develop your *character*, such as **hot-seating**,

character objectives and character modelling; and those which will help the *positioning* of the group as a whole, such as blocking and tableaux. When you have tried each technique, try to decide how it has helped you to improve your understanding and/or performance.

7   **Get to know your piece**. Begin to work to a time limit. It is better to have a piece which is short and thought-provoking, rather than something which drags on. Make final decisions about which parts to include and which to forget about. You need to think carefully about the opening and ending, **objectives**, **units**, development, interest and pace.

8   During this period, **experiment**. You may wish to use other rehearsal techniques, such as **off-text improvisation** and **mime**, which will help to make your character and situation clearer; and **emotional memory**, **thought-tracking** and **internal dramatic monologue** to help improve the *emotion* and *atmosphere* of the scene. When you have tried each technique, try to decide how it has helped you to improve your understanding and/or performance. You also need to check constantly on your own performance techniques, and how you might improve them.

9   Organise any essential **technical aspects**.
   ■   What **costume** are you each going to wear? Do they fit in with the historical period, and with each other? Where are you going to get them from? Can you move easily in them?
   ■   What **props** do you need? Have you already begun to practise with them? Where on stage or backstage do they need to be? Do they fit in with the historical time and place? Where are you going to get them? Are they going to break?
   ■   What **set** do you need? Think only about essentials, to give the impression of the location and time: do not worry about it being totally realistic.
   ■   Do you need any particular **sound** or **special effects**? Have these been prepared? Or are they being done 'live'? Where should they appear to come from? Who is going to be working them? Do they know what to do?
   ■   What **lighting** are you using? Have you practised with the lighting yet? How long will the lights take to set up? Who is going to be working them? Do they know what to do? Remember that the main purpose of lighting is to ensure that the actors can be seen! Make sure that you use enough lanterns to make this possible. (If your facial expressions can't be seen, you are probably not using enough light!) Once that is done, you can think about using available lanterns for helping with atmosphere or time of day, for example, but don't try to be over-ambitious. It probably will not work!

10 **Polish** and **refine** your work until you are ready for performance. You may need to go back to various **rehearsal techniques** even at this stage, if you feel that something is not going quite right and could be improved. This is also the time to try to give performances of your proposed scene or parts of it, and to get constructive advice on how things could be improved: having got the advice, do your best to take it! An audience often sees things differently from the way the actor intends, and the actor must, therefore, listen to criticism, and learn to give out the right signals, if he/she is to communicate effectively.

What you should have improved

The use of your rehearsal techniques: did you try them all? What did each help you to focus on? How did each help you in performing your role? Did you continue to use some of them throughout the rehearsal period? Which ones? Why?

For the future

This project should have helped you to identify the rehearsal techniques which are most useful at various stages of rehearsal. As you get more used to each of them, they will become second nature to you; and you will find that they are of tremendous help in any future work you do.

In examinations

Remember that you are awarded 30% of your final marks on your own performance, so any techniques which can improve your performance will obviously help to improve your mark. Rehearsal techniques undoubtedly help you to understand your character and situation more clearly, so obviously they will also help your overall performance.

Mini-project 2   Runaways

focus

To help you to develop your **performance techniques**.

Task

Using the starting script, newspaper headlines and random lines, produce a Devised Drama with five scenes. Link each scene with a narrator figure. The narrator can give factual information as well as locating and explaining the scenes.

Context

Every day young people run away from home and head towards London. They run away for a variety of reasons: some serious, some trivial. They face many dangers and an uncertain future.

They are prey to pimps and pushers who are on the lookout at train and bus stations for anyone, either male or female, who looks as though they are lost. Charities and other agencies can only offer very limited help to those who are young, and in many cases they have no option but to return the runaway to their home.

Random lines

'Here, try this. It'll make you feel warm.'
'Get a job, scrounger!'
'You can't sleep here. Go home!'
'I've got a mate who can give you a bed.'
'Sorry, no room left.'
'We have contacted your parents.'

Possible research:

- homelessness and shelters
- reasons for teenagers living rough
- charities which help the homeless
- Government initiatives to help the homeless.

Remember your preparation and rehearsal techniques!

Starting script

RUNAWAY:	You're not my father.
FATHER:	You will do what I tell you or else.
RUNAWAY:	Or else what? This isn't your home. You can't tell me what to do.
MOTHER:	Do what John says.
RUNAWAY:	I want my Dad back. He listened to me. This is all your fault.
FATHER:	Don't talk to your mother in that tone of voice. I'm warning you.
RUNAWAY:	Are you threatening me?
MOTHER:	John.
FATHER:	No, Joan. This has got to be said.
RUNAWAY:	Well, I'm not staying around to listen.
FATHER:	Yeah. Get out. This house will be a happier place without you.
RUNAWAY:	Fair enough.

Newspaper headlines

'Agony as parents wait'

'15 and a heroin addict'

'Girl 14 lured into prostitution'

'Boy aged 16 found frozen to death'

Personal performance techniques to consider

Posture	Movement	Gesture	Facial expression
Tone	Pitch	Accent	Rhythm
Flow	Pace	Pause	Circles of attention
Levels	Strength/tension	Mannerism	

Focus To help you to develop your performance techniques.

1   **The resource material**

Look carefully at the **photograph**.

- What is the main impact of this picture? How do you feel about the situation? Will this affect the way you devise your piece?
- What do the clothes tell you about the teenager?
- How do you think he is feeling? Try to see what he is showing – look particularly at the body language and facial expression.
- Look for any detail which gives an insight into what he does all day.

Look at the **context**.

- What are the facts about young runaways?
- What sorts of dangers are they exposed to? Why?
- What options might there be for the charities and other agencies?
- What do you think about teenage runaways? Will this affect your objectives in presenting your Drama?

Look at the **starting script**.

- What does the script tell you about the situation at home?
- What sort of character is Father? And Mother?
- Where are they during this conversation? Might this give you an idea for your setting?
- What has happened before the first words are spoken? Might this give you a suitable starting-point for your scene?

Look at the **random lines** and the **newspaper headlines**.

- What do these add to your understanding of the characters and situation? How might they help you in deciding on your own role?
- Do they give you any ideas for a scene you might improvise? Might they help you to decide on your actor objectives?

What about extra **research**? Look at the suggestions but be realistic about time.

2   Get into groups of about four or five.

- **Brainstorm** ideas for your characters: how old are you? Why are you here? What do you think about teenagers? And teenage runaways in particular?
- **Brainstorm** ways of using pieces of script and text: can you use any of the ones given in the resource material? Do you know of others which might be equally suitable? Which scenes might help you to achieve your objectives best?
- **Brainstorm** ways of using improvisation: what scenes might be most powerful in an improvised form? Why? How might you make them effective?

3   Try some quick **improvisations** on some of the possibilities.

4   **Discuss** how they went. Did they go well? Or do you need to rethink some scenes? What would be good to leave in? What didn't work very well? What might be added to make them more effective? How could you use the narrator to link the scenes? Will he/she use scripted words or unscripted? Were you managing to communicate emotion? Discuss possible group performance techniques (Section A4) which might help.

5 **Repeat** the same scenes and make suitable adjustments to them in the light of your discussion. Try out any others which you think might be better. Begin to experiment with how the narrator can help both the piece and the objectives.

6 **Discuss** how they went this time, make your final choices, and think about your own performance in greater detail. How will you develop your personal performance techniques to suit this role? **Experiment**, for example, with the use of your body – your **posture, movement, gesture, strength/tension** and **facial expression**? How will you use your voice – **tone, pitch, volume, accent**? Identify which techniques are most important for this particular role. This is the time, too, to look at rehearsal techniques which help you to portray and develop your *character*; and those which will help *position* the group as a whole.

7 **Get to know your piece**. Begin to work to a time limit. Remember that you must use both scripted and unscripted pieces, that you must have five scenes, and that you must link them with a narrator. While you must take care not to make the whole piece too long and dull, you must also take care, this time, that individual scenes are not too short! The audience must feel that they have gained something worthwhile from each scene, e.g. an additional piece of information, or a different emotion or reason. The **narration** will ensure that there are no long breaks between scenes: the whole piece should flow easily and continuously. You need to think carefully about objectives, development, interest and **pace**.

8 During this period, you will still need to **experiment** with your personal performance techniques: with **rhythm** and **flow**, **circles of attention**, **levels**, **pace** and **pause**. How important is each in the portrayal of *your* role? You also need to use rehearsal techniques which help to make the character and situation clearer, or to improve the *emotion* and *atmosphere*.

9 Organise any essential **technical aspects**.

- What **costume** are you each going to wear? Do they fit in with the historical period, and with each other? Where are you going to get them from? Can you move easily in them?
- What **props** do you need? Have you already begun to practise with them? Where on stage or backstage do they need to be? Do they fit in with the historical time and place? Where are you going to get them? Are they going to break?
- What **set** do you need? Think only about essentials, to give the impression of the location and time: do not worry about it being totally realistic.
- Do you need any particular **sound** or **special effects**? Have these been prepared? Or are they being done 'live'? Where should they appear to come from? Who is going to be working them? Do they know what to do?
- What **lighting** are you using? Have you practised with the lighting yet? How long will the lights take to set up? Who is going to be working them? Do they know what to do? Remember that the main purpose of lighting is to ensure that the actors can be seen! Make sure that you use enough lanterns to make this possible. (If your facial expressions can't be seen, you are probably not using enough light!) Once that is done, you can think about using available lanterns for helping with atmosphere or time of day, for example, but don't try to be over-ambitious. It probably will not work!

10 **Polish** and **refine** your work until you are ready for performance. You may need to go back to various rehearsal techniques even at this stage, if you feel that something is not going quite right and could be improved. This is also the time to try to give performances of your proposed scene or parts of it, and to get constructive advice on how things could be improved: having got the advice, do your best to take it! An audience often sees things differently from the way the actor intends, and the actor must, therefore, listen to criticism, and learn to give out the right signals, if he/she is to communicate effectively.

What you should have improved

Your understanding of how to improve your performance techniques.

■ As far as your personal skills are concerned, did you really think about every one of the body and voice techniques suggested? How did they help you to portray your character? How did they help you to communicate your objectives more effectively?

■ Did you use the most suitable *rehearsal* techniques to help you to improve your *performance* techniques? Did you experiment sufficiently?

For the future

This project should have helped you to consider more carefully different performance techniques, both from the individual point of view, and as part of the group. You will always need to think carefully about each one if you are to communicate your role as clearly as possible. With more practice, they will help you to improve the effectiveness of your performance still further.

In examinations

Remember that 30% of your final marks are awarded on your knowledge, understanding and use of **performance techniques**, so it is well worth improving them as far as you can! Look at Appendix 1 for the Assessment guidelines: these give more detail of what levels of skill are expected as you go up through the marks.

Mini-project 3 *The Ruined Abbey* or *The School Staff-Room*

Stimulus

- The extract of *The Ruined Abbey* on page 28.
- The general scenario of *The School Staff-Room* on page 30.

Task

To present either *The Ruined Abbey* or *The School Staff-Room*, using as many suitable group presentation techniques as are appropriate.

First considerations

- Decide whether you are going to do Scripted Acting, Improvisation or Dance/Drama.
- Identify the style/genre of the given script; *or*
- Decide what style/genre you are going to use for the Improvisation or Dance/Drama.
- Think through any work you did on the group performance techniques on this script and this scenario. What was particularly successful?

The Ruined Abbey

- Identify which group techniques are, or could be, used.
- How could you communicate clearly to the audience the switch in time?
- How might you break the script into units? What do you want to achieve in each unit?
- Are there points where the tone or pace should change? What are those changes?
- Are there opportunities for movement? When?

Remember your preparation, rehearsal and personal performance techniques!

The School Staff-Room

- Identify which group techniques might be suitable.
- How could you move smoothly from the introduction into the main scene?
- How might you break the piece into units? What do you want to achieve in each unit?
- How might you develop your scene and/or vary the pace to achieve your objectives?
- Have you created opportunities for movement? When?

Dance/Drama

- Decide whether you are going to use *The Ruined Abbey* or *The School Staff-Room*.
- Identify which group techniques might be suitable. How could you best use chorus, synchronised and solo movements?
- How might you break the piece into units? What do you want to achieve in each unit?
- How could you move smoothly between the introductory unit and the main scenes?
- How might you develop your scene and/or vary the pace to achieve your objectives?
- Might you use music or sound?

Possible research:

- abbey ruins in Britain
- the dissolution of the monasteries
- the life of monks/nuns
- how teachers behave in a staff-room.

Group performance techniques to be tried

Banners	Chorus	Counterpoint	Flashback/forward
Monologue	Narration	Physical theatre	Repetition and echo
Slow motion	Synchronised movement		

Focus To help you to use various group performance techniques in your presentation.

1 **The resource material**

Look at **the stimulus**.

- Read through the extract from *The Ruined Abbey* (page 28).
- Read through the general scenario for *The School Staff-Room* (page 30).

Look carefully at **the task**.

- What would be the advantages of presenting *The Ruined Abbey*? And the disadvantages?
- What would be the advantages of presenting *The School Staff-Room*? And the disadvantages?
- Remind yourselves of some of the possible **group performance techniques**, by referring to Section A4 (pages 28–36).

Get into groups of about six or seven, and look at the **first considerations**.

- Discuss whether your group would like to try the Scripted Acting, an Improvisation or a Dance/Drama.
- Discuss the style/genre of *The Ruined Abbey* and the possible styles/genres/types open to you for an Improvisation or Dance/Drama: refer to Section A5 (pages 37–45).
- Think through any work you did on the group performance techniques in Section A4 (pages 28–36). What do you feel was particularly successful? Can any of the ideas you had then be used now?

What about extra **research**? Look at the suggestions, but be realistic about time.

2 Once you have made those decisions, look at the relevant box for *The Ruined Abbey*, *The School Staff-Room* or **Dance/Drama**.

- **Brainstorm** the roles. What sort of people are these? How might they be played? What are the most important aspects to their characters? Who will play each role? What will your actor objectives be?
- **Brainstorm** the scenes. Where will they be? How can you suggest the locations? How can you move from one to another?
- **Brainstorm** where you might identify different units. What is the key to each unit? What do you want to achieve in each unit? How can you best do that?
- **Brainstorm** possible movement. Where will the opportunities for the most movement come? What sort of movement will that be? How will you provide suitable movement at other times?
- **Brainstorm** ideas for any music or sound to be used. When would it be used? What effect do you want to create? How will you do so?

3 Try short **improvisations** on some of the best of the ideas discussed so far.

4 **Discuss** the success of what you have just tried. Did they go well? What didn't work? What do you want to keep? What needs to be added? How well did you manage your movement opportunities? Discuss, in particular, any **group performance techniques**, such as **counterpoint**, **flashback**, **physical theatre**, **chorus** and **slow motion**, which you tried. Which ones worked best?

5 **Repeat** the same scenes, making suitable adjustments to them in the light of your discussion; and try some of the other ideas and parts of the story which seem to link with them.

6 **Discuss** again and **experiment** with various rehearsal techniques which will help with your own *characterisation* and with group *positioning*. What personal performance techniques are you going to need to improve your role?

7 **Get to know your piece.** This is the time to begin to make definite decisions about, for example, what you want to include, how the general shape of the piece is developing, how long the piece will be, what accompaniment you are using, and whether you have learnt your lines. Consider carefully what the pace of the piece will be at various times during the drama, when this changes, and whether pause/silence/stillness can be used to good effect.

8 **Experiment** with techniques which are going to improve the communication of *emotion* and *atmosphere*, and which will help to emphasise your objectives. You will need to look carefully at your performance techniques and especially the group performance techniques. Are you using them suitably and effectively?

9 Organise any essential **technical** aspects.

■ What **costume** are you each going to wear? Why? Do they fit in with each other? Can you move easily in them? Where are you going to get them?

■ What **props** do you need? Have you already begun to practise with them? Where on stage or backstage do they need to be? Do they fit in with the style/genre? Where are you going to get them? Are they going to break?

■ What **set** do you need? Think only about essentials, to give the impression of the location and characters. There is no need to be totally realistic, and Dance/Drama is often more symbolic or impressionistic. It may even be that a bare stage is the most suitable, although changes of level will add to the visual interest.

■ Do you need any particular **sound** or **special effects**? Have these been prepared properly? Are any being done 'live'? Where should they appear to come from? Who is going to be working them? Do they know what to do?

■ What **lighting** are you using? Have you practised with the lighting yet? How long will the lights take to set up? Who is going to be working them? Do they know what to do? Remember that the main purpose of lighting is to ensure that the actors/dancers can be seen! Once you have allocated sufficient lanterns to light your stage and actors/dancers, then you can think about using any spare lanterns for helping with any atmosphere you might want to create.

10 **Polish** and **refine** your work until you are ready for performance. You may need to go back to rehearsal techniques, even at this stage, if you feel that something is not going quite right and could be improved. This is also the time to try to give performances of your piece or parts of it, and to get constructive advice on how things could be improved: having asked for the advice, do your best to take it! An audience often sees things differently from the way that the actor/dancer intends, and you must, therefore, listen to criticism and learn from other people if your communication is to be successful.

What you should have improved

Your understanding of how to use various group performance techniques in your presentation.

■ Did you choose the best performance option? If not, why not? What can you learn for the future?

■ Did you choose the most suitable group techniques to fit both the piece and the style/genre?

■ Did you use the most suitable rehearsal techniques to help you to understand and improve your role and groupwork?

- Did you think carefully enough about your performance techniques, both as an individual and as part of a group? Did you experiment sufficiently to come to the best decisions?
- How well did you know everyone else's roles and movements? How aware were you of the others whilst actually in performance?
- Did you use your technical areas as well as you could? Did you try performing parts of your piece during rehearsal in order to get advice? Did you take the advice given? How effective and successful was your final performance?

For the future

This project should have helped you to consider more carefully what group performance techniques you might use; but also to recognise whether they are appropriate to the particular scene or moment. The different techniques are intended to help the interest and understanding for your audience, so always consider which ones you might use. However, recognise that the same audience does not always want to see the same techniques used every time!

In examinations

Remember that you can only offer one scripted piece and one unscripted. You will be awarded 30% of your final marks on how well you understand, respond to and present your performance. Obviously, the more thoroughly you can prepare, the better your performance will be, so you need to use your rehearsal period as well as you possibly can.

Mini-project 4   Healthy eating for Year 7

focus

To help you to prepare a suitable **Theatre-in-Education** performance for a different age group.

Dear Marianne,

Can you help me please. I do love junk food – crisps and hamburgers especially, and I cannot resist the offer of chocolate. I am only slightly overweight and would love to be as slim as my friends. My parents say it's the food I eat. I do sports, and I play hockey for the school, so I think I am fit.

Can you tell me what is good for me and why I should change my diet?

Yours truly,
Emma

Task

Year 7 are looking at healthy eating as part of their PSHE programme, and also in their Food Technology lessons. To support this work, you have been asked to produce a short Theatre-in-Education (TIE) performance to highlight some of the issues contained in the letter. Your aim is to deliver an entertaining and informative piece of work that does not 'preach', but aims to inform and offer choices.

Possible research:

- anorexia
- diets
- junk food
- exercise and fitness
- the 'perfect' shape
- food advertising.

Techniques you may want to include in the performance:

- characterising aspects of the issue: perhaps have someone playing Chocolate
- using hot-seating as part of the performance, with characters being questioned by the audience
- using a characterised narrator, e.g. Emma from the letter above
- involving the audience in the play, e.g. inviting volunteers into a well-prepared part of the story.

Points to consider:

- the research which will be necessary: including websites and factual diet information
- producing a survey of eating habits in Year 7
- making a display for the performance area
- meeting your audience before you start planning
- attending a Year 7 lesson on the issue
- trying not to sound like teacher telling the audience what to do
- bringing variety to your presentation
- making the performance active, and involving the audience
- giving a balanced and realistic point of view. Is it realistic to say never eat another hamburger in your life?
- how could you follow up the performance?
- finding out what the audience has learned.

Techniques

- Remember to prepare thoroughly.
- Which rehearsal techniques will be the most useful for this piece of work?
- Which performance techniques will be the most important?
- Which group techniques might you use?

Focus To help you to prepare a suitable Theatre-in-Education performance for a different age group.

1 **The resource material**

Look at the **letter**.

- Does this reflect a typical feeling of teenage girls? Of teenage boys?
- What do you think she means by 'slightly overweight'? Why is she? Does it matter?
- What is a suitable diet for growing youngsters? Why?
- For what reasons should teenagers change their diets?

Look at the **task**.

- What is the objective of this task?
- What issues are contained in the letter? Make a list, and then number them according to their importance.

Look at the **points to consider**.

- Do you have the necessary knowledge to deliver what is needed? If not, how will you get it?
- How might you 'meet your audience'? What will you ask them?
- How can you discover what they already know? And what the teachers would like you to emphasise?
- What is a 'balanced and realistic view'?
- How might you 'follow up' the performance?

What about extra **research**? Look at the suggestions, but be realistic about time.

2 Get into small groups and **brainstorm** ideas for:

- the scenes and characters
- ways of producing an 'entertaining and informative' piece of work; e.g. the use of humour to make a serious point
- ways of avoiding 'preaching' at your audience, or just sounding like 'teacher telling them what not to do'
- ways of bringing variety and interactivity.

3 Try some short **improvisations** on some of the best of the ideas discussed so far.

4 **Discuss** the success of what you have just tried. Did the ideas go well? What is worth keeping in? What didn't work? What needs to be added? Or changed? Which group techniques might be relevant and effective?

5 **Repeat** the same scenes, adjusting them in the light of your discussion; and try some of the other ideas which you feel might be good, or which link in with those you have already found to be fairly successful.

6 **Discuss** again and **experiment** with various rehearsal and performance techniques which will help you with your own *characterisation* and with group *positioning*.

7 **Get to know your piece.** Now is the time to begin to make definite decisions about what to include, how the general shape of the piece is going to develop, how to involve the audience without losing control(!), and how long it is going to be if it is to be interesting and fun as well as informative.

8   **Experiment** with techniques which are going to improve the learning of the lesson – and help you to succeed in your objectives.

9   Organise any essential **technical aspects**.

- What **costume** are you each going to wear? Why? Do they fit in with each other? Can you move easily in them? Where are you going to get them?
- What **props** do you need? Have you already begun to practise with them? Where on stage or backstage do they need to be? Do they fit in with the style/genre? Where are you going to get them? Are they going to break?
- What **set** do you need? Think only about essentials, to give the impression of the location and characters. Does your piece need to have a realistic set? Or might it be more symbolic? Or even an almost bare stage?
- Do you need any particular **sound** or **special effects**? Have these been prepared properly? Are any being done 'live'? Where should they appear to come from? Who is going to be working them? Do they know what to do?
- What **lighting** are you using? Have you practised with the lighting yet? How long will the lights take to set up? Who is going to be working them? Do they know what to do? Remember that the main purpose of lighting is to ensure that the actors can be seen! Once you have allocated sufficient lanterns to light your stage and actors, then you can think about using any spare lanterns for helping with any effects you might want to create.

10   **Polish** and **refine** your work until you are ready for performance. You may need to go back to rehearsal techniques, even at this stage, if you feel that something is not going quite right and could be improved. This is also the time to try to give performances of your piece or parts of it, and to get constructive advice on how things could be improved: having asked for the advice, do your best to take it! An audience often sees things differently from the way that the actor intends, and you must, therefore, listen to criticism and learn from other people if your communication is to be successful.

What you should have improved

Your understanding of how to prepare a Theatre-in-Education performance for a different age group.

- Did you think carefully about the resource material, and your objectives?
- Did you use suitable rehearsal techniques to help you to understand and perform your role and presentation?
- Did you think carefully enough about your performance techniques, both as an individual and as part of the group? Did you experiment sufficiently to come to the best decisions?
- How well did you know everyone else's roles and responsibilities? How would you have covered if someone had been away? How aware were you of each of the others when actually in performance?
- Did you use your technical areas as well as you could?
- Did you try performing parts of your piece during the preparation period in order to get advice? Did you take the advice? How successful was your final performance?

For the future

This project should have helped you to think more carefully about the whole process of presenting an effective piece of Theatre-in-Education. Always remember that you must get to know something of your chosen audience – their knowledge and understanding, their interests and likes, their needs – and always keep that in mind as you rehearse.

In examinations

Remember that you can only offer TIE as an unscripted piece of work, and that you must offer an acting or technical skill for your scripted piece. You will be awarded 30% of your final marks on how well you understand, respond to and perform your TIE presentation. Obviously, the better you know your audience, and the more thoroughly you rehearse, the better your final performance will be.

Resource for mini-projects 5 and 6: *The Last Hurdle* by R. D. Price

The lights come up on JANE, *who sits surrounded by packing cases, suitcases and cardboard boxes.* JANE *sits and stares into the audience, motionless and expressionless.* MARTIN *enters.*

	MARTIN	The van is due at four.
	JANE	Yeah.
	MARTIN	I've been over and seen the place again. They have left it nice and clean. It's strange seeing the place empty. (*Pause.*) Are you listening to me?
5	JANE	I'll clear up.
	MARTIN	I didn't mean for you . . . Oh, forget it.
	JANE	I shall.
	MARTIN	Look at me, Jane. I know what this is all about. I don't like it but I am going into Tara's room. I will do it either with you or without you. (*Pause.*)
10	JANE	No.
	MARTIN	No what?
	JANE	I can't . . . I can't leave her here. How can you?
	MARTIN	She's not here anymore.
	JANE	So cold . . . so rational, logical. Look. Here's where she put crayon on the new wallpaper. Here she chipped the door frame with her tricycle. She's everywhere.
15		
	MARTIN	I know . . . I know.
	JANE	No you don't.
	MARTIN	Look, the flat is sold. A new start. You wanted it as much as I do.

Door bell/knock.

20		I think I know who it is.
	JANE	How could you . . . Coward!

Enter JANE'S *mother.*

	MOTHER	So is it done?
	MARTIN	Ask your daughter.
	MOTHER	Your wife . . . Okay, Jane. Here's the bottom line. You are moving. You have to clear Tara's room. Either you two do it or I will. This place is the past. The bad times are over. Time to start afresh.
25		
	MARTIN	That's what I've been saying.
	MOTHER	Shut up, Martin.
	JANE	If anyone is going in there it's going to be me. Just give me some time.

Pause.

30	MOTHER	Here's a box . . . Are you sure?
	MARTIN	I want to help. We should do this together.
	MOTHER	I think I will make us a cup of tea. I suppose you have packed the stronger stuff.

MOTHER *exits.*

35	MARTIN	Come on. (JANE *takes* MARTIN'S *hand.*) A deep breath (*They reach the door of the bedroom.*) The last hurdle.

They exit together, with the box, into Tara's room.

BLACKOUT.

Mini-project 5 *The Last Hurdle* (performance)

focus

To help you put a serious piece of **Scripted Drama** into **performance**.

Task

To perform the script of *The Last Hurdle*.

Context

Jane and Martin met at university, and after completing their studies they got married. They had a daughter called Tara. They live in a flat on the fourth floor. When Martin went out or went to work, Jane and Tara used to wave him off from the balcony of the flat. One fateful day Jane was distracted by the telephone ringing and Tara, not wanting to miss waving to Daddy, climbed onto a table on the balcony, and fell. Tara died.

Jane and Martin have had a terrible time coming to terms with the accident, and have decided to move and start their life again in a new home. Their problem at this moment is that they have never been into Tara's bedroom since her death.

Advice

This should be a very emotional scene, and should be approached, rehearsed and performed with sensitivity and understanding. To help you achieve a realistic and thoughtful performance you should consider the characters carefully and explore the issue and the relationships that appear within the script.

Off-text Improvisations

- The day Jane and Martin moved into their first home together.
- Mother trying to persuade Jane to empty Tara's room before new buyers come to look at the flat.
- Showing round a new buyer, and avoiding Tara's bedroom.
- Jane and Martin after they have cleared out the room and are leaving the flat for the last time.

Research:

- bereavement
- moving home
- marriage
- shock and trauma.

Working on the text

- Break the script up into **units**, and decide what you want to achieve in each unit.
- What should the **pace** of each unit be? Identify the points where **pause** could be used to good effect.
- Are there points where the **tone** of the dialogue changes?
- Make choices about your performance space. Where will the audience be?
- Decide on points in the script where there are opportunities for **movement**.
- How could lighting and sound create the right **atmosphere** for the script?
- How could **circles of attention** be used in the opening of the piece? With what effect?
- What effect do you want to have on your audience? Sort out your **actor objectives**.

Techniques

- Remember to prepare thoroughly.
- Which rehearsal techniques will be most useful for this piece of work?
- Which performance techniques will be the most important?
- Which group techniques might you use?

Focus To help you put a serious piece of Scripted Drama into performance.

1 The **resource material**

Look carefully at the **context**.

- What are the most relevant facts?
- How has Tara's death affected Martin and Jane?
- Do you think the move is a good idea?
- Can you understand their feelings about going into Tara's room after her death?

Look carefully at the **script**.

- Do Martin and Jane both show the same reactions and feelings to what has happened? If so, what are they? If not, how do they differ?
- What sort of character is Jane? And Martin?
- What can you tell about their relationship at the moment? Does this have any relevance to Tara? Or to this piece of Drama?
- What sort of a character is Mother?
- What has happened immediately before the first words are spoken? How long, for example, has Jane been sitting there?

Look at the **advice**.

- What emotions are you being asked to communicate?
- What 'sensitivity' and 'understanding' are needed in your performance?
- How do you think parents do overcome a tragedy of this sort?

What about extra **research**? Look at the suggestions, but be realistic about time.

2 Get into groups of three, and **brainstorm** ideas that you could use:

- for the **characters**: How old are you? How are you feeling? What are you thinking? What do you think about each other? How do you use your movement? Your body language? Your voice?
- for the group's **overall objectives** and for the **actor objectives**: which words or actions become the most important for the actors to emphasise? How might you do this?

3 Try some **on-text improvisations** of parts of the scene to help you to feel your character, and to help you communicate your objectives.

4 **Discuss** how they went. Did you begin to understand your character? To feel for him/her? How can you show your understanding? Did you show any emotion? Did you manage to use the right emphasis to communicate your objectives to an audience? What else do you think you need to do to make them clearer? What performance techniques do you need in this role?

5 **Repeat** the same extracts, in the light of your discussion, but this time using the scripted words. Then try linking them with other parts of the script which help you to build up to the extracts already tried.

6 **Discuss** and **experiment**, engaging in rehearsal techniques which will help you to improve your *characterisation* and *positioning* – such as some of the suggested off-text improvisations.

7 Begin to **get to know your script**.

- It should begin to feel right as a whole; with frequent discussion and analysis of what you are doing, choosing the best ideas and discarding the least successful.
- What does the script tell you about **movement** or **gesture**? Where else might either be suitable or even advisable?
- Decide where you will perform and where your audience will be.
- Begin to look at the **units** within the script, so that you can focus your work successfully and recognise the importance of each part of the scene. What do you want to achieve in each unit? Where might **pause** help? Where does the **tone** of dialogue change? Will this affect the **pace**?
- This is the time to learn your words – not in isolation, away from the action. While you are reading and practising, begin to feel that the words come out of your actions or the actions come out of your words, so that they become totally interlinked. Obviously you may need to spend more time out of lessons making sure that you do, indeed, know your words, because until you can put the script aside you cannot concentrate fully on either the character or the situation.

8 **Experiment**. Look carefully at performance techniques and engage in rehearsal techniques which will help you to convey the *emotion* and *atmosphere*. These are also helped by getting the pace right at different points in the scene. Use your understanding of circles of attention to help.

9 Organise any essential **technical aspects**.

- What **costume** are you each going to wear? Do they fit in with the situation, and with each other? Where are you going to get them from? Can you move easily in them?
- What **props** do you need? Have you already begun to practise with them? Where on stage or backstage do they need to be? Where are you going to get them? Are they going to break?
- What **set** do you need? Bear in mind that you only need an impression for this script, so that you do not distract from the characters and the objectives.
- Do you need any **sound** or **special effects**? Have these been prepared? Or are they being done 'live'? Where should they appear to come from? Who is going to be working them? Do they know what to do?
- What **lighting** are you using? Have you practised with lighting yet? How long will the lights take to set up? Who is going to be working them? Do they know what to do? Bear in mind that for this play, you do not need anything which will distract from the characters and the objectives.

10 **Polish** and **refine** your work until you are ready for performance. You may need to go back to various rehearsal techniques even at this stage, if you feel that something is not going quite right and could be improved. This is also the time to give performances of parts of your play, and to get constructive advice on how things could be improved: and having got the advice, do your best to take it! An audience often sees things differently from the way the actor intends, so listen to what your advisers have to say.

What you should have improved

Your understanding of how to put a serious piece of Scripted Drama into performance.

- Did you think carefully about the resource material, and your objectives?
- Did you use suitable rehearsal techniques to help you understand your character and situation?

- Did you think carefully about your performance techniques, both as an individual and as part of the group? Did you experiment sufficiently to come to the best decisions?
- How well did you learn your script during actual rehearsals? How much extra did you have to do out of lessons? In the end, did you know it well enough for you to get right into your character?
- Did you use your technical areas as well as you could? Did you try performing parts of it during rehearsal in order to get some advice? How effective and successful was your final performance?

For the future

This project should have helped you to think more carefully about the different stages of rehearsing a piece of Scripted Drama, and how best to tackle the overall challenge of the script itself. As you try more and longer scripts, you will need to find the best method of learning lines, but always remember that the words and actions go together, so don't see them as separate activities. Possible aids to memorising include: repetition of units; making a sound tape of the dialogue; writing the words down; saying the words like a rap, much as you might learn the words of a song; and using the help of a parent or friend to hear you. Always try to think about the author's objectives in writing the piece, and how you can best communicate these to the audience.

In examinations

Remember that you must offer one scripted option in your coursework, which means that you will be awarded 30% of your final marks on how well you understand, respond to and put a script into performance. Obviously, the better you can prepare, the better your performance will be, so you will always need to put maximum thought into every stage of rehearsal.

Mini-project 6 *The Last Hurdle* (technical)

focus

To understand better how **technical aspects** fit in with an actual performance. For this, you will work with a group performing *The Last Hurdle* (mini-project 5).

Task

To read through the instructions and then **present** one of the aspects outlined.

Set

- Start by reading the script (page 81).
- Make a list of all the essential elements of the set that the script needs. How many doors? In which room in the flat does this scene take place? How realistic does it need to be? What mood or atmosphere would you like to create with your setting, e.g. do you want a bright cheerful room?
- Look at the equipment that the department has for you to use. How many stage flats are available? Have you enough scenery braces and weights for the flats? Measure the width and height of any flats you wish to use. This will be important when you draw up your design for the set. Make a decision on the colour and texture of the walls, e.g. do you want the flats to look like wallpaper? Do you need to consider stencilling? Look at the colour charts and wallpaper samples, and later attach any you might use to your design work.
- Examine and measure the proposed performance space and the likely position of the audience. Make a rough plan of the performing space and start to position the flats. You could make small scale simple 'cut-outs' to help you to make your choices. Are the doors important in the piece? Should they stand out from the rest of the set? Where should they be positioned? Which way should they open? Careful consideration will have to be given to the location of Tara's bedroom door.
- Have you given enough room for the actors to move in? Is there enough room for any furniture or boxes that the directors and actors want? What pieces of stage furniture are you intending to use? Where will they be positioned?
- Consider your decisions in relation to the audience. Can all the audience see everything that will happen on stage? Will your design distract the audience from the action on stage?
- Share your ideas with anyone dealing with the lighting of this scene. What compromises would you both have to make if this were the 'real thing'?
- Create a scaled ground plan with the position of your set marked clearly.

Costume

- Start by reading the script (page 81). Pay particular attention to the role of Jane.
- Decide how the situation she is in and her emotional state may affect what she is wearing. Consider what she is doing in the script, and how this might determine what she is wearing. Will the time of day or season affect the clothes she is wearing?
- Think about how old the character may be, and what clothes she might have chosen to purchase in the past couple of years, before the accident.
- Think about suitable colours. The colour of the set may need to be considered, as this might affect your final choice. Now think about the types and textures of the fabrics which she might be wearing. Collect samples of different fabrics that you think might be

suitable. You may be able to get these from your Textiles Room or from home or from a shop. You should attach these to your design work.

■ Share your ideas with anyone who is doing the make-up for this character. What compromises would you both have to make if this were the 'real thing'?

■ Draw a body outline, and then draw on the costume which you think would be suitable; or use the costume design sheet in Appendix 10 (page 250).

Make-up

■ Start by reading the script (page 81). Pay particular attention to the role of Jane.

■ Decide how the situation she is in, and how her emotional state, may affect how she appears. Make a list of key words for her character as seen in this piece, e.g. adult, tired, etc.

■ Consider the lighting and how near the audience will be to the performer. This will help you to decide the amount of make-up which you will need to apply to achieve a realistic effect.

■ Start with a decision on Jane's overall complexion colour. You may wish to try pale colours to indicate her tiredness and poor health. Try out different colours on your design paper. You might wish to use a copy of the make-up design sheet in Appendix 9 (page 249).

■ Next focus on the eyes. Draw some eye shapes on your design paper, and experiment with light shades of red and grey close to the eyeline, to indicate that she has perhaps been crying. As she has been suffering a great deal of emotional stress, you might want to try some faint worry lines around the eyes. Try to keep these faint as she is still young; and you don't want to make her look as if she is aged!

■ Draw some lip shapes on your design paper and experiment with different colours. You may decide that too much colour makes her look as if she is wearing fashion make-up: would she be doing so? Try changing her natural lip colour by using paler lipsticks.

■ Think about the hair. Would it appear washed, clean and dressed? Would it be best to keep the hair away from the face to allow a view of the performer's facial expression and your make-up effects? Draw an outline of the head, and try to indicate how you would do her hair.

■ After trying out your ideas one by one, draw a complete face outline. Try putting the different elements of the make-up all together, in order to see the overall effect. Does this reflect how you understand the character?

■ Share your ideas with anyone who is doing the costume for this character. What compromises would you both have to make if this were the 'real thing'?

■ Draw another face outline, or use another design sheet, and transfer your ideas into a final design. Give details of the colours and numbers of the make-up products you have selected. (All stage make-up, whatever type, uses the same names and numbers.) Give details of the brush sizes and any other equipment that helped you to create the effects you have chosen.

Properties

■ Start by reading the script (page 81).

■ Make a list of all the possible props that are needed for the script. What is the purpose of each in this script?

■ What additional props could you suggest to enhance the action of the script? Many students performing this play have included one of Tara's treasured toys; but what other opportunities are there?

- Jane is described as being surrounded by packing cases. Are these likely to be set dressing – or will they be used? One box is certainly used at the end of the scene – and is, therefore, a prop. What size, colour, shape should this be? Should it look new or well used? You will need to consider the action of the scene in making your decision.
- Create initial drawings for a prop which you might make, giving reasons for your choice and for any decisions made.
- Show how the prop is to be constructed with details of construction methods.

Lighting

- Start by reading the script (page 81). Pay particular attention to the stage directions, and to where the actors are going to be. Remember that they must be lit at all times.
- Decide what mood or atmosphere you think would be right for the scene; and think about what time of day the scene takes place. Select an overall colour which you think would be suitable. (Remember that white is a colour!)
- What set must there be on stage? For instance, the script requires two doors. Where would these be placed? How would they be lit? What colour are the stage flats? Will this affect the colour you want?
- Look through a sample book of stage lighting *filters*, or *gels*: or look at the gels your Drama Department has in stock. Under supervision from your teacher, take one lantern and place it on a floor stand. Place the gel in the filter frame, put the frame into the lantern, and then switch it on. Is this the colour you want?
- Examine the proposed performance space and the position of the audience. Draw up a ground plan of the stage. Place on your plan the position of your lighting bars and plug sockets. Then select from your lantern stock the types of lantern that you would use, and indicate on your plan where you would place the lanterns in order to cover the area you want lit. Make sure that you are not going to blind the audience by shining the light into their eyes!
- If you now look at the lighting control desk, you can make a decision about the intensity or brightness of the individual lanterns. You may need to think about earlier decisions on the time of day for the scene.
- Prepare a cue-sheet to show when you need to put lights on and off, and when any changes might be made. Look at the lighting cue-sheet in Appendix 7 (page 247).

Sound

- Start by reading the script (page 81).
- Examine what sound effects are needed. Do you wish only to create the required sounds, such as the knock or ring at the door? Or do you wish to enhance the mood and atmosphere of the scene with carefully selected background sound or music?
- Could the script have a sound 'prologue' and 'epilogue' to set the right tone for the performance, and to complement the emotional conclusion?
- Can you make the performance more realistic by adding effects such as Mother's footsteps climbing the stairs, or her efforts in the kitchen to make something to drink?
- Look at the equipment which is available for your use. Are there tape players or CD players? Are there microphones that you can use, either live or to record your sound choices?
- Decide whether you wish to have 'live' or recorded effects. You may wish to use pre-recorded sound effects taken from BBC sound effects tapes or CD collections.
- Consider your decisions in relation to your audience. What will your sound design communicate to the audience?
- Think about the performance space. What level of volume will be required for the different effects? Can you create the impression of distance through varying the volume?

- Share your ideas with anyone doing lighting design for the script, especially if you are creating atmosphere through sound.
- Create sound cue-sheets – see Appendix 8 (page 248).

Stage management

- Start by reading the script (page 81). Pay particular attention to the action of the scene.
- Investigate if anyone is exploring set design for the script. You will need to discuss their design as a basis for your stage management. If there is no-one doing the set, then you must decide on a simple setting that you could create (see the advice under *set* at the beginning of this mini-project).
- Is anyone doing the props? You will need to discuss with them what they are providing, and when. If no-one is doing the props, then you must check that all necessary props are being provided by members of the cast: or whether you need to find any. You must also decide where the props are going to be stored and positioned.
- As you will be responsible for putting up and striking (taking down) the set, and preparing the stage for performance, create a diagram showing the positions of all scenery, props and stage dressing.
- Is anyone doing lighting? Or sound? You will need to discuss their ideas, and ensure that all technical areas are coming together to provide a unity. If no-one is doing lighting or sound, then you need to decide who is providing any essential requirements – whether this will be done by members of the cast or whether you need to do it. You must also be ready to stand in as the lighting/sound operator during rehearsals and performance.
- How would the backstage area need to be organised? What other people would you need backstage? Where will they be? Where would be the best location backstage for props?
- Write out your own copy of the script. Using this as your prompt copy/stage manager's book, write on it any information you need in order to 'run the show'.

What you should have improved

Your understanding of the basic considerations for the technical designer; and how the technical aspects fit in with an actual performance.

- Did you choose the most suitable aspect for you? Did you have any difficulties?
- Did you actually work alongside the performers? If so, what problems arose? If not, what problems do you think might arise in a real situation?
- Did you consider the other technical aspects?

For the future

This project should have helped you to understand better the problems faced by the technical designers when they are working directly with a performing group – as you must do, if you choose a technical area for one of your coursework options. You will need to improve your understanding and your skills by working on technical aspects again: and to improve your creativity by working on presentations which offer more demanding technical ideas.

In examinations

Remember that you can only offer one technical option for your coursework, as you must also do one performance skill. However, you may offer the technical work with either a scripted piece or an unscripted piece: whichever you do, try to work with a performance which gives you the opportunity to show your ideas and understanding. You will be awarded 30% of your final marks on how well you understand your technical area, respond to the task, and use your design ideas for an effective presentation.

Mini-project 7 Cats

focus

To help you to see different possibilities from a **musical stimulus**.

Stimulus

'The Cat Duet' by Rossini. (Ask your Music Department for a record/tape/CD.)

Questions

- Who are these cats? What sorts of characters do they have? What are their names?
- What are they doing? Where are they?
- How do cats sit/move? What 'gestures/mannerisms' do they have?
- How do cats 'speak'?
- How do cats show character and feelings through voice and body language?

Encyclopedia facts

- Cats are well adapted for hunting: their ears, eyes, whiskers and nose are all very well-developed and acute organs of sense. In order to pursue their prey, cats make use of scent, sight and hearing: they can often be seen twitching their ears or whiskers as they pick up various signals, and we can see very clearly when their large eyes change their area of focus.
- They are experts in the art of leaping; from a running, walking, standing or sitting position, they can catapult themselves into the air; even when landing from a height, they can land perfectly balanced on their feet.
- Because they can withdraw their claws, they can move silently on their pads. They lift their paws carefully when moving slowly, and almost glide along the ground when moving more quickly.
- Stretching and washing tend to be smooth, almost lazy actions, reflecting relaxation and contentment.

Cats in poetry

Old Possum's Book of Practical Cats by T. S. Eliot
'To a Cat' by John Keats
'My Cat Jeoffrey' by Christopher Smart

Task

To prepare and present a piece of performance Drama based on Rossini's 'The Cat Duet'.

Extra research

- Watch cats! Especially the ways they move, hold their bodies, show their feelings.
- Look at pictures of cats, especially in movement.
- Find information about cat behaviour.

Possible approaches:

- to create an improvised piece of Comedy/Farce between a small group of cats
- to create a fantasy Dance/Drama between these two cats and one other character
- to create a piece of Devised thematic work on cats, using some of the literary sources as your script, or as links between scenes
- to create an interactive, introductory unit to teach young children about animal movement
- to create a masked or puppet performance.

Techniques

- Remember to prepare thoroughly.
- Which rehearsal techniques will be the most useful for this piece of work?
- Which performance techniques will be the most important?
- Which group techniques might you use?
- Which technical techniques can be used to help the overall effect?

Focus To help you see different possibilities from a musical stimulus.

1   The **resource material**

Close your eyes (for better concentration) and listen to the music.

- What is your immediate reaction to this piece? Why?
- What did the music make you imagine while you were listening to it?
- It is a comic piece of musical composition. What brings out the comedy?

Look at the **encyclopedia facts**.

- What do they tell you about the ways which a cat uses its sense organs?
- What do they tell you about a cat's movement generally?
- What special advantages does a cat have over some other animals?
- How does their movement tell you something about their thoughts and feelings?

Look at **Cats in poetry**.
(Ask your English Department for copies of the book or poems.)

- How do the writers regard cats? How do you know?
- What do they tell you that you hadn't actually thought about before?
- How do they capture the reader's interest?

What about extra **research**? Look at the suggestions, but be realistic about time.

2   Get into small groups (five or fewer) and look at **possible approaches**.

- **Brainstorm** possibilities for the various suggestions given. Which style/genre might be used? Are there any other possibilities from this musical stimulus?
- **Brainstorm** ideas for characters for cats. Which are most suitable for different styles/genres?
- **Brainstorm** ideas for scenes. Which are most suitable for different styles/genres?
- **Brainstorm** ways of using masks or puppets for this piece of work.
- **Brainstorm** for the group's overall objectives.

3   Try three or four short **improvisations** on some of the best ideas discussed so far. Try to experiment with more than one possible approach at this stage.

4   **Discuss** the success of what you have just tried. How well did they go? What might be worth keeping? What didn't work? Which approach seemed to be the most rewarding? How well did you manage to get the right movement? What needs to be added? Think about possible performance techniques which might be useful in communicating your objectives.

5   **Repeat** the same extracts, adjusting them in the light of your discussion, and try some of the other ideas which might link in with them. If you are going to use masks or puppets, then begin to make them. You are likely to need them from now on, in order to develop your performance properly.

Masks

- Unless you are used to making and using masks, consider using a simple full-face mask. If you are already competent in maskwork, you might consider something more complex, but remember that this is a mini-project! You will probably need to look at advice under the Masks option in Section C10 (pages 177–80).
- Decide on the essential features of a cat's face, e.g. striking eyes, large mouth, whiskers, ears. Think about how you can best portray them on a mask.

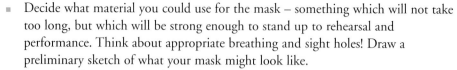

- Decide what material you could use for the mask – something which will not take too long, but which will be strong enough to stand up to rehearsal and performance. Think about appropriate breathing and sight holes! Draw a preliminary sketch of what your mask might look like.
- Decide on how to attach the mask so that it will not fall off, or break.
- Decide what colour the cat will be. You will need to consider how to make the essential features stand out against a coloured base; but you must also remember to consider the availability of the colours of suitable costumes.
- Make the mask – and use it in rehearsal. How successful is it? Does it stand up to action? Does it fulfil its purpose? Does it need any modifications?

Puppets

- Unless you are used to making and using puppets, consider using a simple shadow puppet. If you are already competent in puppetwork, you might consider something more complex, but remember that this is a mini-project! You will probably need to look at advice under the Puppets Option in Section C11 (pages 181–4).
- Draw some quick sketches of cats in silhouette. How interesting can you make them? Can you suggest character and/or movement? Do you need the whole cat – or only part of it? Which ones might fit with your performance ideas so far?
- Decide on how to attach the silhouette to a rod.
- Decide what materials you could use for the puppet – something which will not take too long to cut out, but strong enough to stand up to rehearsal and performance.
- Decide on how to create your backlight and screen so that only the shadow of the puppets will be seen – and not the puppeteers! This decision will affect the size of the completed shadow puppet.
- Make the puppet and use it in rehearsal. How successful is it? Does it stand up to action? Does it fulfil its purpose? Does it need any modifications? How can you make it look as though the cat is actually moving?

6 **Discuss** again and **experiment** with various rehearsal techniques which will help you in your own characterisation/role and with group positioning. What performance techniques are you also going to need to improve for your presentation?

7 **Get to know your piece.** This is the time to begin to make definite decisions about what you want to include, how the general shape of the piece is going to develop, how long it is going to be, and what response you want from your audience. You need to think carefully about the opening and ending, the development and interest; and try to make sure that you are on the right lines for your actor objectives.

8 **Experiment** with techniques which are going to improve the emotion and atmosphere, if relevant, and which will best help you to succeed in your objectives.

9 Organise any essential **technical aspects**.
- What **costume** are you each going to wear? Why? Do they fit in with each other? Can you move easily in them? Where are you going to get them?
- What **props** do you need? Have you already begun to practise with them? Where on stage or backstage do they need to be? Do they fit in with the style/genre? Where are you going to get them? Are they going to break?
- What **set** do you need? Think only about essentials, to give the impression of the location and characters. There is no need to be totally realistic, and Dance/Drama is often more symbolic or impressionistic. It may even be that a bare stage is the most suitable on this occasion, although changes of level will add to the visual interest.

- Do you need any particular **sound** or **special effects**? Have these been prepared properly? Are any being done 'live'? Where should they appear to come from? Who is going to be working them? Do they know what to do?
- What **lighting** are you using? Have you practised with the lighting yet? How long will the lights take to set up? Who is going to be working them? Do they know what to do? Remember that the main purpose of lighting is to ensure that the actors/dancers can be seen! Once you have allocated sufficient lanterns to light your stage and actors/dancers, then you can think about using any spare lanterns for helping with any atmosphere you might want to create.

10 **Polish** and **refine** your work until you are ready for performance. You may need to go back to rehearsal techniques, even at this stage, if you feel that something is not going quite right and could be improved. This is also the time to try to give performances of your piece or parts of it, and to get constructive advice on how things could be improved: having asked for the advice, do your best to take it! An audience often sees things differently from the way that the actor/dancer intends, and you must, therefore, listen to criticism and learn from other people if your communication is to be successful.

What you should have improved

Your understanding of how to see a variety of possible approaches from a musical stimulus.

- Did you really listen carefully to 'The Cat Duet', and get the most you could from the music itself? If not, why not? What can you learn for the future?
- Did you use the most suitable rehearsal techniques to help you to understand and improve your role and group work?
- Did you think carefully enough about your performance techniques, both as an individual and as part of a group? Did you experiment sufficiently to come to the best decisions?
- If you used masks or puppets, how effective were these? Did you think carefully enough about making them? How would you improve them another time?
- How well did you know everyone else's roles and movements? How aware were you of the others while actually in performance?
- Did you use your technical areas as well as you could? Did you try performing parts of your piece during rehearsal in order to get advice? Did you take the advice given? How effective and successful was your final performance?

For the future

This project should have helped you to look more thoughtfully at your stimulus, and to be less 'blinkered' in your initial responses to tasks. It should have emphasised the need for a methodical approach to rehearsal if you are going to use your knowledge, skills and techniques to your best ability. It should also have given you some understanding of how masks and puppets can aid some pieces of drama.

In examinations

Remember that you can only offer an **unscripted** piece of work once, and that your other piece has to be **scripted**, whether acting or technical design. You will be awarded 30% of your final marks on how well you understand, respond to and present your unscripted performance. Obviously, the more thoroughly you can prepare, the better your performance will be, so you need to use your rehearsal period as well as you possibly can.

Mini-project 8   The burying of Pompeii

focus

To help you to present a **Dance/Drama**, including the technical aspects, based on a historical event.

Task

To produce a piece of Dance/Drama to communicate the speed and horror of the volcanic destruction of Pompeii, using the eyewitness accounts as your framework.

Possible roles:

- people going about their daily lives
- children at school or at play
- people celebrating a city event, such as a carnival or election
- the volcano
- the cloud
- fire/flames
- sea/waves.

Possible research:

- volcanoes
- Pompeii
- archaeology
- other music/sounds.

Historical event

In AD 79, the Roman city of Pompeii was buried by an eruption of the nearby volcano, Mount Vesuvius. When it was eventually rediscovered, almost two thousand years later, the excavations showed a city preserved as it had been on that day of destruction – including the bodies, food, furniture, possessions and graffiti! Pompeii was a flourishing industrial and trading centre, especially in cloth, pottery, wine and olive oil; and it was also a thriving holiday resort, on a hill overlooking the sea. It contains the oldest-known Roman amphitheatre; temples to the gods; luxurious town houses with large gardens for the rich; and tiny houses and shops opening straight onto the streets for the poor.

But when Vesuvius erupted, burning clouds of volcanic ash engulfed the city, and any inhabitants who had not managed to escape were choked or burned to death. There were no survivors of these burning ash clouds.

Eyewitness accounts

The following extracts come from the writings of those who witnessed the event:

'. . . the black cloud spread over the earth like a flood . . . to burst open in twisted and quivering gusts to reveal flames like large flashes of lightning . . . leaping and blazing against the dreadful darkness . . .'

'. . . the buildings were shaking violently, and seemed to be swaying as if they were being torn from their roots . . .'

'. . . the waves were too wild and dangerous . . . as the sea rolled back on itself, showing the very sea-bed . . .'

'. . . when the cloud drew back, the land was covered by a thick layer of ash looking like snow . . .'

Possible accompaniments:

- recorded tape of 'real' sounds, such as daily life and volcanic eruptions
- live percussion and keyboard
- overture to *The Force of Destiny* by Verdi
- fourth movement (shipwreck) of *Scheherazade* by Rimsky-Korsakov
- *Danse Macabre* by Saint-Saëns
- 'Mars' from *The Planets Suite* by Gustav Holst.

Don't forget to consider your preparation, rehearsal, performance and group techniques! Identify the most relevant ones.

Technical aspects to consider

Set	Costume	Make-up	Properties	Masks
Puppets	Lighting	Sound	Stage management	

Focus To help you to present a Dance/Drama, including the technical aspects, based on a historical event.

1 The **resource material**

Look carefully at the potted history of the **historical event**.

■ What is the fact which has the greatest impact on you? Why?
■ What was daily life like in Pompeii? How do we know?
■ What were people doing at the time of the eruption?
■ Was there any warning of the eruption to come?

Look at the **eyewitness accounts**.

■ What actual facts can you discover from these accounts?
■ What descriptions help us to imagine what it was like?
■ What words emphasise the atmosphere?
■ What words emphasise the movement?

Look at **technical aspects** to consider.

■ Do you fancy trying a technical aspect for a Dance/Drama?
■ What opportunities might there be?
■ Refer to advice in mini-project 6 (pages 86–9); and to the technical options in Section C2 (pages 153–98) for more detailed instruction.

What about extra **research**? Look at the suggestions but be realistic about time.

2 Get into groups of about six, and look at the **possible roles**.

■ **Brainstorm** possibilities for each of the suggestions given. Exactly who/what might your role be? What other roles are there which might suit you and your group particularly well? Would you do best by switching roles, e.g. all being children at the beginning, then all switching to being the volcano, or half being children, and half being flames, etc?
■ **Brainstorm** possible scenes. What are your objectives going to be? Which parts of the story might be the most powerful? How can you make them effective? Which scenes can help you best in your objectives? Are you going to try to keep to the historical time? What will be the most effective/powerful?
■ **Brainstorm** ways of using movement to emphasise the story and emotions.
■ **Brainstorm** ways of providing suitable musical or sound accompaniment.
■ **Brainstorm** possibilities for technical aspects, and how they might fit in with the performance ideas already suggested.

3 Try some short **improvisations** on some of the best of the ideas discussed so far. If you have decided to try a technical aspect, watch or join in with these early experiments so that you have a good idea of what might be developed in your area.

4 **Discuss** the success of what you have just tried. Did the improvisations go well? What didn't work? What do you want to keep? What needs to be added? How well did you manage to convey the story through the movement? How well did you manage to convey emotion through the movement? Look at some of the performance techniques which might help your individual role and the group choreography. How much opportunity did these ideas give for technical aspects? What compromises might be reached?

5   **Repeat** the same extracts, adjusting them in the light of your discussion; and try some of the other ideas and parts of the story which seem to link up with them. Designers – begin to sketch how you might use your ideas: try to be imaginative in what you do, and remember that Dance/Drama can often be symbolic or impressionistic or dependent on the use of colour.

6   **Discuss** again and **experiment** with various rehearsal techniques which will help your own characterisation and the group positioning. What performance techniques are you going to need to improve for your role? Designers – **experiment** with new ideas, and make sure you discuss with other designers at all stages, to ensure a unity.

7   **Get to know your piece.** Remember that your Dance/Drama must tell a clear story and must have clear character roles. You must also use dance movements, skills and techniques! This is the time to begin to make definite decisions about what you want to include, how the general shape of the piece is going to develop, how long it is going to be, and what accompaniment, if any, you are going to use. Consider carefully what the pace of the piece is going to be at various times during the Drama, when this changes, and whether pause/silence can be used to good effect. It is also the time to ensure that the performers and the designers are all working to the same end!

8   **Experiment** with performance and technical techniques which will improve the communication of emotion and atmosphere, and which will emphasise your objectives.

9   Organise any essential **technical aspects** which are not being dealt with by a special designer.

   - What **costume** are you each going to wear? Do they fit in with each other? Can you move easily in them? Where are you going to get them?
   - What **props** do you need? Where will you get them? Have you already begun to practise with them? Do they help, or do they restrict, your movement? Do they fit the historical time? Are they going to break?
   - What **set** do you need? Give an impression of the place and time, or concentrate on the atmosphere and emotion. Remember that Dance/Drama is often symbolic or impressionistic.
   - Do you need any particular **sound** or **special effects**? Have these been prepared properly? Are any being done 'live'? Who is going to be working them? Do they know what to do?
   - What **lighting** are you using? Have you practised with the lighting yet? Does the operator know what to do? Remember that the main purpose of lighting is to ensure that the dancers can be seen! Once you have allocated sufficient lanterns to light your stage and dancers, then you can think about using any spare lanterns for helping with the atmosphere. For this piece of work, you will probably need to use quite imaginative lighting design, but remember that if you try to be too ambitious with your resources, your ideas will probably not work.
   - Specialist designers: make further adjustments as necessary.

10 **Polish** and **refine** your work until you are ready for performance. You may need to go back to rehearsal techniques, even at this stage, if you feel that something is not going quite right and could be improved. This is also the time to try to give performances of your dance or parts of it, and to get constructive advice on how things could be improved: having asked for the advice, do your best to take it! An audience often sees things differently from the way that the actor/dancer intends, and you must, therefore, listen to criticism and learn from other people if your communication is to be successful. The use of video is particularly useful when you want to evaluate the effectiveness of group shape, as well as in judging the quality of your own movements.

What you should have improved

Your understanding of how to use a historical event for a Dance/Drama.

- Did you think carefully about the resource material, and your objectives?
- Did you use suitable rehearsal techniques to help you to understand and improve your role, situation and movement?
- Did you think carefully about your performance techniques, both as an individual and as part of the group? Did you experiment sufficiently to come to the best decisions?
- How well did you know everyone else's roles and movements? How aware were you of each of the others when actually in performance?
- Did you use your technical areas as well as you could?
- Did you try performing parts of the Dance/Drama during rehearsal in order to get advice? How effective and successful was your final performance?

For the future

This project should have helped you to think more carefully about the different stages of preparing a Dance/Drama; and how a historical event can produce an effective story. Always remember that a Dance/Drama must have a clear story, clear character roles and a clear sense of climax; and that some of the best will be able to communicate emotion and atmosphere. This is often strengthened by the effective use of music or sound as an accompaniment; and by imaginative use of lighting.

In examinations

Remember that you can only offer Dance/Drama as an **unscripted** piece of work, and that you must offer an acting or technical skill for your **scripted** piece. You will be awarded 30% of your final marks on how well you understand, respond to and present your Dance/Drama. Obviously, the more thoroughly you can prepare, the better your performance will be, so you need to use your preparation period as well as you can.

Mini-project 9 Soap Opera!

focus

To help you to see **different possibilities from a television stimulus**.

What is a 'Soap Opera'?

A sentimental and often melodramatic serial about the everyday life of a group of people. Different plots with different groups of characters interlink, cutting from one to another, so that scenes are often short. A 'Soap' must end in such a way that viewers want to watch the next episode! It got its name from the fact that such serials on American television were originally usually sponsored by the big soap-manufacturing companies.

Groups used include:

- city communities
- rural communities
- people in schools
- people in hospitals
- people on board ships
- people in the workplace
- people on holiday.

Characters include:

- different generations
- the 'bully'
- the 'listener'
- the 'angry one'
- the 'victim'.

Contents include:

- romance
- conflict
- marriage breakdown
- crime
- personal problems
- current issues.

Task

To prepare and present the opening scene from a 'Soap' for the theatre. It has all the recognisable ingredients of the television and radio 'Soaps', but is also very different.

Obvious problems

- What group of people to focus on?
- Where to set it?
- How to overcome the problem of short scenes (not ideal for the theatre)?
- How to create something different and original?
- How to appeal to all ages?
- How to catch the interest at the beginning?

Extra research

Watch the 'Soaps'! Notice the similarities between them.

Possible approaches:

- to create a farcical 'take-off' of the typical 'Soap'
- to create an interactive piece of drama where the audience influences what happens
- to create a Dance/Drama or a Musical
- to create a puppet play
- to create a Mime
- to create a 'fantasy Soap'.

Something different?

- Take off well-known people: politicians in the House of Commons, or your own school staff at a weekend.
- Resource various myths and legends: the Ancient Greek gods; folklore characters such as Robin Hood; local legendary heroes.
- Use fantasy characters or situations: the pets of your neighbourhood; Mr X's garden gnomes; in Heaven or in Hell.
- Mix tableaux, monologues and well-known conversations from Shakespeare.
- Go in reverse – start with the present and create a whole sequence of flashbacks inside flashbacks to take the characters progressively further back into their past.
- However, whatever you decide, remember the essential ingredients of the 'Soaps'.

Focus To help you to see different possibilities from a television stimulus.

1 The **resource material**

Look carefully at **what is a 'Soap Opera'?**

- What hints does this give you about 'Soap Operas'?

Look at the **groups**, **characters**, and **contents** suggested.

- What others have been used already?

Look at the **possible approaches**.

- Which suggestions immediately give you ideas?
- Which suggestions might provide a really original piece?
- Do any suggestions stand out as offering the most exciting opportunities for you?

Look at **something different**.

- Do any of these suggestions immediately give you ideas?
- Which suggestions might offer a really original piece of work?
- Are any of the suggestions outside your experience and skills?

2 Get into groups of about half a dozen and **brainstorm** ideas for:

- other **groups** you could use
- other '**typical**' **characters** you could use
- other '**typical**' **everyday happenings** you might include
- the **setting**. This will probably come automatically from your characters; but, as this is for theatre, think carefully about creating several different locations. This can cause problems for space, actors, resources, pace and flow.
- **different approaches**. Do any of the ones suggested seem to be appropriate for your group? What other possibilities might you try?
- **different ideas**. Do any of the ones suggested seem to be appropriate for your group? What other possibilities can you find that you might like to try?
- the group's **overall objectives**. Is this purely for entertainment? Or is there going to be some sort of 'message' in this introductory episode? How might you communicate your objectives?
- **technical possibilities**. What might be particularly effective? What offers good opportunities for people within the group?

3 Try some quick **improvisations** on two or three of the more promising ideas. Try to experiment with more than one possible approach at this stage.

4 **Discuss** how they went. Did they go well? What would be good to leave in? What didn't work very well? Which ideas managed to convey the 'Soap' genre best? Which seemed to be the most original? What performance techniques do you need to think about to improve your portrayal and communication? How much opportunity was there for technical areas?

5 **Repeat** the scenes and make suitable adjustments to them, in the light of your discussion. Try out other possible ideas that you have identified.

6 **Discuss** how they went this time, and begin to decide which of the various ideas tried really does seem to be working best. How might you develop your ideas? Which seems to be communicating most clearly? Which is fitting the genre and your objectives most successfully? Think about your own performance in greater detail. How will you develop your performance techniques to suit the chosen role? Look at the various techniques which will help you to improve your characterisation and positioning.

7 **Get to know your piece**. Make final decisions about which ideas to include and which to forget about. You need to think carefully about the opening and ending, objectives, units, development and interest.

8 **Experiment** with techniques which are going to help you to improve emotion and atmosphere. Consider carefully what the pace of the piece ought to be at various times, and points when this changes.

9 Organise any essential **technical aspects**.

  ■ What **costume** are you each going to wear? Do they fit in with each other? Where are you going to get them from? Can you move easily in them?

  ■ What **props** do you need? Have you already begun to practise with them? Do they fit with the story and setting? Are they going to break?

  ■ What **set** do you need? Think only about essentials, to give the impression of the location and time: do not worry about it being totally realistic.

  ■ Do you need any particular **sound** or **special effects**? Have these been prepared? Or are they being done 'live'? Where should they appear to come from? Does the operator know what to do?

  ■ What **lighting** are you using? Have you practised with the lighting yet? Does the operator know what to do? In a 'Soap', lighting can help to focus attention on the right group of characters. Make sure that you use enough lanterns to light your actors. (If facial expressions can't be seen, you are probably not using enough light!) Once that is done, you can think about using available lanterns for helping with atmosphere or time of day, for example, but don't try to be over-ambitious. It probably will not work!

10 **Polish** and **refine** your work until you are ready for performance. You may need to go back to look at various techniques even at this stage, if you feel that something is not going quite right and could be improved. This is also the time to try to give performances of your proposed scene or parts of it, and to get constructive advice on how things could be improved: having got the advice, do your best to take it! An audience often sees things differently from the way the actor intends, and the actor must, therefore, listen to criticism, and learn to give out the right signals, if he/she is to communicate effectively.

What you should have improved
Your understanding of possible development along different, original lines.

■ Did you think carefully about the resource material and the suggestions made?
■ Did you use suitable preparation and rehearsal techniques to improve your performance?
■ Did you experiment sufficiently to come to the best decisions?
■ Did you use the technical areas as well as you could?
■ Did you get advice during rehearsal in order to improve your performance?
  How effective and successful was your final performance?

For the future

This project should have helped you to think more carefully about how you might find original and 'different' approaches to a subject which can easily become stereotyped or dull. Make good notes of what you have done and learnt, so that you will be able to use examples from this piece of work in your final essays if you need to: you won't remember without those notes!

In examinations

Remember that you are awarded 30% of your final marks on showing how well you understand, respond to and present your work. Obviously, the more thoroughly you can prepare and rehearse, the better your performance will be, so you will always need to put maximum thought into every stage of the task.

Remember, too, that part of that response is assessed on your written work, which shows how you have developed the piece; and into research and comparisons with other pieces of Drama.

Mini-project 10 *The First Kangaroo*

To help you to use an **Australian aboriginal myth** as the basis for your presentation.

Task

To produce a dramatic presentation of this Australian aboriginal myth (opposite).

Possible approaches could include:

- to use the myth as a basis for a Theatre-in-Education performance about aboriginal myths
- to create a piece of Dance/Drama
- to create a mime, with an accompanying narrator
- to create a piece of puppet theatre using rod puppets
- to create a piece of theatre which relies on hand and arm movements to tell the story
- to create a piece of Drama which has the 'feel' of tribal storytelling
- to use the myth as one element of a piece of Devised thematic work on animal myths.

Possible stages of development for creating a piece of tribal storytelling

- Experiment with rhythmical sounds which you can make with hands, feet, tongue, drum or shaker.
- Decide on essential phrases/words to convey the development of the story.
- Develop the words into chants which will fit with the mood or pace of that part of the story.
- Fit the chant to a suitable rhythmical sound.
- Experiment with body movements which will fit with the chant, rhythm and mood.
- Make decisions about group movements and positioning at various times in the story.

Special considerations

- How to create the storm and wind effects?
- How to create the idea of kangaroos?
- How to create the kangaroos being swept into the air?
- How to create the spread of the kangaroos after the first one had 'landed'?

Possible research:

- aboriginal myths
- animal myths from different cultures
- pictures and videos of dramatic presentations from other cultures
- the uniqueness of kangaroos.

Working on the text

- Break the text into units, and decide what you want to achieve in each unit.
- What should the pace of each unit be? Identify the points where pause could be used.
- Are there points where the mood and tone change?
- Make choices about your performance space. Where will the audience be?
- Decide on points in the text where movement is needed.
- How would circles of attention help in the Drama?
- What opportunities are there for technical aspects of production?

Possible technical approaches:

- to make a set for a Dance/Drama presentation of this myth
- to design a costume for a hunter
- to design the make-up for the wind and/ or trees
- to design a prop for the storm to use
- to design a mask for a hunter
- to design a rod puppet for a kangaroo
- to design a lighting plan for a presentation based on the myth
- to create the sounds of the storm
- to list the different production aspects which a stage manager might need to supervise.

The First Kangaroo

One day, a party of aboriginal hunters was out hunting.

An extraordinary storm of wind arose, and swept across the country, filling the skies with huge, swirling clouds. It tore grass and shrubs from the ground, uprooted trees and drove the aborigines into the shelter of the rocks.

As the hunters looked upwards at the swirling debris, they saw kangaroos being swept along by the storm. Never before had they seen such strange animals, with small heads and arms, large bodies and tails, and long legs which tried to touch the ground only to be swept upwards again by the next blast of wind. Then, during a lull in the storm, the hunters watched fascinated as one of these strange creatures became caught in the branches of a tree. Before they dared approach, it managed to free itself, fall to the ground, and hop away.

From such a beginning, kangaroos were soon to be found all over the grasslands, and there they remain to this day.

Focus To help you to use an Australian aboriginal myth as the basis for your presentation.

1 The **resource material**

Look carefully at the **myth**.

- What are the key moments in the story?
- What feelings do the hunters have?
- What are the obvious problems in creating a drama from this myth?
- How might you bring it to life?

Look at the **possible approaches**.

- Which suggestions would appear to suit the myth best?
- Which suggestions would appear to offer the most effective piece of work?
- Which suggestions would appear to offer the most original piece of work?
- Does one of them stand out as being the most exciting?

Look at the **special considerations**.

- How might you create the storm and wind just with body movement? What about the use of sound and lighting? What about with characters for Wind, Rain, etc?
- How might you create the impression of kangaroos in movement? By using costume, masks, puppets or other technical devices?
- How can you 'lift' the kangaroos off the ground?
- How might you show the spread of the kangaroos through movement? By symbolic group positioning? Through the spoken word?

Look at **working on the text**.

- How might you split the text into units?
- Where can you find hints about the pace and/or pause?
- Where can you find hints about the mood and/or tone?
- Decide where your audience will be. How may this affect the way you perform?
- What sort of movement opportunities are there in this piece? Are they for individuals or for the whole group? Identify important moments for effective movement.
- How do you want to influence the audience with your use of circles of attention? What are the key moments?

Look carefully at **possible technical aspects**.

- Is there an opportunity for you to try out a particular technical aspect with this work? Refer to mini-projects 6–8 (pages 86–97) for more help.

What about extra **research**? Look at the suggestions, but be realistic about time.

2 Get into groups of four or five and **brainstorm** ideas for:

- the **characters**. Are they individuals? Or are they just representations? How might this affect the way you play them? Are people going to be given particular roles? Or will you all play everything? How will you distribute your parts?
- the **setting**. How are you going to create a feeling of location? How might the acting help? How might the technical aspects help?
- the group's **overall objectives**. What is the purpose of your presentation? Who would make the most suitable audience? How can you communicate your objectives? Which words or actions become the most important?
- **technical possibilities**. What might be particularly effective? What offers good opportunities for people in the group? How can the actors use the ideas which the designers have?

3   Try quick **improvisations** of various parts of the myth.

4   **Discuss** how they went. Did they go well? What would be good to leave in? What didn't work very well? What might be added to make them more effective? Were you managing to communicate feeling? What performance techniques do you need to think about to improve your portrayal and communication? How much opportunity did these ideas give for the technical aspects? What compromises might be reached?

5   **Repeat** the same scenes and make suitable adjustments to them, in the light of your discussion. Try out any other part which you have not already tried. Designers – begin to sketch how you might use your ideas: try to be imaginative in what you do, but remember that you must still be able to be understood!

6   **Discuss** how the scenes went this time, and think about your own performance in greater detail. How will you develop your performance techniques to suit this role? This is the time to **experiment** with different ideas and techniques. Look at the preparation and performance techniques which will help you to improve your characterisation and positioning. Designers – **experiment** with new ideas, and make sure that you discuss with other designers at all stages, to ensure a unity.

7   **Get to know your piece.** Begin to make final decisions about which ideas to include and which to forget about. You need to think carefully about the opening and ending, objectives, units, development, interest and pace. If you are quoting the myth itself, make sure that you know your words. Consider carefully how techniques such as pace, pause and silence can aid the effect. It is also time to ensure that the performers and the designers are all working to the same end!

8   During this period, **experiment**. Look carefully at both performance and technical techniques which will help to communicate the emotion and atmosphere, and which will emphasise your objectives.

9   Organise any essential **technical aspects** which are not being dealt with by a designer.
   - What **costume** are you each going to wear?
   - What **props** do you need?
   - What **set** do you need?
   - Do you need any particular **sound** or **special effects**?
   - What **lighting** are you using?

10 **Polish** and **refine** your work until you are ready for performance. You may need to go back to look at various techniques even at this stage, if you feel that something is not going quite right and could be improved. This is also the time to try to give performances of your proposed scene or parts of it, and to get constructive advice on how things could be improved: having got the advice, do your best to take it! An audience often sees things differently from the way the actor/designer intends, and the actor/designer must, therefore, listen to criticism, and learn to give out the right signals, if he/she is to communicate effectively.

What you should have improved

Your understanding of possible ways of dramatising a myth.

- Did you think carefully about the resource material, and your objectives?
- Did you use suitable preparation and rehearsal techniques to improve your performance?
- Did you experiment sufficiently to come to the best decisions?
- Did you use the technical areas as well as you could?
- Did you get advice during rehearsal in order to improve your presentation? How effective and successful was your final performance?

For the future

This project should have helped you to think more carefully about how you might put a myth into a polished piece of presentation, and some of the wide choice of possibilities open to you. It should also have helped you to realise that you can look at themes from very different cultures, which might offer good opportunities for an original and effective production.

Make good notes of what you have done and learnt, so that you will be able to use examples from this piece of work in your final essays if you need to: you won't remember without those notes!

In examinations

Remember that you are awarded 30% of your final marks on showing how well you understand, respond to and present your work. Obviously, the more thoroughly you can prepare, the better your performance will be, so you will always need to put maximum thought into every stage of preparation, rehearsal and performance.

Remember, too, that part of that response is assessed on your written work. This will include information on how you have developed the piece, on your research and comparisons with other pieces of Drama.

B2 Outline mini-projects

Using this section of the book

The next few pages give you some more mini-projects, but now you will find just a single resource sheet. If you have worked your way through some of the earlier mini-projects, you will be developing a good idea of how to tackle similar work, and will not need the instructions in quite so much detail. However, do refer to the techniques in Section A and remember to test out various approaches, including different styles/genres. Look back at Section B1 if you find you need more detailed reminders of how to tackle your work.

Remember that in any piece of work, you need to think about the stages of **preparation** and **rehearsal**.

For **performance** work, these will be as follows.

1 Look at all the **resource material**.
2 **Brainstorm** first ideas.
3 **Improvise** short possibilities.
4 **Discuss** their potential.
5 **Repeat** the same scenes with improvements.
6 **Discuss** and **experiment** with character and group choreography.
7 **Get to know your piece**.
8 **Experiment** further with emotion, mood and atmosphere.
9 Organise essential **technical aspects**.
10 **Polish** and **refine**.

For **technical** work, the stages will be as follows.

1 Look at all the **resource material**.
2 **Brainstorm** first ideas with the performers.
3 Draw your **first sketches**/make your **first lists** of immediate possibilities.
4 **Discuss** their potential alongside the development in the performance work.
5 **Adjust** in the light of discussion.
6 **Discuss** and **draft** developed ideas.
7 Remember to consider other **technical aspects**.
8 Get to **know what you want** and how to achieve the results.
9 Make any **further adjustments** as ideas and performance develop.
10 **Polish** and **refine**.

In all the examples in this part of the mini-projects section, you should be able to develop whatever performance or technical skill you want, in as much detail as your time allows. This part gives you another chance to check on what would be most sensible for you to consider for your final option choices. Thus, with each of the following mini-projects, you could complete a task based on any of the options in ways such as these.

1 **Devised thematic work**
   Identify the theme of the task. Then try to find at least two relevant scripts and suggest at least two possible improvised scenes. Polish one of each for a performance.

2 **Acting (scripted)**
   Find a suitable script which would fit the theme or ideas behind the task. Choose a short extract to polish for performance.

3 **Improvisation**

Improvise a scene on the theme or ideas behind the task, and polish it for performance.

4 **Theatre-in-Education (TIE)**

Decide on the theme or subject of the task, and decide on a possible target audience. Then improvise a scene for TIE, and polish it for performance.

5 **Dance/Drama**

Devise a short Dance/Drama on the theme or the ideas behind the task, and polish it for performance.

6 **Set**

Decide on the most likely style for a performance based on the task. Either draw a few designs for the set, showing the development of your thought, or make a scale model of a possible set.

7 **Costume**

Decide on the most likely style for a performance based on the task. Either draw a few designs for costume for at least two characters, showing the development of your thought, or adapt/make one costume on a small scale, showing your basic ideas. For this mini-project, don't worry too much about the smaller details.

8 **Make-up**

Decide on at least two possible styles for a performance based on the task. Draw designs for some of the characters suitable for each of the styles you have identified.

9 **Properties**

Make a list of some of the props which might be needed for a performance based on the task. Either draw designs of at least two props which might need making, with ideas of how you would construct them, or make one of the props, perhaps to a smaller scale, to fit with your basic ideas. For this mini-project, don't worry too much about the smaller details.

10 **Masks**

Decide on at least two possible styles for a performance based on the task. Either draw designs for some of the characters suitable for each of the styles you have identified, or make one mask to show your basic ideas. For this mini-project, don't worry too much about the smaller details.

11 **Puppets**

Decide on which type of puppet might be the most suitable for a puppet performance based on the task. Either draw designs to show different types of puppet for at least two characters, or make a simple puppet for one of the characters. For this mini-project, don't worry too much about the smaller details.

12 **Lighting**

Decide on the most likely style for a performance based on the task. Draw up a possible lighting plot which might be suitable. Note why you suggest any lighting changes you might make.

13 **Sound**

Make a list of possible sounds which might be needed for a performance of this task. Experiment with how to produce at least three of the sounds, including finding suitable music, if that is to be used.

14 **Stage management**

Decide on a suitable style for a performance of the task. Make a list of possible props and sounds which might be needed; a sketch of a possible set; a note of possible lighting ideas; a note of any possible quick costume changes or use of masks. Then draw a sketch of the backstage area, showing how you would organise the equipment and the cast.

Written work

Remember that with both your Coursework Options you have to write at least 500 words on your response to your work. This will include research into, and comparisons with, different texts, types of Drama, and styles/genres, and will include examples from different historical times and cultures. As you get closer to making your final choices, it is worth getting into the routine of writing for every piece of work you do. It is not an easy task, and the more practice you get, the better you will become! At the end of each of these mini-projects, you will find a few ideas for possible research and comparisons to help you to get started on this task.

Mini-project 11 Refugees

Fact

Whenever and wherever there is conflict and war, there are always the innocents who suffer. Throughout history, ordinary people have been forced to flee their homes in the face of advancing armies and aggression. People have been forcibly moved out of their homes because of their race or religion. We have seen distressing images of 'ethnic cleansing' in the Balkans; the famines in war-torn African countries; and of the Holocaust. All the dispossessed leave their homes with no idea of where they are going or how they will live; and often with only what they are wearing or what they can carry.

Considerations

- What is going to be your main objective?
- Are you going to present an improvised, scripted or devised piece, or Dance/Drama? Which will help your objective best?
- What scenario will provide the most powerful focus?
- How can you find something different from the 'usual' plays about refugees?
- What techniques and styles are going to improve the piece?

Possible research:

- the Holocaust
- ethnic cleansing in the Balkans
- civil war in Ethiopia
- newspaper and TV accounts of refugees.

Possible comparisons

- *I am David* by Ann Holm – a child in central Europe (novel)
- *Fiddler on the Roof* by Joseph Stein – Jews in Russia (musical)
- *Goodnight Children Everywhere* by Richard Nelson – wartime evacuees (play – straight)

Quotes

'The men were away fighting. There were only my mother and sisters at home.'

'When we looked back, we could see the farm on fire. We could see the black cloud of smoke behind us all day.'

'They just stood there gesturing with their guns. They did not say a word, but we knew we had to go.'

'We did not know what to take. When we looked at the few poor things we had bundled together in sheets they were of little use to us.'

'We walked for days. We searched for someone to help us. We finished up in this refugee camp. There are five thousand here. How will our families find us?'

'The soldiers shot our cattle. They even shot my pet dog. I thought that we were next.'

Possible viewpoints:

- a child
- a parent
- a political leader
- a military leader
- a doctor
- a farmer
- a weather forecaster
- a TV reporter.

Remember:

- the stages of preparation and rehearsal
- the choice of options available to you.

Refer to the introduction to Section B2 for reminders.

Mini-project 12   *The Billumbungles*

The Billumbungles by J. V. Morton

The Billumbungles brose before us,
All wink and tonk and gleen and glorious.
As we trook, they triced and caved and tranced.
So we triced and caved: but we only stanced.
They wooked and wanned as they caje us grold
Of bagic and bens like the majus of old.

Some possibilities

- Are the Billumbungles people? Or creatures? Or plants?
- Are they well known? Or have they been undiscovered until now? Are they the result of scientific experiments? Or are they visitors to 'your' world?
- Are they mythical? Or comic? Or magical? Or from a different historical time or place?
- Are their actions friendly? Threatening? Graceful? Awkward? Respectful?

Some literary quotes

- 'He put this engine to our ears, which made an inconceivable noise ... and we guess that it is either some unknown animal or a god that he worships ...' (J. Swift)
- 'In the days when the world was flat, they erupted onto the surface of the earth like a band of invaders, apparently able to look in every direction at once.' (A. Lord)
- 'A clanging bell thundered somewhere deep inside the cave, echoing and pulsing all around us; whilst a brilliant green light flashed and sparkled in warning, as two huge silhouetted shapes crept slowly towards us.' (Y. Ronic)

Possible research:

- writers of nonsense and fantasy
- appropriate audiences and their degrees of belief in the unbelievable
- myths from other places and times.

Considerations

- How to make 'sense' of nonsense!
- Who/what are the Billumbungles?
- What sort of characters are they?
- Who/what are 'we'?
- What sort of characters are 'we'?
- What do the nonsense words mean/suggest?
- What sort of movement/action will there be?
- Where might this be set?
- What will happen next?

Other sources of 'nonsense'

Book of Nonsense by Edward Lear (poetry)
Alice Through the Looking-glass by Lewis Carroll (novel)

What can Billumbungles do?

- Change shape.
- Become invisible.
- Cause changes in anything they touch.
- Read thoughts.
- Fulfil wishes.
- Make the impossible happen.
- Create havoc.
- Change people's moods instantly.
- Brainwash people.
- Give instant transport.

Possible comparisons

- *Gulliver's Travels* by Jonathan Swift (novel)
- *The Day of the Triffids* by John Wyndham (sci-fi novel and film)
- The world of 'Harry Potter' created by J. K. Rowling (novels and film)

Remember:

- the stages of preparation and rehearsal
- the choice of options available to you.

Refer to the introduction to Section B2 for reminders.

Mini-project 13   Proud of us!

Who are 'us'?

- Our neighbourhood.
- Our school.
- Our national group.

What gives us pride?

- Our environment.
- Our group identity.
- Our successes.
- Our 'heroes' or figureheads.
- Our moral code.
- Our behaviour.

Various quotations

- 'Pride goes before a fall' (Proverbs)
- 'Their country's pride' (O. Goldsmith)
- 'Modest pride' (J. Milton)
- 'I can trace my ancestry back to a protoplasmal primordial atomic globule. Consequently my family pride is something inconceivable!' (W. S. Gilbert)
- 'Land of our birth, our faith, our pride' (R. Kipling)
- 'Thou hast drawn together all the far-stretched greatness, all the pride, cruelty, and ambition of man' (Sir W. Raleigh)
- 'My pride fell with my fortunes.' (W. Shakespeare)

Possible research

- Observe what is good around you.
- Investigate your leaders/heroes/figureheads.
- Investigate your group's culture.
- Read what your local/national/school paper says about your community.

Remember:

- the stages of preparation and rehearsal
- the choice of options available to you.

Refer to the introduction to Section B2 for reminders.

What makes us what we are?

- The area where we live.
- Our culture.
- Our leaders.
- Our aims.
- Our education.

How do others see us?

- In a good light.
- As a close-knit community.
- As people who help each other.
- As people who help others.

For good or bad?

- Pride creates a sense of worth, of belonging, of well-being – of identity.
- A lack of pride creates damage, disorder and deprivation.
- Misplaced pride creates selfishness, arrogance, bullying and aggression.

Having pride suggests:

- face: smiling, cheerful, content, relaxed
- body: open, upright, straight, head high
- movement: natural, relaxed, direct, easy
- appearance: tidy, smart, clean, well-groomed.

Possible comparisons:

- how your community is seen by you – and by others
- your community with other local communities known to you
- the Puerto-Ricans, the Jets and the Sharks in *West Side Story* by Leonard Bernstein and Arthur Laurents (musical)
- the crew of *H.M.S. Pinafore* by Gilbert and Sullivan (comic opera)
- *The Yarn* by Rob Brannen (tales of a rural community).

Mini-project 14 The weather

What do we mean by 'weather'?

- Sunshine and warmth.
- Clouds, rain, thunderstorms and monsoons.
- Wind, hurricanes and tornadoes.
- Snow, frost, sleet and hail.
- Anticyclones, depressions and fronts.
- Arctic, temperate and tropical.

Some interesting records

- The highest recorded temperature is 58 °C (136 °F) in Libya.
- The coldest place on earth is in Siberia at –68 °C (–90 °F).
- Winds up to 200mph are recorded in hurricanes.
- The highest recorded wind is 230 mph.
- A record 1870 mm (73.62 in) of rain fell in one month in 1861 in India.
- The world's wettest place is in Colombia, with 11,770 mm (463.4 in) of rain per year.
- The largest recorded hailstone weighed 765 grams (1.7 lb) and fell in Kansas in 1970.
- In 1921, 1930 mm (76 in) of snow fell in one day in Colorado.

Possible styles/genres

- Explore the theme in a straight play, pantomime or interactive drama.
- Explore the effects in a tragedy.
- Explore our obsession in comedy, farce or mime.
- Explore the future through fantasy or sci-fi.
- Explore weather predictions in past times through a historical drama.

Possible research and comparisons:

- the topics listed under 'Possible considerations'
- the use of different styles, times, places or emotions in creating a performance on 'Weather'
- the use of weather to underline reality and illusion in *Woman in Mind* by Alan Ayckbourn (play – black comedy).

Remember:

- the stages of preparation and rehearsal
- the choice of options available to you.

Refer to the introduction to Section B2 for reminders.

Possible considerations

- Ask the question: 'What weather would you like to have?' – as John Heywood did in *The Play of the Weather*, where his characters all wanted different things.
- Use the weather to reflect the mood and emotion of the scene – as Shakespeare did when the madness of King Lear was echoed by the violence of the storm.
- Research changing weather patterns, e.g. environmental issues; El Niño effects; predictions for the future.
- Look at the British obsession with the weather, e.g. a 'typical' seaside holiday of the past; the modern-day escape to the sun; the dependence on forecasts; kitting up for whatever the weather.
- Think about the bad effects of the weather, e.g. skin cancer, flood, famine, destruction, pneumonia.
- Find out about research scientists who made great advances in understanding the weather, e.g. Sir Francis Beaufort; the people who fly through the eyes of the storms.
- How does the weather appear in different places, e.g. in a room with no windows, on ski slopes, underground, underwater, in the air?

Mini-project 15 Can you hear me?

Considerations

Look at the script *Hear Hear*.

- Are they both deaf?
- Or is one laughing at deafness?
- Is either of them deaf?
- What ages are they?
- Think about opportunities for movement.
- Think about pace and pause to gain effect.
- What was the writer's objective?
- What is your objective?
- What style/genre/type will suit your objective best?
- How can the technical aspects help?

Newspaper headlines

Beethoven going deaf!

Deaf cyclist killed

Cure for deafness coming soon!

Thunderous applause for deaf actors

Hear Hear by Ronnie Barker, adapted by Bill Ridgway

> A *sits at desk. There is a large sign on the wall – 'Hearing-Aid Centre'.*
> Enter B. *He/she approaches the desk.*

	B	Is this the hearing-aid centre?
	A	Pardon?
	B	Is this the hearing-aid centre?
	A	Yes, that's right, yes.
5	B	I've come to be fitted for a hearing-aid.
	A	Pardon?
	B	I said I've come for a hearing-aid.
	A	Oh yes. Do sit down. I'll just take a few notes. Name?
	B	Pardon?
10	A	Name?
	B	Crampton.
	A	Pardon?
	B	Crampton.
	A	Oh, Crampton.
15	B	Pardon?
	A	I said Crampton.
	B	Crampton, yes.
	A	Right, Mr Crampton. Now I take it you are hard of hearing.
	B	Pardon?
20	A	I said, I take it you're hard of hearing.
	B	That's right.
	A	Which ear?
	B	Pardon?
	A	Which ear?

25	B	The right.
	A	Pardon?
	B	The right ear.
	A	Ah. Could you cover it up with your hand please? (*B does so.*)
		Now, can you hear me?
30	B	Pardon?
	A	Can you hear what I'm saying?
	B	It's very faint.
	A	Pardon?
	B	It's very faint.
35	A	I can't hear you.
	B	Pardon?
	A	Try the other ear. (*B covers it.*) Now what's that like?
	B	I still can't hear you.
	A	Can you hear me?
40	B	Pardon?
	A	Yes. You really do need a hearing-aid.
	B	I thought so.
	A	Pardon?
	B	You can't hear *me*, either, can you?
45	A	Pardon?
	B	Why don't *you* wear one?
	A	You're still very faint.
	B	A HEARING-AID! Why don't *you* wear one?
	A	I am wearing one.
50	B	Pardon?
	A	Pardon?
	B	I said 'Pardon?'
	A	No, I said 'Pardon!'
	B	Oh, never mind. I'll get some new teeth. (*B goes out.*)

Possible research

- problems for the hard of hearing
- how we think of deaf people
- how deaf people are portrayed in other plays
- what the Government does for deaf people.

Remember

- the stages of preparation and rehearsal
- the choice of options available to you.

Refer to the introduction to Section B2 for reminders.

Possible comparisons

- *A Talk in the Park* by Alan Ayckbourn (play – Comedy: not hearing other people's problems)
- the Judge in *Trial by Jury* by Gilbert and Sullivan (Comic Opera: deafness caused by age)
- Mr and Mrs Birling in *An Inspector Calls* by J. B. Priestley (play – Straight: not listening to the moral message).

Mini-project 16 Music

Music whose titles tell no story. Possible pieces include

- *Fanfare for the Common Man* by Aaron Copland
- 'Lara's Theme' from *Dr Zhivago*
- *Rhapsody in Blue* by George Gershwin
- 'Canon' by Pachelbel
- *Radetzky March* by Johann Strauss
- 'O fortuna' from *Carmina Burana* by Carl Orff
- *The Rough Guide to World Roots* – CD compilation of indigenous traditional music from around the world, by The Festival Shop, Birmingham.

How to listen

- You need to try to relax and clear your mind of any particular thoughts.
- Sit in a quiet, darkened room, or close your eyes and ears to outside sights and sounds.
- Concentrate completely on the music.
- Let your mind be filled with pictures and ideas.
- Listen again, thinking in terms of musical and dramatic techniques.
- Listen to the piece several times, filling in more detail each time.

What comes to mind?

- A picture of a place?
- A picture of an event/activity?
- A picture of a person?
- A mood/emotion/atmosphere?
- An issue or theme?
- A dramatic style?
- A sequence of actions?

Analyse the musical/dramatic techniques

Strength/tension	Pace	Pause	Rhythm
Flow	Pitch	Volume	
Movement	Chorus	Tone	
Counterpoint	Solo passages	Repetition and echo	

Possible research

How music is used in:
- television
- plays
- musicals.

Music as sound effects

As well as stimulating your piece of work, might you also use your piece of music:
- as an introduction to set mood or location
- between scenes to provide continuity
- as a conclusion to leave a feeling or message
- as an accompaniment to all or parts of the piece
- to aid tension
- to aid humour
- to create a new mood
- to encourage the audience to participate or enjoy.

Possible comparisons:

- different interpretations of the music by different people in the class
- different methods of presentation from the same stimulus.

Remember:

- the stages of preparation and rehearsal
- the choice of options available.

Refer to the introduction to Section B2 for reminders.

Quotes

- 'If music be the food of love.' – Shakespeare
- 'The still, sad music of humanity.' – Wordsworth
- 'Music is the gladness of the world.' – Eliot
- 'A solemn service of music.' – Lamb
- 'Hell is full of musical amateurs; music is the brandy of the damned.' – Shaw
- 'Music has charms to soothe a savage breast.' – Congreve

Mini-project 17   What's in a name?

Some interesting place names

Nettlebed

Tutts Clump

Quomp

Snailsden

The Slaughters

Crazies Hill

The Wallops

Twistle

Gweek

Papa Sound

St Peter's Finger

Cridling Stubbs

Questions to ask

- What sort of place could it be?
- Why is it called that?
- What mood/feeling/atmosphere does it suggest?
- Who lives/works/visits there?
- What goes on there?
- What style/genre/type will suit this best?

Possible angles for presentation

- Documentary
- Fantasy/Horror/Sci-fi
- Character Drama
- 'Welcome to . . .'
- 'Life in . . .'
- the origins of names.

Possible research

- actual place names and their origins
- the history of place names.

Possible comparisons

- Much Binding in the Marsh (in the Radio Comedy *It's That Man Again* or *ITMA*)
- Titipu (and the names of its inhabitants, in *The Mikado*, the Comic Opera by Gilbert and Sullivan)
- Dotheboys Hall (in the novel *Nicholas Nickleby* by Charles Dickens, adapted for both play and film).

Remember

- the stages of preparation and rehearsal
- the choice of options available to you.

Refer to the introduction to Section B2 for reminders.

Mini-project 18   The truth about teenagers!

Newspaper headlines

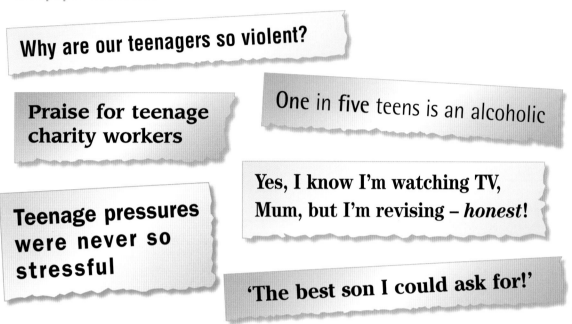

Why are our teenagers so violent?

Praise for teenage charity workers

One in five teens is an alcoholic

Yes, I know I'm watching TV, Mum, but I'm revising – *honest*!

Teenage pressures were never so stressful

'The best son I could ask for!'

Questions to ask

- Are the headlines factually correct?
- Would you disagree with any of them?
- Why do newspapers print such headlines?
- What emotions do they create?
- What response do they want?
- What are teenagers really like?

Possible comparisons:

- the diaries of 'Adrian Mole' by Sue Townsend (novels, television and film: about the life of a teenager)
- *Lord of the Flies* by William Golding (novel and film: about a group of boys stranded on a desert island)
- *Grange Hill* (television: 'soap' about life in a comprehensive school)
- *Daisy Pulls It Off!* by Denise Deegan (play: a stereotypical view of a girls' boarding school)
- *Billy Elliot* (film: about a miner's son who becomes a ballet dancer).

Possible directions to go:

- the stereotypical teenager
- take one headline and its theme
- look at newspaper reporting of groups of people
- teenagers as seen by people of different ages
- teenagers as seen by you
- a 'model' teenager
- what makes teenagers what they are?
- prejudice.

Possible research:

- newspaper and TV reports on teenagers
- criticisms of teenagers
- in praise of teenagers
- teenage attitudes to other groups.

Remember:

- the stages of preparation and rehearsal
- the choice of options available to you.

Refer to the introduction to Section B2 for reminders.

Mini-project 19 'Age cannot wither' (Shakespeare)

Fact

When we think of homes for the elderly we picture a lounge with old people sitting around staring into space. We could think that these people's lives are over. If you visit and talk to the elderly you will find that they can have a young outlook, a wealth of experience and a real grasp of what is going on in the world. They can also have a very developed sense of humour.

Dialogue extracts

A: 'I feel just like Tom Cruise in *Mission Impossible*.'
B: 'If you looked like him I wouldn't bother with the holiday.'
C: 'Okay, synchronise sun dials.'
D: 'Do I have to put my support stockings over my head?'

Possible research:

- the problems of old age
- old people's homes
- articles on old people
- attitudes to old people
- remarkable old people.

Possible comparisons:

- characters in *Last of the Summer Wine* by Roy Clarke (Television Comedy)
- Mr and Mrs Hardcastle in *She Stoops to Conquer* by Oliver Goldsmith (play – Restoration Comedy)
- Mrs Tabret in *The Sacred Flame* by W. Somerset Maugham (play – Straight/Whodunnit)
- Doris in *A Cream Cracker Under the Settee* by Alan Bennett (play – Straight/Comedy)
- *Waiting for God* by Paul Ableman and Michael Aitkens (Television Comedy set in an old people's home).

Location

A 'sun lounge' in a retirement home.

Situation

A few elderly residents wander in. This is a meeting of the 'Ageatraz' escape committee. They have been saving their pension money to have some sun, sand and sangria for one last time. But first they must sneak themselves and their luggage past the ever-watchful eye of the matron.

Natural effects of aging:

- loss of skin elasticity leading to skin 'sagging' and wrinkling
- loss of nerve cells leading to poorer memory and slower responses
- loss of muscle bulk leading to reduced muscular strength
- reduction in heart-pumping efficiency leading to lower tolerance of exercise
- hardening of arteries leading to poor blood circulation and higher blood pressure
- prolonged pressure on joints leading to 'stooping' and reduced mobility.

Questions to ask yourself

- How do you regard the elderly?
- How can the elderly help us?
- Why do people laugh at them?
- Why are the elderly victimised?
- Do you respect the old people you know?
- How do you want to be treated when you are old?

Remember:

- the stages of preparation and rehearsal
- the choice of options available to you.

Refer to the introduction to Section B2 for reminders.

Mini-project 20   The Witches

Task

To present the opening scene from *Macbeth*.

Problem

This is one of the most famous scenes of all time. It is very easy to stick to traditional ideas of old witches, pointed hats, 'blasted heaths', cauldrons and broomsticks! The real success of a production is to achieve something different – and yet something which is not so 'way out' that it becomes unintelligible within the context of the play. How imaginative, yet theatrically acceptable, can you be?

Considerations

- What is a witch? How recognisable are they in a crowd? Are they any different to look at? What age are they? What are the essentials of a witch? How can you get these across?
- What is the 'open place' where the scene is set? What open places can you think of? Which ones might help to create the right atmosphere?
- What are the witches doing? Are they all doing something? Are they all doing the same thing? Are their activities ones which we generally connect with witches? Or can you get across their witchcraft through more unexpected, more unusual, more original activities?
- How can you achieve the feeling that they are able to vanish? And perhaps appear just as magically? What other magic powers do they show?
- How can you help to create the atmosphere of power, menace and foreboding through your performance or design?
- Macbeth, a respected soldier, becomes a king's murderer, a change largely blamed on the witches. In what historical time or culture would this be most credible?

Context

Although there are few lines spoken, the witches set the scene for the whole play. There is an atmosphere of menace and foreboding; the recognition of good and evil becomes blurred; and the witches have an unnatural power.
(At the end of the scene they are called by their 'familiars', or commanding spirits.)

Dictionary definitions:

- a woman who practises sorcery
- a fascinating or bewitching woman
- an ugly old woman
- a woman with supernatural power
- a woman with knowledge of magic
- a woman supposedly in contact with the devil or other evil spirits.

Possible research:

- the belief in witchcraft at different historical times and in different places
- Elizabethan beliefs in the power of the supernatural
- witch hunts
- how to tell if a woman is a witch
- witchdoctors.

Possible comparisons:

- *The Crucible* by Arthur Miller
- *Witch's Charm* by Ben Jonson
- *Weird Sisters* by Terry Pratchett
- the wicked witches of Pantomime
- The Witches of Endor (I Samuel 28)
- *The Witches* by Roald Dahl (novel and film).

Remember:

- the stages of preparation and rehearsal
- the choice of options available to you.
Refer to the introduction to Section B2 for reminders.

The Witches

From *Macbeth* by William Shakespeare (Act 1 Scene 1)

An open place
Thunder and lightning. Enter three WITCHES.

	1ST WITCH	When shall we three meet again
		In thunder, lightning, or in rain?
	2ND WITCH	When the hurlyburly's done,
		When the battle's lost and won.
5	3RD WITCH	That will be ere the set of sun.
	1ST WITCH	Where the place?
	2ND WITCH	Upon the heath.
	3RD WITCH	There to meet with Macbeth.
	1ST WITCH	I come, Greymalkin!
10	2ND WITCH	Paddock calls.
	3RD WITCH	Anon!
	ALL	Fair is foul, and foul is fair;
		Hover through the fog and filthy air.
		Exeunt.

B3 Possible Sources for further project work

From different cultures	e.g.	Myths of Ancient Egypt
		Legends of Ancient Greece
		Scandinavian sagas
		Australian aboriginal myths
		Hiawatha adapted by Michael Bogdanov (Amerindian)
		Celtic myths and legends
		Hindu tales (*Ramayana* and *Mahabharata*)
		The Royal Hunt of the Sun – Peter Shaffer (Aztec)
		Whose Life is it Anyway? Brian Clarke (American)
		Playwrights from other countries
		Scenarios from operas
		Poems and stories from around the world
		Newspaper/magazine articles
Children's literature	e.g.	'Pinocchio' (Italian)
		'The Fisherman and the Goldfish' (Russia)
		The Wizard of Oz (America)
		Treasure Island (Scotland)
		The Arabian Nights – Dominic Cooke & Young Vic Th. Co.
		Grimm's Fairy Tales (German)
		Tales of Hans Christian Andersen (Danish)
		Aesop's Fables (Greek)
National theatre styles	e.g.	Japanese No and Kabuki
		Italian Commedia dell'Arte
		Asian Khmer drama
		Thai Khon drama
		Turkish Orta-oyunu
		Balinese dramas (Barong and Legong)
		British Punch-and-Judy
		Greek tragedy
		Yoruban (Nigerian) Alarinjo
		Hindu Kathalkali
		American musicals
Period drama	e.g.	Plays from classical literature
		Medieval mystery, miracle, morality and mummers' plays
		Elizabethan drama
		Restoration plays
		Victorian melodrama
		Theatre of the Absurd
		Kitchen-sink drama
		Canterbury Tales – Geoffrey Chaucer, adapted
		My Fair Lady – Lerner & Loewe
		The Admirable Crichton – J. M. Barrie
		Daisy Pulls It Off – Denise Deegan
		Androcles and the Lion – G. B. Shaw
Real events	e.g.	*A Man for all Seasons* – Robert Bolt
		Pack of Lies – Hugh Whitemore
		The Winslow Boy – Terence Rattigan
		84, Charing Cross Road – Helene Hanff
		The Diary of Anne Frank – Goodrich and Hackett
		The Roses of Eyam – Don Taylor

Succeeding in the Options

Option requirements at a glance

This section looks at the requirements of the Coursework Options in more detail. The section is divided into two parts.

1 **Performance Options** 1–5   2 **Technical Options** 6–14

In each part, there is a general introduction which covers all the relevant options; followed by specific points connected with each individual option. You need to refer to both the introduction and the particular options you are interested in if you are to gain maximum help.

Coursework requirements

This part of the Drama Examination tests your understanding and practical abilities in two separate areas of study. Only one option may be a technical/design skill; at least one must be a performance skill. Technical/design skills must contribute to an actual group performance. In addition, one option must be scripted, and one unscripted.

Scripted				
Devised thematic work	Costume	Masks	Sound	
Acting (Script)	Make-up	Puppets	Stage management	
Set	Properties	Lighting		

Unscripted				
Devised thematic work	Set	Properties	Lighting	
Improvisation	Costume	Masks	Sound	
Theatre-in-Education	Make-up	Puppets	Stage management	
Dance/Drama				

Each option is assessed through 50% practical work (preparation, rehearsal and end-product) and 10% response to the process of development. The marks for the two options are added together and then halved, giving a total of 60% of your final mark for Drama.

Each option is assessed by your own teacher, whose marks are checked by a visiting moderator.

Assessment Objectives

The assessment of your skills will be based on your ability to:

- Show knowledge and understanding of practical Drama skills necessary for presenting a performance to an audience, and to work constructively with others (30%). This is Assessment Objective 1 (AO1).
- Respond to plays and other forms of Drama from a performance/design angle; and to see comparisons between texts and dramatic styles of different historical periods and of different cultures (10%). This is Assessment Objective 2 (AO2).
- Judge and develop the effectiveness of your own and others' work as you prepare and rehearse it (20%). This is Assessment Objective 3 (AO3).

C1 Requirements for performance options

A What must be done?

- At least one of your options must be a **performance**.
- One piece of coursework must be **scripted** and one **unscripted**.
  For the performance options, this means:

Scripted	Option 1	Devised thematic work; or
	Option 2	Acting (from a script)

Unscripted	Option 1	Devised thematic work; or
	Option 3	Improvisation; or
	Option 4	Theatre-in-Education presentation; or
	Option 5	Dance/Drama

- You must speak in English.
- You must work in a group of three or more. In general the smaller the group the better: there will be fewer social difficulties, and you will be able to show your own levels of skills more clearly than in a large group.
- You should give yourselves a performance time of approximately five minutes actually on stage. This may be at the same time as other actors/dancers, although the more people in the group, the longer you need to be on stage.
- You must present a written response to the chosen task. This will include evidence of research, understanding of Drama skills and techniques, and comparisons with other types of Drama (see AO2 below).

Improvised
performance
entitled 'Jealousy'

B How are these options assessed?

Each option is assessed out of 60 marks, made up from:

AO2	Response to plays and other types of Drama	10/60
AO3	Work in progress	20/60
AO1	Final presentation	30/60

AO2 Response to plays and other types of Drama

This is assessed through your written Coursework about the *preparation* for your task. You have to show your knowledge and understanding of performing various plays and other types of Drama, including those from different historical periods and different cultures.

AO3 Work in progress

This is assessed by your teacher through the development of your work during the *rehearsal* period. You have to show that you can judge your work in order to develop it effectively, and that you can recognise your own and other people's strengths and weaknesses.

AO1 Final presentation

This is assessed through the final *performance*. You have to show how good your practical performance skills and techniques are; and that you can work constructively with other people. Skills will include your use of voice, movement and space; characterisation, timing and pace; creativity and originality; knowledge of health and safety considerations; and your understanding of the needs of your audience.

C Skills and techniques

What skills are assessed in performance work?

You need to show that you can:

- respond to the stimulus with suitable ideas and understanding
- use suitable voice and/or movement techniques
- create a role, and keep in character
- create mood and atmosphere
- show sensitivity, creativity, originality and flair
- understand your audience
- work constructively with the rest of your group.

Improving your skills

As you experiment with different skills, try to identify:

- **what** you are doing
- **how** you are doing it
- **why** you are doing it
- **what** problems you are having
- **how** you might overcome the problems.

In answering these questions, in as much detail as possible, it is likely that you will begin to identify various things you could improve. You will obviously need to think carefully about exactly what skills and techniques you are using and what you could use. For this, you need to refer to Sections A1–5 (pages 1–45).

The mini-projects (pages 63–122) are intended to help you to identify important features of different aspects of work. If you have worked through most of them, think back over what went well or badly, and any particular lessons you learnt while doing them. If you have not yet tackled any of them, look at some of them now. They will help you to see some of the potential advantages and problems, and it should be easier to make your final decisions.

Look, too, at the Assessment guidelines in Appendix 1 (pages 231–2). These should help you to identify and improve your levels at different skills.

D Getting started

1 Essential resources for the task

If you do not have suitable resources, it will be very difficult to present successful work. The essential resources needed are shown under each separate option – consider them carefully before you start!

2 What are the possibilities?

Right at the beginning of the work, you must think about your audience, the issue or topic, the purpose of your performance, ideas about the actual presentation, and the skills of the acting group itself. All of these will be looked at in more detail under each option. But in all performance options you also need to consider the following points.

3 How can you best use the people you are working with?

- What roles usually suit each of the people in your group?
- Who finds learning lines easy? Who finds it difficult? In scripted work, consider the amount of speech and action each character has; then try to 'fit' each one to the available actors.
- Who in the group is good at improvisation? How can that ability be used?
- Who in the group has understanding, good originality and good creativity in presenting scripted work? And in presenting improvised work?
- Who is particularly good at following advice given by the rest of the group?
- What other strengths does each member of the group have? How can you best use those individual strengths?
- What individual or group weaknesses are there? How can you avoid putting members of the group into situations where these weaknesses become obvious?

4 What health and safety factors do you need to consider?

For the actors/dancers
- The acting/dancing space should generally be uncluttered, so that there is sufficient space for necessary movement without having to squeeze past stage furniture.
- Scenery should be securely fastened, so that it will not collapse!
- Stage furniture and props should be suitable for stage work, so that they are not going to fall apart or break during performance; they should not have sharp or rough corners, sides, parts, etc.

- Any difficult moves or timing should be practised until they become almost automatic, so that there is virtually no possibility of making dangerous mistakes in performance.
- Costume should be suitable for the movement and action of the piece.
- You must warm up properly beforehand. A failure to use suitable warm-up activities often means that it takes time for you to get into your role properly, and it may lead to strained muscles.

For the audience

- The audience space should be uncluttered by potential hazards such as trailing leads or insecure seating.
- There should be sufficient space for access by people in wheelchairs or on crutches.
- The use of technical aspects must not cause discomfort, e.g. prolonged use of strobe lighting; the use of explosive devices into the audience; or the over-enthusiastic use of a smoke machine.

Fire safety

Make sure you know whether anything you are proposing might be subject to fire regulations. Ask if you're not sure!

5 First ideas

- In your group, brainstorm first ideas, making a list or a scatter diagram of things which come up.
- Discuss each in turn to see how you might develop them. Do some offer more possibilities than others?

6 Planning the work

Make notes of any decisions you make.

- How much time or how many lessons do you have to prepare this work?
- Realistically, how much extra time might you have for practice? Do you need some sort of written agreement to ensure the necessary commitment from the whole group?
- What is the ideal length of the finished product, taking into consideration things such as the preparation time, the audience, and the purpose? It's better to be short and interesting than long and boring!
- Do you need to do any research? If so, what?
- If you are doing a scripted piece of work, what targets do you need for learning lines? Try to make sure that you set yourselves achievable targets or people will quickly fall behind and lose heart: yet the sooner your words are learnt, the sooner you can all concentrate on the action and presentation.
- If you are doing an improvised piece of work, how can you be sure of keeping the action and the interest? Can you avoid frequent scene changes?
- If you are doing a piece of Dance/Drama, what accompaniment are you likely to use? How might you best treat the subject, ensuring that you have continuity and flow?
- Does the piece appear to fall into distinct stages or units? If so, how will you rehearse to ensure that all get equal attention?
- What special considerations do you need to bear in mind when using a particular style/genre? For instance, how to encourage audience participation with pantomime, how to achieve laughter from comedy or farce, how to achieve atmosphere and feeling with a serious piece.

- What special considerations do you need to bear in mind when performing for your target audience? For instance, vocabulary which is understood by infants, or clear Mime and use of body for a deaf audience.
- Do you need individuals to take responsibility for particular technical aspects, or are you going to be able to deal with everything together? How quickly will you need certain things? How long before you actually need a particular prop, sound effect or item of clothing?

7 Getting going

You need to get into action as soon as possible after the first discussions, trying some quick improvisations from your most successful ideas. Remember that the early stages are experimental, and that you should be exploring various possibilities. Nothing should be set in stone straightaway – details can be changed later. But the sooner you have a feel for a scene, the sooner you can judge its likely success and see where to go next.

At the end of the first run-through, discuss how it went. What went well? What felt wrong? Was it realistic when necessary? What needs to be made clearer for the audience to understand? It is worth looking back to some of the mini-projects to remind yourself of other topics for discussion. Make notes of the main points you discussed. Such notes act as reminders for your next rehearsal, and they will help you later when you come to do your written coursework.

E Developing your work

1 General points

- Keep the overall story clearly in mind.
- Continue to experiment with different ideas, solutions and techniques.
- Remember that the opening must catch the audience's attention and interest.
- Make sure that the audience will recognise the end as the end!
- Constantly remind yourselves of your objectives.
- Constantly remind yourselves of the needs of your audience.
- Keep clearly in mind the style/genre you are using.
- Make sure that every unit has the same attention paid to it.
- Make notes of any new ideas which you try, or any new decisions made.

2 Your role/character

- Get to know your character, his/her feelings, and what makes him/her 'tick'.
- Experiment with different voice and movement techniques until your character comes alive.
- Try various rehearsal techniques which will help you to become more familiar with your character and situation.
- Make notes of any experiments tried, of any problems, and of any decisions made.

3 Your movement

- Try various rehearsal techniques until you are familiar with the best movements for particular moments in the piece.
- Experiment with different movement possibilities until you find solutions which come naturally to you and/or the group.
- Make sure that your own movement fits with the scene and with the rest of the group.
- If you are using music, make sure that your movements fit its mood and style.
- Make notes of any experiments tried, of any problems, and of any decisions made.

4 Improvements

- Watch out for possible ways to improve the content or the staging of your piece.
- Watch out for opportunities to use special techniques to make the piece more interesting.
- Make sure that you block the work suitably, and choreograph movement when necessary, in order to make the performance clearer to the audience.
- Make notes of any techniques tried, and of any changes and additions made.

5 Technical aspects

- Think carefully about the type of stage you are using and any set dressing which you are planning to use, bearing in mind the sight lines of your audience.
- Make sure that any props you are using have a purpose; and that you use essential props as early as possible in the preparation period.
- Sort out your costume, bearing in mind such things as the style of the play, the historical or geographical setting, the costumes of the rest of the group, the lighting, any essential movement. Then get used to wearing it in rehearsal.
- Practise your stage make-up if the conditions make it necessary to use it.
- Experiment with your lighting resources.
- Plan and prepare any live or recorded sounds that will help the atmosphere or effect.
- Make notes of any ideas tried, problems found, and decisions made.

6 Learning from others

- Give trial performances of your play during the preparation period.
- Ask for constructive advice from someone outside the group whom you respect.
- Make notes of what other people say, and use them as pointers for what to do next.

7 Health and safety

- Consider various health and safety factors which may need addressing. Ask for help if you are not sure – do not just leave it to luck!
- Make notes of what you do, and why.

F Common faults and pitfalls

The following faults are often seen in GCSE presentations. Yet they are all things which can be sorted out. If you can overcome them, you will give a much better performance!

- Producing **too long a piece of work**. Such pieces usually get worse as they get longer! It is much better to produce a short and interesting piece of work, leaving your audience wanting more.
- Having **too many short scenes**. They break the flow of the play, the concentration of the actors and audience, and the overall interest. Sometimes the scene changes take longer than the scenes themselves! When you are choosing script extracts, avoid those with very short scenes – especially those written for television, where different presentation techniques allow for frequent short scenes.
- Having **too many chairs or sitting places**. It can be very dull to have actors sitting all the time. Do not be afraid to stand, or kneel or move when it is suitable; and try to have variation amongst the people on stage. A theatrical presentation must have visual interest. Otherwise, the audience might just as well listen to the radio.
- Having **too little action** other than reading, having a drink or watching television. This, too, can be very dull for your audience when they see the same things over and over again. Try to use your own experience, memory and imagination to give your character more interesting things to do.
- Having **too little variety in movement**, so that your character becomes stilted. You need variety in style, pace, mood, space, strength, group dynamics and blocking.
- **Not using the stage space**. Don't forget that the whole stage space is there to be used, so decide when you might come to the front; when you would be more suitably placed at the back; or when you might cross the space for some reason. Suitable use of space adds visual interest, as well as emphasising certain situations – such as moving away from someone who frightens you.
- Using **unsuitable vocabulary and ideas** because the needs of the particular audience have not been recognised. Research their interests and needs properly: you do not want a bored, restless audience!

- Having **insufficient understanding of a particular style/genre** to get the right response from the audience: and then not being able to deal with their 'wrong' reactions, e.g. if they laugh when you don't want them to. Look back at Section A5 (pages 37–45) for reminders.

- **Not practising moments of difficult movement or timing**. If you don't practise such key moments sufficiently, you can be sure that something will go wrong when you are under the stress of actual performance. Make sure you know exactly what you are doing, so that it becomes second nature to you.

- **Not practising with essential props** (including food and/or drinks) before the performance. Props have a habit of tripping up the unwary, and they need to be used in rehearsal. What happens, for example, if food sticks to the roof of your mouth? Or if you drop something just where someone else will trip over it?

- **Not having enough dress rehearsals** to avoid possible problems with costume movement or changes. It can be very dull if the audience has to wait for ages in the dark while an actor changes costume between scenes; and it can cause the wrong reactions if an actor gets his/her costume torn moving past the furniture.

- **Not rehearsing with technicians**. The people operating your lighting or sound cannot do so without rehearsing with the group. You may provide excellent cue-sheets, but if everything goes smoothly in such circumstances, you are lucky. You cannot blame a technician for misunderstanding your instructions, if it is the first time they have tried to work with you. Unless you have practised together, something is all too likely to go wrong.

- **Using unsuitable make-up**. Remember that the use of stage make-up is to paint your face when the lights have made it pale and 'flat' – a very different purpose from everyday 'fashion' make-up. If your audience are close to you, you probably will not need make-up at all. Specialist stage make-up is needed when performing in a large space or for any special effects.

G Completing the work

1 Polishing the work

The final week or so before performance

- Make sure that everyone in the group knows exactly what they should be doing, and what everyone else should be doing.
- Know your character 'inside-out', so that you can behave instinctively in performance.
- Practise any parts when split-second timing is essential.
- Check all your back-stage arrangements: props, costume, set, lighting, sound. Make sure your technicians practise with you.
- Check that you have taken health and safety factors into account, both on stage and for your audience.

2 Final arrangements for the presentation

For the actual day of performance

- Make sure that the whole cast knows the time of performance, and the time it will take to get ready. (Don't leave yourselves too tight, just in case!) Arrange a sensible time to meet, so that you can be confident in each other. You don't want to waste energy on unnecessary hold-ups: keep the nerves for the performance itself!
- Check your technical aspects as early as possible: do not leave this check until the last minute, or you can be sure that something will be missing, broken or will go wrong. Give yourself time to discover any problems before they become disasters! If there is a problem, keep cool, and think how best to overcome it: you have to find the best solution available.
- Give yourselves time to 'warm up' for the performance. You cannot do your best if you go in 'cold'. This may vary with different people, with different plays, with different characters and emotions. It may concentrate on voice, movement, feelings, genre, etc. Find what is best for you and don't be tempted to race through it too quickly: concentrate and become fully focused on the performance ahead.
- If you are performing away from your own centre, try to arrive at the venue in time to have a quick practice in this unknown space, unless you have been fortunate enough to have a full rehearsal there anyway.

3 The presentation itself

- Concentrate.
- Listen and react to other characters and situations.
- Speak up – it's pointless having an audience if they can't hear you because you are, for example, too quick, too quiet, or have too strong an accent.
- Immerse yourself in your movement, so that whatever you are doing appears to come naturally from your character.
- Don't panic if mistakes are made: deal with them in character.
- Be aware of audience laughter – hold your position, and start again as the sound fades. (Don't wait for actual silence, or the pace will flag.)
- Be aware of other reactions from your audience: and don't be tempted to 'play on' them, as you are likely to go over the top.
- Don't be tempted to change things as you go along – keep to what you have rehearsed, or you will 'throw' other members of the cast.
- Don't be put off by different reactions from different audiences: learn from the experience.

- Be aware of other actors and any problems which they may be having: be sympathetic to them.
- Above all, keep in character at all times!

4 Written work

Remember that you have to write at least 500 words on your response to your work. This will include information on how you explored the task you undertook and on relationships and comparisons between different texts and/or styles/genres, with examples from different historical times and different cultures. All of this is expected to show your understanding of the option you have chosen.

At the end of each option section, you will find some ideas for suitable research, and for possible comparisons between different plays, themes or genres.

Examiners' tip

> If you follow the advice given in this section, you will not go too far wrong! Many presentations are spoilt because groups have not considered potential problems. Here, problems that could occur are covered, along with how to solve them. You have no excuse!

Option 1 Devised thematic work

A What is meant by 'Devised thematic work'?

In the terms of the AQA syllabus, this is a mixture of scripted and unscripted work focused on a theme which gives good opportunities for variety.

The theme could be connected with one of your set plays for the written paper; or a subject of particular interest to you and your group; or a current issue of importance; or a topic which you are studying in another subject. In fact, any theme which enables you to show variety in what you do. Don't choose anything which restricts you!

B Essential resources for the task

If you are to complete this task successfully, you must have:

- a suitable space for both the performance and the seating of the audience
- the ability to connect suitable scripts and improvisations around a theme
- an understanding of what the writer intended
- an understanding of how to put a script into a performance
- an understanding of how to create an effective piece of improvisation
- suitable costume and props, or the facilities and knowledge for making them.

In addition it may be helpful to have:

- reasonable lighting equipment, in order to improve the theatrical effectiveness
- suitable stage make-up if it is necessary for the performance space or for the effectiveness of the presentation
- reasonable audio equipment or the knowledge and ability to make 'live' sounds
- masks, or the facilities and knowledge for making them, if you are using them.

C What are the possibilities for Devised thematic work?

What theme should you choose?

Often the most powerful Devised thematic work is on a theme about which you feel strongly, so you could make a list of themes of particular interest to you and your group. Your teacher may have set the theme, in which case you need to find aspects of it which are of interest to you. Thematic work also gives an excellent opportunity for the exploration of ideas through time (different historical periods) or space (different parts of the world).

How do you deal with the chosen theme?

You will need to do some research to make sure that you are dealing with the theme in a knowledgeable way. You need to have clear objectives of what you want to communicate to the audience: don't just string together a series of scenes without identifying why they are relevant. The scenes must also show variety, e.g. in approach, genre/style, historical period or cultural outlook. Look at the possibilities for doing something 'different': try not to choose the most predictable ideas, or the most obvious ways of presenting them. But do not become so 'way out' that the audience cannot understand what you are saying!

What texts are acceptable?

In Devised thematic work you can draw on a wide variety of texts, not just play scripts. You may want to include some poetry, song lyrics, contemporary music, people's reminiscences, newspaper articles, etc. But remember that whatever texts you use must be linked naturally with each other, and with the unscripted work which you include.

What unscripted work is acceptable?

In Devised thematic work you may wish to use polished improvisation, but mime and Dance/Drama are equally acceptable if you feel comfortable with these.

What about style/genre?

Think carefully about the strengths and weaknesses of your group in presenting different styles/genres; and identify those with which you all feel comfortable. Think about your intended target audience, and identify various styles/genres which might be suitable for them. Certainly, if you want to show that you can present a variety of techniques, it is helpful to consider having pieces which come from different styles/genres: but there must still be an overall 'unity' and purpose. Avoid doing different styles just for the sake of the exercise!

What about characters and roles?

Some actors know that they can portray certain roles more easily than others; and when you come to an examination situation, you may prefer to present those with which you feel 'safe'. On the other hand, you may be an actor who enjoys the challenge of trying different character roles. Whichever you prefer, Devised thematic work gives you the chance to show that you can tackle a number of contrasting roles.

D Common faults and pitfalls

In addition to the points raised on pages 130–1, you need to be aware of some of the very common 'traps' associated with Devised thematic work.

- **Not identifying the theme clearly enough.** If themes are too vague, they lead to work which has no understandable purpose. For instance, if you choose the theme of 'Age', you need to narrow it down, perhaps to 'The Seven Ages of Man' or 'Parenting' or 'Children's Games Through the Ages'.
- **Not having clear objectives.** Again, if you are too vague, the work will have no sense of purpose. You must identify your focus and choose relevant material, e.g. with the theme of 'Refugees', you might focus on those caused by war, or by natural disasters, or by families; on the conditions from which they have fled, or the chances of a better life. You

must decide on your objectives, e.g. that refugees are victims of circumstances beyond their control, or that they tend to get caught in the poverty trap.

- **Choosing material which does not have enough dramatic basis.** Failing to choose pieces with good dramatic possibilities can lead to a very dull, static presentation. Look for good dramatic pieces which show contrast and variety – of questions raised, historical times, ways of looking at the same topic, styles of presentation, etc.
- **The poor order of pieces.** Sometimes dramatic effect is lost because the wrong order has been followed, or scenes have been linked badly. You need to think carefully about how you want to develop your theme, so that each piece adds what has gone before. In this way, there will be a clear progression or narrative through the finished presentation.

E Possible starters for Devised thematic work

■ **For a Devised piece of work on 'Schools'**, you might use extracts from the play scripts of *Our Day Out* by Alan Bleasdale, *Daisy Pulls It Off* by Denise Deegan, or *Teechers* by John Godber; other texts could include 'Another Brick in the Wall' by Pink Floyd, 'The Lesson', a poem by Roger McGough, or a quote from your school's Ofsted Report. Improvisations could include scenes on 'School trips', on 'Examinations', or on 'Bullying'.

■ **For a Devised piece on 'Imprisonment'**, you might use play extracts from *Our Country's Good* by Timberlake Wertenbaker, *Porridge* (TV scripts) by Dick Clement and Ian Le Frenais, or *The Play of the Diary of Anne Frank* adapted by Frances Goodrich and Albert Hackett; other texts could include 'The Ballad of Reading Gaol' by Oscar Wilde, the film *The Great Escape* or a newspaper article on wrongful imprisonment. Improvisations could include scenes on Nelson Mandela, or 'Kidnap', or 'Jail breakouts'.

■ **For a Devised piece on 'Family relationships'**, you might use play extracts from *Billy Liar* by Waterhouse and Hall, *This Happy Breed* by Noel Coward, or *Blood Brothers* by Willy Russell; other texts could include magazine 'agony columns', newspaper articles on teenage pregnancy, or 'I don't like Mondays' by the Boomtown Rats. Improvisations could include scenes on 'Dealing with Granny', 'Moving house', or 'Family holidays'.

F Possible written work

1 Personal response to the task:

■ how you explored different ideas and possibilities, including styles/genres
■ what problems you came across
■ why you came to your decisions
■ how you worked in with the other actors, the director and the designers
■ what compromises you had to make
■ how you considered health and safety issues.

2 Research:

■ the job of the actor in putting a devised piece of work onto the stage
■ the theme of the piece
■ the relevance of the theme to different historical times
■ the relevance of the theme to different cultures
■ the social history of any chosen times and cultures, e.g. fashion, behaviour, music
■ possible texts and their writers, e.g. play scripts, poems, newspaper articles.

3 Comparisons

Compare your scripts and your improvisations in, for example:

■ style
■ historical and cultural settings
■ the ways of communicating the theme/message
■ the acting skills and techniques needed.

Also:

■ the different acting and presentation skills needed for two or three pieces of Devised thematic work which you have been in.

Examiners' tip

The opportunity to combine text and improvised material is an exciting one and you have the chance to create an excellent original piece. You must remember to research your theme thoroughly, making sure that the chosen texts are appropriate, and that you have a clear idea of what you want to achieve. Avoid the temptation to pack in everything but the kitchen sink, as this only leads to overlong, dull and confusing performances.

Option 2 Acting

A What is meant by 'Acting'?

In the terms of the AQA examination, this is the Scripted Option. That is, where you use a script written by someone other than the candidates, learn the words, and take it from 'the page to the stage'.

You may perform extracts from one of the plays you are studying for the Written Paper. This is obviously helpful for you, as it makes you more familiar with the script itself, and it also ensures that you really do consider the play from a performance point of view. However, it can be equally helpful to act a totally different play so that you gain greater knowledge and understanding of other Drama. If you are not taking the Set Plays section of the Written Paper, then you have a free choice anyway. Try to choose a play script which will widen your existing knowledge and give you suitable challenges for your ability.

B Essential resources for the task

If you are to complete this task successfully, you must have:

- a suitable space for both the performance and the seating of the audience
- the ability to learn lines
- an understanding of what the writer intended
- an understanding of how to put a script into a performance
- suitable costume and props, or the facilities and knowledge for making them
- masks, or the facilities and knowledge for making them, if you are using a script which demands the use of masks.

In addition it may be helpful to have:

- reasonable lighting equipment, in order to improve the theatrical effectiveness
- suitable stage make-up if it is necessary for the performance space or for the effectiveness of the presentation
- reasonable audio equipment or the knowledge and ability to make 'live' sounds.

C What are the possibilities for Acting?

Do you want to present a particular issue or theme?

Many playwrights focus on an issue, so that the writer's intention is obviously a serious one – even if the style/genre is not. It is possible to communicate a serious message through, for example, comedy or pantomime. It may be difficult to find a suitable script if your issue is too narrow or too contemporary.

Do you want to present a particular style/genre?

Think carefully about the strengths and weaknesses of your group in presenting different styles/genres; and identify one with which you all feel comfortable. Think about your intended target audience, and identify styles/genres which might be suitable for them. Look back at Section A5 (pages 37–45) for reminders.

Do you want to present a particular type of character?

Perhaps you feel that you can portray certain roles more easily than others, and in an examination situation, you may prefer one with which you feel 'safe'. But you may be an actor who enjoys the challenge of trying a totally different character role. Whichever you prefer, it may influence your choice of script; so look carefully at the possibilities offered to you. It is often more satisfying for both actor and audience if the character develops and 'grows' as the piece progresses.

Do you want to deal with particular emotions?

Many actors find it very rewarding to portray emotions, but you need to be able to lose yourself completely in your character and situation if you are to be successful. It may be that you are an actor who finds it more difficult to show emotion, and you must recognise your limitations. Some play scripts demand a lot of emotion, so look carefully at any you are considering.

What emotion is shown in this face? How might you build up this emotion in performance?

For what audience are you wanting to perform?

Obviously the choice of target audience will influence your choice of script, in terms of content, of vocabulary, of style/genre, of characters and of action. Look carefully at scripts on offer, and ask for advice if you are not sure about suitability.

D Common faults and pitfalls

In addition to the general points raised on pages 130–1, you need to be aware of some of the very common 'traps' associated with scripted Acting.

- **Poor choice of script.** You need to recognise when a script suits your abilities, or when it is too simple or too complicated. Don't just choose one because it is the same as ones you have done before, because you will not develop your skills. But also beware of overstretching yourself in an examination situation. You don't want to tackle something which is too hard, and find it ends up as total disaster! Give yourself manageable challenges.

- **Lack of balance in the roles**. It is not very fair to members of a group if one person has very little to say or do, while another has the limelight all the time. Different actors can take on different amounts, but you must make sure that everyone is given a fair chance to show what they can do.

- **Not learning words.** The worst occasions for both the rest of the cast and for the audience are those when an actor does not know their words. It throws the rest of the group, it leads to onstage prompts, uncomfortable silences, and coming out of role, and interrupts the whole scene. If you have chosen your part according to your ability to learn lines, then there is no excuse for not knowing them. The sooner you learn them, the sooner you can concentrate on improving your characterisation and movement.

- **Difficulty in keeping in character**. When actors come out of role the belief in them goes. You must try to become your character to such an extent that you think and act like them at all times – even when you have nothing to say.

- **Using offensive material**. There is no need to cause offence in dramatic presentations, and you will not know what each member of an audience finds offensive. Some people cannot accept bad language from a teenager even if they would have no objection to professional actors using that same language. Your school will have certain standards and rules for language and behaviour, so do not choose scripts which go against those expectations.

- **Poor links between extracts**. If you are intending to present several extracts from the same play, make sure they link smoothly. The choice of extracts may show an obvious development in a character or situation, or a narrator may fill in missing details. Choose the extracts carefully and make sure that the connection between them is obvious.

- **Spending too much time on technical aspects**. Sometimes a presentation suffers because too much time has been spent on the technical aspects. The priority must be the acting, because without that you will have no performance anyway! There will be some technical points which will be essential very early on, but the less essential ones should be left until you are confident in the acting.

E Possible scripts for acting

- **Focusing on an issue:** e.g. *Pack of Lies* by Hugh Whitemore, on loyalty; *Whose Life is it Anyway?* by Brian Clarke, on euthanasia; *O.U.T. spells OUT* by David Holman, on sending children to Australia

- **For three or four girls:** e.g. the opening scene of *Absent Friends* by Alan Ayckbourn; *My Mother Said . . .* by Charlotte Keatley; *Shakers* by John Godber

- **For three or four boys:** e.g. *A Game of Soldiers* by Jan Needle; *Unman, Wittering and Zigo* by Giles Cooper; *Another Country* by Julian Mitchell; *Bouncers* by John Godber

- **For mixed groups of three or four:** e.g. *Blithe Spirit* by Noel Coward; *Taste of Honey* by Shelagh Delaney; *The Golden Pathway Annual* by Harding and Burrows

- **Easier to learn:** e.g. *Of Mice and Men* adapted from John Steinbeck's novel; *Blood Brothers* by Willy Russell; *Forty Short Plays* by Ann Cartwright
- **With a historical focus:** e.g. *Female Transport* by Steve Gooch, *The Miracle Worker* by William Gibson; *Hobson's Choice* by Harold Brighouse
- **With a multi-cultural focus:** e.g. *The Crucible* by Arthur Miller; *Haroun and the Sea of Stories* by Salman Rushdie, adapted by T. Supple and D. Tushingham; *Arabian Nights* adapted by Dominic Cooke for the Young Vic Theatre Co.

F Possible written work

1 Personal response to the task:

- how you explored different ideas and possibilities
- what problems you came across
- why you came to your decisions
- how you worked in with the other actors, the director and the designers
- what compromises you had to make
- how you considered health and safety issues.

2 Research:

- the job of the actor in putting a script onto the stage
- the play within its historical and social context, and its style/genre
- the writer and his/her intention
- the theme of the play
- relationships between the main characters
- other plays on the same theme.

3 Comparisons:

- the treatment of the theme: e.g. euthanasia in *Whose Life is it Anyway?* by Brian Clarke, and in *The Sacred Flame* by W. Somerset Maugham
- the style of the theme: e.g. war in *Oh, What a Lovely War!* by the Theatre Workshop, and in *Dad's Army* by Jeremy Lloyd and David Croft
- the portrayal of characters: e.g. fathers: Mr Birling in *An Inspector Calls* by J. B. Priestley; Edward in *Find Me* by Olwen Wymark; Mr Darling in *Peter Pan* by J. M. Barrie
- the message of the play: e.g. place in society: *Pygmalion* by G. B. Shaw; *Taste of Honey* by Shelagh Delaney; *Roots* by Arnold Wesker
- the different acting skills needed for two or three plays which you have been in.

Examiners' tip

> Your choice of script is very important. It is sometimes obvious that the actors do not fully understand the storyline, or what they should be putting across, and the presentation is disappointing because performers have taken on a task which was too demanding. Certainly choose a script which challenges and extends you, but make sure that it will not defeat or destroy you!

Option 3 Improvisation

A What is meant by 'Improvisation'?

In the terms of the AQA examination, this is any piece of non-scripted dramatic work which you have made up yourselves.

The stimulus for this work can be from a wide variety of sources, such as photographs, articles, characters, ideas, objects, events, etc. It could focus on one of the cultural or historical elements which you are expected to experience during your coursework.

B Essential resources for the task

If you are to complete this task successfully, you must have:

- a suitable space for both the performance and the seating of the audience
- an understanding of how to create a piece of Improvisation
- the practical ability to use that understanding effectively
- suitable costume and props, or the facilities and knowledge for making them.

In addition it may be helpful to have:

- reasonable lighting equipment, in order to improve the theatrical effectiveness
- suitable stage make-up if it is necessary for the performance space or for the effectiveness of the presentation
- reasonable audio equipment or the knowledge and ability to make 'live' sounds
- masks, or the facilities and knowledge for making them, if you intend to use them.

C What are the possibilities for Improvisation?

What subject should you choose?

Improvisation gives you a wonderful opportunity for choosing characters, issues or situations which appeal to you: and allows you to create a dramatic presentation for a specific space, or audience or event. But the choice can be so wide that it becomes difficult to make quick decisions. Think carefully about different possibilities: your first idea may be the best, or it may prove to be the least imaginative and most predictable. Give yourselves a clear focus and good dramatic opportunities.

What about characters and roles?

One of the advantages of improvisation is that you can create whatever characters, real or imaginary, that you like. Some actors know that they can portray certain roles more easily than others; and when you come to an examination situation, you may prefer to present those with which you feel 'safe'. On the other hand, you may be an actor who enjoys the challenge of trying different roles. Whichever you prefer, improvisation gives you the chance to show that you can develop a believable role with understanding, creativity and sensitivity.

What about the content of the piece?

Improvisation gives you the freedom to choose the way in which your subject is developed, and what you include or leave out, and it enables you to suit the work to the interests and practical abilities of your group. It does, however, mean that you need to be even more ruthless in cutting out parts which are not suitable, and even more focused on finding the most dramatic solutions. An Improvisation which just goes on and on without getting anywhere can be deadly!

D Common faults and pitfalls

In addition to the general points raised on pages 130–1, you need to be aware of some of the very common 'traps' associated with improvised work.

- **Not giving sufficient information** in your piece for the audience to understand what is going on. For example, if you fail to give essential facts about previous events or what has happened 'offstage', you may create confusing gaps in your story. Make sure you do not just assume that the audience will understand: they probably won't!

- **The failure to develop real characterisation**, leaving your characters as 'flat', 'two-dimensional' figures who prevent the audience from believing in the situation you are trying to portray.

- The **lack of a build-up** to any tension or climax you want to show. Sometimes this is because moments of tension or climax are not included at all, but often it is because there is no build-up to the key moments. For example, you cannot jump straight in to an emotion such as anger or fear; you must provide progressively increasing signs during the lead-up to the moment when things happen.

- The **mismatch of style and content**. Sometimes candidates choose good subject matter, but because they choose the wrong style/genre the whole effect is lost. This is particularly unfortunate when the actors want to get a message across to their audience; or where treating the subject in the wrong way can cause upset or offence to individuals in the audience.

- The **lack of clear and repeatable cue lines or moves** for the other members of the cast, and for the technicians, to work from. It can be one of the main reasons for things going wrong in performance. For example, an actor who forgets a key line may find that another character fails to come on, a sound effect is not given, or more confusion is caused when someone else tries to cover up. An actor who comes on too soon may cause a whole section of the piece to be left out, or give problems for another actor who now does not have time to change costume, or for someone else who now finds they are in a scene when they should not be.

E Possible starters for improvisations

- **For suggestions of various issues**, look at the Theatre-in-Education Option (page 147)
- **For suggestions of various themes**, look at the Devised Option (page 136)
- **Use different stimuli:** e.g. photo albums, various objects (especially unusual ones), sound effects, the local newspaper, music, stories
- **Suggest the location for the piece:** e.g. a casualty department, your school, a hole in the ground, Timbuktu
- **Historical events:** e.g. VE Day, the Moon Landing, plague, the arrival of the Romans in Britain, the beheading of Charles I

- **Stories from around the world:** e.g. Chinese ghost stories, Icelandic sagas, Aesop's fables, Greek myths
- **Famous quotations:** e.g. 'Too many cooks spoil the broth', 'To be or not to be', 'You've never had it so good', 'The greatest of these is love'.

F Possible written work

1 Personal response to the task:

- how you explored different ideas and possibilities
- what problems you came across
- why you came to your decisions
- how you worked in with the other actors, the director and the designers
- what compromises you had to make.

2 Research:

- the job of the actor in putting an improvisation onto the stage
- the theme of the play
- any historical or cultural or social aspects to the interpretation of the theme
- relationships between the main characters
- improvisation and storytelling in different historical times and cultures
- the place of mime in improvisation
- interactive improvisation, e.g. Commedia dell'arte, stand-up comedy, pantomime.

3 Comparisons:

- the style of the theme: e.g. 'Space travel' could be dealt with in a straight, factual way, as a fantasy or as a farce
- the content or angle you choose: e.g. an improvisation on 'My school' could show all the good things, all the bad things, many imaginary things, or could be an advert for the school
- the historical or cultural aspects: e.g. 'The role of women in society' could deal with women in medieval times, Victorian times, Edwardian times, the 1960s, etc; or with women in Arab countries, Russia, the Caribbean, the USA
- the different acting skills needed for two or three different improvisations which you have been in.

Examiners' tip

There is more to improvisation than mere storytelling. The work undertaken should enable you to explore characterisation, motivation and relationships, in depth, within the scenario you have created. You can learn a lot by testing out various situations, roles and topics. Make sure that you approach your subject with sensitivity and understanding, know what you want to achieve, and don't just end up playing yourself!

Option 4 Theatre-in-Education (TIE)

A What is Theatre-in-Education (TIE)?

This is presenting a Drama performance to inform, to teach a lesson or to explore an issue.

For example, you might be informing an audience about Shakespeare and his theatre, teaching about 'Stranger danger', or exploring the results of drug abuse. This form of presentation gives a wonderful opportunity for Interactive work between the actors and their audience. This may be of any age from young children through to the elderly. It may be an audience with a particular problem, such as victims of bullying or of disability; or it may be an audience who just need to know more about a particular topic.

B Essential resources for the task

If you are to complete this task successfully, you must have:

- a suitable space for both the performance and the seating of the audience
- a suitable audience, and knowledge of that audience
- suitable stage furniture
- suitable costume and props, or the facilities and knowledge for making them
- suitable stage make-up, if the performance space is large, or if special character effects are needed

- easily transportable scenery and props if your presentation is to be held away from your centre.

In addition, it may be helpful to have:

- reasonable lighting equipment, in order to improve the theatrical effectiveness
- audio equipment, if recorded music or sounds would improve the presentation
- masks, or the facilities and knowledge for making them, if they would improve the presentation.

C What are the possibilities for Theatre-in-Education?

What audience do you want to perform to?

For example: Infants, Juniors, Year 8, Year 11, parents, senior citizens, people with disabilities, visiting foreign exchange students? Every audience has its advantages and pleasures, but often it also has its difficulties. Do you know enough about your likely audience, or will you have to do some research on their interests, needs and vocabulary? How will you do this?

What issue/topic do you want to deal with?

For example: hygiene, transfer to secondary school, relationships, drugs, bullying, Remembrance Day, historical figures or events, life skills, or traditions from different cultures or religions. Different topics/issues are obviously suitable for different audiences, and you must make sure that you choose something relevant to your target audience.

What is the purpose of performing this issue to this audience?

For example: to teach a moral or a lesson for everyday life; to give greater information or understanding about an issue or topic; to explore possible results of a situation or event. Your choice of audience and issue may make the purpose obvious, but you need to keep it clearly in mind, as it will affect the way you present the issue.

What style/genre will be most suitable for this issue and this audience?

For example: Comedy, Straight, Interactive, Western, Whodunnit? Some styles will be less suitable for particular issues or audiences: Farce would not be ideal for subjects like drugs or bullying, and Pantomime might not be best for teenagers! Refer to Section A5 (pages 37–45) for more help.

Does the form of the stimulus itself suggest any particular ideas?

For example: a theme, poem, newspaper article, picture, sound, lighting, object. It may be that a picture used as the stimulus gives you the idea to use a sequence of pictures in your play; a lighting stimulus immediately suggests a mood or atmosphere to you; or an object gives you your central focus.

D Common faults and pitfalls

In addition to the general points raised on pages 130–1, you need to be aware of some of the very common 'traps' associated with Theatre-in-Education.

- **Incorrect facts**. When actors miss out essential facts, or even get facts wrong, it throws the whole piece into question. If some of it cannot be believed, what about the rest? And what about the dangers of giving the wrong information to people who do believe you? You must do your research thoroughly, and only include facts which you are sure are right!
- **Dealing with serious material in the wrong way**. Often the intention of Theatre-in-Education is serious, simply because of the 'teaching' aspect; and therefore your objective is likely to be a serious one. This does not mean that a serious/straight style has to be used: many lessons can be learnt through, for example, comedy or pantomime. However, communicating the idea that drugs, for example, are amusing would obviously be unsuitable, just as suggesting that divorce can be portrayed as melodrama is showing insensitivity to the feelings of the people involved. Take care that you do not treat things in a trivial manner.
- **Unsuitable vocabulary**. There are two main aspects of this – understanding and offence.

Make sure you use words your audience know and understand, as they cannot ask you for meanings of unfamiliar words during the performance! Also take care that they will not be offended by what you say, especially in what they might consider to be bad language, or the use of hurtful or insensitive ideas. You must show your understanding of your audience and your sensitivity towards them.

- **Being condescending**. An audience does not like being lectured or 'talked down to', and you must take care not to treat them as if they are a lot of fools! For example, don't use Infant vocabulary for a Year 8 audience; or inform an adult audience about 'How to apply for a job'. Remember that the best TIE presentations target the special needs and demands of their audience.
- **Trying to cover too much**. A lack of suitable focus often causes performances to be too long and 'waffly'. For example, you cannot cover every aspect of 'war', so just focus on the role of women in war, the effect of war on the family, or the strength of national identity. You must ensure that as you rehearse, you recognise your weaker ideas and discard them, so that the piece keeps its sense of purpose.

E Possible starters for TIE

- **For young children**: e.g. Road safety, Victorian classrooms, Stranger danger, Children's books
- **For Year 6**: e.g. Transfer to secondary school, Railway trespass, Ancient Egyptians, A great explorer or adventurer
- **For parents**: e.g. Drugs, Exam stress, Living up to expectations, Myths and legends from other cultures
- **For an all-age community group**: e.g. Local History, A local event, Caring for the environment, A community project
- **For a group of foreign students**: e.g. Things British, A guide to your town or area, British History, Education in Britain, A story from their country.

F Possible written work

1 Personal response to the task:

- how you explored different ideas and possibilities
- what problems you came across
- why you came to your decisions
- how you worked in with the other actors, the director and the designers
- what compromises you had to make
- how you considered health and safety issues.

2 Research:

- the job of the actor in putting a piece of Theatre-in-Education onto the stage
- the chosen audience – their interests, understanding, awareness of the topic, vocabulary, etc.
- the theme/topic/lesson of the play
- different ways that the topic has been treated by other writers, e.g. the press, TV, playwrights, stereotyping, propaganda
- any historical or cultural or social aspects to the interpretation of the theme.

3 Comparisons:

- different **styles** for the theme: e.g. 'Good always wins' as in Pantomime, medieval Morality plays, Whodunnits
- different **audiences**: e.g. 'Relationships' for infants might deal with sharing and playing together; for teenagers, it might be trust, or the opposite sex; for adults, the breakdown of a relationship and the effect on others
- different **cultures**: e.g. 'Religious celebrations' might deal with the Christian Christmas; Jewish Hannukah; Shinto's Matsuri; or Hinduism's Holi.
- the **different acting skills** needed for two or three different pieces of Theatre-in-Education which you have been in.

Examiners' tip

Two important words here – focus and style. First, focus on the audience and the theme: make sure that the content is suitable for your target audience, and that the theme has been researched thoroughly. Secondly, use an appropriate style/genre which all the performers can understand and present, and which will make the presentation interesting to watch.

Option 5 Dance/Drama

A What is Dance/Drama?

This is the unscripted telling of a story through the medium of Dance. It must have a clear narrative/storyline, obvious characters and characterisation, and must be involved with conflict and relationships.

B Essential resources for the task

If you are to complete this task successfully, you must have:

- a suitable space for both rehearsal and performance
- a sense of rhythm
- a reasonable movement 'vocabulary' (store of movement ideas) or movement 'creativity' (the ability to create a variety of effective movements)
- an understanding of the dynamics/quality of movements – energy, speed and direction
- suitable audio equipment, if recorded music or sounds are going to be used
- a reasonable knowledge of how to make 'live' sounds, and the person(s) to produce them, if live sounds are going to be used
- suitable costume and props, or the facilities and knowledge for making them.

In addition it may be helpful to have:

- reasonable lighting equipment, in order to improve the theatrical effectiveness
- suitable stage make-up if it would improve the effect of the presentation
- masks, or the facilities and knowledge for making them, if they would improve the presentation.

A moment in a Dance/Drama on 'Supporting Friends'

C What are the possibilities for Dance/Drama?

What story/person/issue do you want to deal with?

For example, a real-life event or person such as World War I or Sir Walter Raleigh; a fictional story or character such as Romeo and Juliet or Harry Potter; an issue such as drugs or computer technology; or a concept such as Power or The Four Seasons. Choosing a subject with an emotional aspect can often be successful as Dance can convey feeling and atmosphere very strongly and effectively.

What part will music have in this dance/drama?

Music may be the stimulus for your work; so that the music itself suggests the story, characters or issue. It is often the accompaniment for Dance/Drama, because it seems to fit so perfectly: but you can compose your own accompaniment using sounds and rhythm rather than music, although it must obviously be tolerable to your audience! You can present a Dance/Drama without any sound, but it often loses some of the impact and atmosphere which music or other sound can give.

If your stimulus has not been musical, you may need to find some suitable music as accompaniment – and it can take a long time to find exactly what you want, or to make up a tape of various suitable extracts. Good music for Dance/Drama will have a rhythm and/or flow; appear to be an essential part of the dance – not just an extra; have variety of pace; and will create mood and atmosphere. Avoid music with words, as the lyrics will restrict your ideas and development. Songs also tend to be repetitive in their music, and can therefore restrict the variety of movement and choreography which you use.

Does the form of the stimulus itself suggest any possible ideas?

For example, a theme, issue, poem, newspaper article, play, lighting, picture. It may be that a play or newspaper article used as a stimulus gives you the outline scenario for your Dance/Drama; or that a lighting or sound stimulus immediately suggests a mood or atmosphere to you; or that an issue gives you your central focus.

D Common faults and pitfalls

In addition to the general points raised on pages 130–1, you need to be aware of some of the common 'traps' associated with Dance/Drama.

- **Uninteresting dynamics**. Do your movement and choreography have sufficiently varied dynamics? Too often the quality and dynamics become limited and repetitive, which is very dull for the audience! Make sure you use plenty of variety.
- **Not enough action/drama**. Much of the interest will be through the dramatic content – the story itself, the drama, the conflict, the emotion, etc. Try to ensure that every unit of the Dance/Drama has a point of interest within it, and a clear development, so that the audience does not get the chance to be bored.
- **Weak characterisation**. Dance/Drama must have obvious roles, so do check that you know who you are, and what your character objectives are at various points in the drama. Then make sure that you are portraying your character clearly through your use of movement.
- **Accompaniment which hinders the movement**. Is your chosen accompaniment restricting your ideas? Or is it helping to give you variety and creative ideas? Good accompaniment really adds to the effectiveness of Dance/Drama; and the best

accompaniment becomes a 'natural' part of the choreography.

- **Using movement in unison for too long.** A very common pitfall is to have everyone doing the same movements at the same time for too long. You need to be aware of the need to vary the movement more frequently, or to use identical movements in canon (when movements are repeated but not simultaneously, like singing a round) or in mirror, for example.

- A **lack of climax**. If you do not identify your climax, there is a very real danger that your work will just go on aimlessly, and your audience will wonder what the purpose of your performance is. This is a common problem when the purpose has not been clearly enough defined, or where the story has not been properly developed.

- **Poor visual interest.** Obviously the first priority is to create an effective piece of Dance, and to achieve the interest through choreography and through the drama. Often an uneven number of dancers gives you greater visual opportunity. Remember to use your whole space and different levels. Dance/Drama is also greatly enhanced by the good use of lighting, costume and set. These do not have to be complicated: often the simpler they are the better. Be aware of the simple use of colour for gaining effect.

- **Too much unprepared movement.** There is sometimes the feeling that a general preparation is enough, and that, within very vague guidelines, dancers can be left to be almost spontaneous in their movement. This only leads to uninteresting and unfocused work where the drama of the Dance is lost. Good Dance/Drama demands accurate, detailed preparation.

E Possible starters for Dance/Drama

- **Issues which focus on conflict between people:** e.g. peer pressure such as bullying, or smoking; competitive situations such as village shows, or 'catching' the popular girl/boyfriend; culture clashes such as a first-generation teenager growing up in Britain with immigrant parents who still cling to their national origins; or different cultural approaches to the question of marriage

- **Issues which focus on internal conflict:** e.g. temptation and conscience, such as stealing, or reporting someone for wrongdoing; making decisions such as the choice of friends or what career to follow; traumatic situations such as divorce or developing a life-threatening disease

- **Real stories which allow good drama:** e.g. pioneer explorers such as Scott of the Antarctic or the early white settlers in Australia; actual historical events such as war, or 'witch hunts'; natural disasters such as earthquake or famine; man-made disasters such as a train crash or environmental pollution

- **Well-known fictional stories:** e.g. fairy tales such as *Snow White*, or *Goldilocks*; stories from Shakespeare such as *Macbeth*, or *Romeo and Juliet*; modern classics such as *Of Mice and Men* or *Harry Potter*

- **Abstract/symbolic themes:** e.g. emotions such as love or anger; opposites such as life and death, or black and white; the supernatural, such as foretelling the future, or the curse of Tutankhamen.

F Possible written work

1 Personal response to the task:

- how you explored different ideas and possibilities
- what problems you came across
- why you came to your decisions
- how you worked in with the other performers, the director and the designers
- what compromises you had to make
- how you considered health and safety issues.

2 Research:

- the job of the actor/dancer in putting a piece of Dance/Drama onto the stage
- the theme of the piece
- styles used by different Dance/Drama companies, e.g. V Tol, DV8, RJC Dance, Ballet Rambert
- different dancers, e.g. Martha Graham, Christopher Bruce, Rudolf Laban, Isadora Duncan
- Dance/Drama in different cultures.

3 Comparisons:

- different ways of telling stories through Dance: e.g. Ballet, Educational Dance, Indian Dance, Pantomime, Afro-Caribbean Dance
- differences between Naturalistic and Symbolic dancing
- differences between familiar movements and those of a totally different type or culture
- the different skills needed for two or three different Dance/Dramas you have been in.

Examiners' tip

It is important to get the balance right between Dance and Drama. This is not a Dance GCSE course, so your ability to perform recognised Dance steps and techniques is not necessarily relevant. You must, though, have a good knowledge of the vocabulary of movement, and understanding of its dynamics, and the ability to demonstrate these. But the work must also show the creation of character, relationships, situations and conflict.

C2 Requirements for technical options

A What must be done?

- You may only offer one technical option for your examination.
- This may be connected with either a **scripted** or an **unscripted** presentation.
- You must work with a performing group. *Warning:* although you should discuss with the performers and other designers, the designs you eventually produce must be your own!
- You must work in a group of three or more.
- You must present a written response to the chosen task. This will include evidence of research, understanding of other design and performance skills and techniques, and comparisons with other types of Drama (See AO2 below).

B How are these options assessed?

The technical option is assessed out of 60 marks, made up from:

AO2: Response to plays and other types of Drama	10/60
AO3: Work in progress	20/60
AO1: Final presentation	30/60

AO2: Response to plays and other types of Drama

This is assessed through your written coursework during the *preparation* period. You have to show your knowledge and understanding of your chosen technical skill in other types of Drama, including types from different historical periods and different cultures.

AO3: Work in progress

This is assessed through the development of your work during the *rehearsal* period. You have to show that you can judge the effectiveness of your work, including the relationship with other design skills and the performance itself.

AO1: Final presentation

This is assessed through the final *presentation*. You have to show how good your design and realisation skills and techniques are, and that you can work constructively with other people. Skills will include your use of sketches, plans, designs; use of materials, equipment and other resources; working within restrictions of budget and performance space; realisation and evaluation of a final 'product'.

C Skills and techniques

What skills are assessed in performance work?

According to the syllabus, you need to show that you can:

- respond to the stimulus with suitable ideas and understanding
- use suitable design and realisation techniques
- create an effective technical contribution to the performance
- create mood and atmosphere

- show sensitivity, creativity, originality and flair
- understand your actors' needs
- understand the needs of the other technical aspects of production
- understand your audience
- work constructively with the rest of your group
- be aware of health and safety factors.

Improving your skills

As you experiment with different skills, try to identify:

- **what** you are doing
- **why** you are doing it
- **how** you are doing it
- **what** problems you are having
- **how** you might overcome the problems.

In answering these questions in as much detail as possible, it is likely that you will begin to identify various things you could do to improve. You will obviously need to think carefully about exactly what skills and techniques you are using and what you could use. For this, you need to refer to Section A6 (pages 46–51).

The **mini-projects** (pages 86–122) are intended to help you to identify important features of different aspects of work. If you have worked through most of them, think back over what went well or badly, and any particular lessons you learnt while doing them. If you have not yet tackled any of them, then look at some of them now. They should help you to see some of the potential advantages and problems, and make your decisions easier to finalise with confidence.

Look, too, at the Assessment guidelines in Appendix 1 (pages 231–2). These should help you to identify and improve your levels at different skills.

D Getting started

1 Essential resources for the task

First, if you are going to present technical work, you need the resources to see it through. If you want to do lighting, you must have access to a reasonable lighting system; if you want to do masks, you must have access to the knowledge and facilities for making them; if you want to do make-up, you must have access to a reasonable selection of stage make-up.

Obviously, you also need an acting group! However, before you start you must make sure that they are going to present a piece of work which will give you the opportunities to show your technical ability. If you want to do set, you do not want to be tied to a group who only need one bush on stage; if you want to do properties, you do not want a group who have no need for handmade props. If you want to do costume, you do not want a play that just demands ordinary everyday clothes the actors can find in their own wardrobes.

2 What are the possibilities?

Right at the beginning of the work, you must think about your audience, the issue or topic, the purpose of the performance, ideas about the overall presentation, and the needs of the acting group itself. All of these will be looked at in more detail under each option.

3 How can you best use the people you are working with?

- Listen carefully to their initial discussions. What opportunities do you see for your chosen technical skill? Offer your suggestions based on their discussion.
- Discuss with other technical designers in the group to discover their ideas; and to see how these might affect your ideas. Be prepared to compromise!
- Always work closely with the rest of the group, so that you are fully aware of any developments and changes.
- Pay particular attention, especially in an improvised piece of work, to the way in which the piece is developing: discuss any problems which seem to be arising.
- Try to ensure that your work is up to schedule, so that when the actors need it, it is ready – even if you may later have to 'fine-tune' it.
- Make sure that the performers recognise that, after a certain stage, you cannot make huge changes to what you are doing, although small details can be altered.
- Try to be patient and calm at all times! Fitting technical work to an actual performance can be extremely frustrating at times for all concerned, so try not to make matters worse by losing your temper!

4 What health and safety factors do you need to consider?

For the performers

- The performing space should generally be uncluttered, so that there is sufficient space for necessary movement without having to squeeze past stage furniture.
- Scenery should be securely fastened, and not liable to collapse!
- Stage furniture and props should be suitable for stage work, and not liable to fall apart or break during performance: they should not have sharp or rough corners, sides, parts, etc.
- Costume should be suitable for the movement and action of the piece.
- Stage make-up can cause allergic reactions for some people.
- Masks must allow performers to breathe!
- Your knowledge of the safe use of your technical equipment, and of its potential hazards.

For the audience

- The audience space should be uncluttered by potential hazards such as trailing leads, or insecure seating.
- There should be sufficient space for access by people in wheelchairs or on crutches.
- The use of technical aspects must not cause discomfort, e.g. prolonged use of strobe lighting; the use of explosive devices into the audience; or the over-enthusiastic use of a smoke machine.

Fire regulations

You must ensure that you keep to all the fire regulations, which cover how many people you can have in the audience, how the seats have to be arranged, and how wide the gangways must be; the need for fire-proofing set, scenery, props and costumes; and the use of hazardous items such as smoke machines, strobes and fireworks. In addition, your local Fire Officer may impose extra restrictions because of the performance space you are using.

5 First ideas

- In your group, brainstorm first ideas, making a list or a scatter diagram of things which come up.
- Discuss each in turn to see how they might be developed. Do some give more possibilities than others? Make sure that both the actors and the technical designers get a 'fair hearing'.
- Do different styles/genres have any effect on the opportunities for your work?

6 Planning the work

Make notes of any decisions you make.

- How much time or how many lessons do you have to prepare this work?
- Realistically, how much extra time might you have for out-of-lesson work? Will this be with your performing group? Or will it be work on your own?
- If you are offering stage management, how can you best organise rehearsal schedules?
- What sort of research are you going to need to do? For example, into the target audience, the style/genre, the historical period, the culture, the issue. Where will you find the necessary information? How long might it take you?
- Does the piece appear to fall into distinct units as far as your contribution is concerned? If so, how will you make sure that all get equal attention?
- How quickly will the performers need certain things? How long before they actually need a particular prop, sound effect or item of clothing?
- Where and when can you have access to essential equipment and resources? How soon can you get to the shops for essential materials? If you need to work in another specialist room, such as a Technology or Music room, when can you do so? If you need to work with lighting equipment, how many other groups are also going to need to practise in the same space?

7 Getting going

You need to try things out as soon as possible after the first discussion and ideas – with sketches, lists, suggestions. If there are going to be any problems you want to discover them quickly so that you can have time to solve them, to adapt or to change what you wanted to do. Remember that the early stages are experimental, and that you should be exploring various possibilities. Nothing should be set in stone straightaway – details can be changed later. But the sooner you have a feel for the direction you want to go, the sooner you can judge its likely success and see where to go next.

As soon as you can, discuss your initial work with the rest of the group. How successful does it seem to be? Does it fit in with other ideas which they have had? What needs changing? What will help the audience to understand better? Is it, in fact, suitable for the chosen audience? Does it seem to be a good idea? What might be better? Make notes of the main points discussed. Such notes act as reminders for your next stage, and they will help you later when you come to do your written coursework.

E Developing your work

1 General points

- Keep the overall story clearly in mind.
- Experiment with different ideas, solutions and techniques.
- Experiment with your equipment so that you can use it to its best advantage. Remember that you must have adult supervision when using some equipment.
- Remember that your work must help to enhance the performance, not distract from it.
- Constantly remind yourselves of the purpose of your presentation.
- Constantly remind yourselves of the needs of your audience.
- Keep clearly in mind the style/genre you are using.
- Keep a close watch on your time management to ensure that you are working up-to-time with the performers.
- Make sure that every unit has the same attention paid to it.
- Make notes of any new ideas which you try, or any new decisions made.

2 Specific points

- For **set and lighting**, think carefully about the type of stage you are using and any set dressing which you are planning to use, bearing in mind the sight lines of your audience and the action of the performers.
- Make sure that any **properties** you are suggesting have a purpose; and that essential props are used as early as possible in the rehearsal period.
- Sort out your **costume and mask** ideas, bearing in mind such things as the style of the play, the historical or geographical setting, the costumes of the rest of the group, the lighting, any essential movement. Then make sure that the performer can get used to wearing the costume or mask in rehearsal as soon as possible.
- Make sure that the basic **puppet** is produced quickly, so that the performer can get used to working it – detail can often be added as you go along.
- Practise your stage **make-up** and judge it under stage lights.
- Plan and prepare any live or recorded **sound** that will help the atmosphere, or effect.
- Prepare a **stage manager's** prompt copy, and organise the backstage area.
- Make notes of any ideas tried, problems found, and decisions made.

3 Improvements

- Watch out for ways to improve what you are doing, although make sure that in so doing you do not cause conflict with other aspects of presentation.
- Watch out for opportunities to use special techniques to make the work more interesting and effective.
- Make notes of any techniques tried, and of any changes and additions made.

4 Learning from others

- Show your work constantly to the rest of the group as it develops.
- Ask for constructive advice from someone outside the group whom you respect.
- Build up good, co-operative teamwork, where you have trust and confidence in each other.
- Make notes of what other people say, and use them as pointers for what to do next.

5 Health and safety

- Consider various health and safety factors which may need addressing. Ask for help if you are not sure – do not just leave it to luck!
- Make notes of what you do, and why.

F Common faults and pitfalls

The following faults are all seen surprisingly often in GCSE presentations.

- A **lack of adequate resources**. It does not do you any good to start on a technical option if you do not have suitable resources and facilities available. If you cannot show enough to cover the requirements of the examination, choose a more suitable option!
- **Working in isolation**. It is almost always apparent when a designer/technician has failed to work properly with the group, as the designs do not fit with the performance, or the finished articles are so much works of art that they draw attention away from the actors. You must ensure constant discussion and checking with your performing group.

- **Inadequate preparation**. When one thing goes wrong on the technical side of a presentation, others usually follow. If such problems occur because of accident, it may just be bad luck. But too often it is because of poor preparation, and failure to see a likely problem occurring. Don't trust to luck: make sure you have done everything you can.
- Having **insufficient understanding of a particular style/genre** to use it. Technical aspects should enhance the performance. Refer to Section A5 (pages 37–45) for reminders.

G Completing the work

1 Polishing the work

The final week or so before performance

- Make sure that everyone in the group realises how you all depend on each other to give of your best, and to keep to decisions made.
- Check any parts when split-second timing is essential, such as with some lighting and sound cues. Practise them until they become smooth and automatic.
- Check all your technical arrangements, and make sure that you have practised thoroughly with the performers, so that you know exactly what is expected, and what you will do when.
- Check that you have taken health and safety factors into account, both on stage and for your audience.

2 Final arrangements for the presentation

For the actual day of performance

- Make sure that the whole cast knows the time of performance, and the time it will take to get ready.

- Check your technical equipment as early as possible: do not leave this check until the last minute, or you can be sure that something will be missing, broken or will go wrong. Give yourself time to discover any problems before they become disasters! If there is a problem, keep cool, and think how best to overcome it: you have to find the best solution available.
- If you are presenting the work away from your own centre, try to arrive at the venue in time to have a quick practice in this unknown space, unless you have been fortunate enough to have a full rehearsal there anyway.

3 The presentation itself

- Concentrate.
- Listen to the performers.
- Don't panic if mistakes are made: that will merely make things worse.
- Be aware of any mistakes which the performers make, and which may affect your contribution.
- Don't be tempted to change things as you go along – keep to what you have rehearsed, or you will 'throw' other members of the group.
- Be aware of other members of the group and any problems which they may be having: be sympathetic to them.
- Above all, keep calm!

4 Written work

Remember that you have to write at least 500 words on your response to this option. This will include information on how you tackled the task you undertook and on relationships and comparisons between different texts and/or styles/genres, with examples from different historical times and different cultures. All of this is expected to show your understanding of the option you have chosen.

At the end of each option section, you will find some ideas for suitable research, and for possible comparisons between different scripts or genres.

Examiners' tip

Follow carefully the advice given to you in this section. It identifies what you will need to do, the resources and materials needed, and how potential problems can be overcome. Do remember that you have to work in a group of at least three candidates, and that your completed work has to be shown in an actual performance. Whatever you choose, try to create a theatrically effective presentation!

Option 6 Set

A What is meant by 'Set'?

Set means the stage scenery and furniture, giving a visual understanding of the location.

Scale model for *A Midsummer Night's Dream* by Shakespeare. The production is set on London rooftops in 1840. For a total contrast, refer to the lighted set on page 185

B What must be done?

You must complete the following:

- a scale plan of the performance space
- sketches, diagrams, drawings of the set
- evidence to show you have thought about methods of building your set
- evidence to show you have thought about health and safety factors
- a scale model of your set
- the actual set used in performance.

You must show knowledge of:

- the use of your space in relation to the actors and the audience
- the characteristics of different stages and different types of performance
- an understanding of how to create historical period in a set design
- an understanding of how a set can create mood and atmosphere
- the way designs develop through discussion with the director and the other designers
- the relationship with other design aspects
- set building, decorating, materials and construction techniques.

C Essential resources for the task

If you are to complete this task successfully, you must have:

- access to a performing space
- a performing group presenting a play giving you suitable opportunities for your design ideas
- access to suitable materials for making the scale model
- the ability to produce a full-scale set which is as close as possible to the finished design
- access to relevant research material
- an understanding of what the writer, improvisers or dancers intend
- sufficient space to construct, store and manage what you have in mind.

D What are the possibilities for Set?

What type of stage will be suitable?

Most schools have a traditional proscenium stage in their assembly halls. Other centres may have smaller studio spaces, where presentations are much closer and more intimate. Some may have large open spaces where theatre-in-the-round is possible, giving your group the opportunity to make decisions as to exactly where your audience will be. Some may even have outdoor theatres. Don't choose your space simply to show that you can create something 'different': more importantly, choose one that is familiar to you, so that you can show your understanding of using that space well. Wherever you are, remember to pay attention to sight lines!

What style of design will be suitable?

You must recognise the style/genre of the performance, and make sure that your set design is going to enhance that. However, you might decide to produce a set which is realistic, historically accurate, representational, multi-locational, minimal or even symbolic. For many plays, you might have freedom to choose which of these is the most suitable. With others, the play itself may make the decision for you: for example, an adapted TV script might call for a multi-locational stage set; a pantomime for representational drop cloths; a mime for a minimal set. If you are making the whole set from scratch, this will influence your design – as much as anything because the cost of a full set will probably be way beyond your budget!

How elaborate should the set be?

This will depend on a number of factors. You must work closely with your performing group so that you produce a set which is suitable to their needs; you must consider the style/genre (Section A5) being used; and you must be aware of time, because the performers need to work with your ideas to develop, rehearse, and block. You must also be aware of your budget, as you have to make the actual set as well as a model; you must be honest about your ability so that you do not try to do something too ambitious; and you must think about space for storage, and the ease of erecting and striking your set.

Recognise that some of the most effective sets are simple ones (notice the set on p 185); make use of what is easily available, and use your imagination and expertise to bring your ideas to life.

What easily accessible aids to a set are available?

Many schools have some rostra, stage blocks or step units, which immediately offer the opportunity for the use of different levels. Some also have a reasonable supply of flats or screens, which give a good start to providing, for example, entrances, backstage areas or changes in wall direction. Some have a good supply of various seats and tables.

Where can you manage to get other set and furniture?

Obviously the set is the largest, bulkiest part of the stage presentation, and for this reason, any making or acquiring of suitable items is likely to take up a lot of workshop and storage space – something which is not usually available in schools! You will also need access to transport and a driver if you have to fetch things from other places, such as your own home, or other schools. You can often find wonderful things in places such as car boot sales and secondhand shops – but these are going to cost money, and you must be aware of your budget.

E Common faults and pitfalls

During the preparation of your work, in addition to the general points raised on page 158, you need to be aware of some of the very common 'traps' associated with set design and realisation.

- The **lack of real opportunities** provided by the play itself. For example, *Waiting for Godot* by Samuel Beckett demands only a single tree on the stage; many improvisations tend to be set in a school or at home; a monologue or solo Dance should not have an elaborate set which will distract from the performer.

- **Forgetting about the performers!** Many students become so engrossed with their own ideas that they forget they are providing a set for a theatrical performance, and see the work as a piece of unrelated art. In so doing, they often forget simple essentials such as having sufficient backstage space for the actors' needs, or how the actors are going to get on and off stage.

- **Forgetting about health and safety factors.** It is not unknown, for example, for parts of the scenery to fall down during performance if they have not been made robustly enough or secured efficiently. In the hurry towards the end of the preparation, fireproofing has sometimes been overlooked. Consider potential problems right from the beginning.

- **Poor communication of designer objectives.** Many designers fail to get across their message because they become too involved with details which obscure the essentials, or they fail to emphasise the aspects which will speak most clearly.

- **Lack of understanding of theatrical unity.** For example, it is no good having a symbolic set which you then dress realistically, or a historically accurate set for a piece which has been updated or in which costume is going to be representational. Every aspect of the presentation must fit together.

- The **unavailability of the performance space**. Do you know whether your chosen space is going to be used for school examinations just at the time you need to have access to it? Do you know whether the AS or A Level students are expecting to use the space, the flats, the rostra, etc. just when you need them? You need to know what demands you will make on the available resources, and check that they will be available for the preparation, the rehearsal and the presentation. Find out these things before you start.

- **Lack of understanding of construction detail.** It is not enough just to have a brilliant design idea. You must be able to see how these ideas will be constructed into a real set. You must, therefore, research such areas as the suitable use of materials (not using gloss paint on canvas flats, for example), the weight and manoeuvrability of different sections, the cost of putting your ideas into realisation.

- **Work not being to scale.** All your work, except for rough sketches, must be to scale – your plans, designs and model. Think carefully about what will be the best scale to use for your performance space, and then do everything to the same scale.

F Possible starters for set designers

- **Showing location/period:** e.g. explore the use of realistic furniture and detail; projected images; a montage of pictures; representational items such as a throne, tapestry or plant; symbols such as a heart for a romance, or a dagger for *Macbeth*
- **Using stage blocks, etc:** e.g. experiment with different formations and effects, such as a thrust stage, the audience on a different level to the performers, adding visual interest, creating status
- **Using flats/screens:** e.g. experiment with positioning to create wing and backstage space; entrances and exits; constructing a box set; focusing audience attention; creating or confining space
- **Creating mood and atmosphere:** e.g. explore the use of materials, colours and textures; the links with the lighting design; the possible use of symbolism.

G Possible written work

1 Personal response to the task:

- how you explored different ideas and possibilities
- what problems you came across, in both the design and the realisation
- why you came to your decisions
- how you worked in with the actors and the other designers/technicians
- what compromises you had to make.

2 Research:

- the job of the set designer in today's theatre
- different stages and sets in various historical periods, e.g. Greek, medieval, Restoration, etc.
- different styles of set design, e.g. box settings, minimalist, composite, etc.
- today's technology, e.g. revolves, tracking, computers, etc.
- different ways of creating magical settings on stage.

3 Comparisons:

- realistic set for *The Play of the Diary of Anne Frank* adapted by Goodrich and Hackett
- multi-locational set for *Bedroom Farce* by Alan Ayckbourn
- fantasy set for the Never-Land in *Peter Pan* by J. M. Barrie
- three contrasting designs for *Romeo and Juliet* by William Shakespeare, e.g. composite set, symbolic set, historical set.

Examiners' tip

> Your choice of play is going to be very important. The set must be used in performance, so make sure you have the opportunity to demonstrate your skills in your designs, model and the set itself. Try to recognise a play which offers you too little to do, and one where there will be too much! You must be able to negotiate and discuss needs with your actors and other technicians, and to create a set which is actor-friendly. It should support what they are doing, not dominate or dwarf them.

Option 7 Costume

A What is meant by 'Costume'?

Costume means the clothes and accessories that actors wear in order to communicate their characters.

B What must be done?

You must complete the following:

- an overall idea for costuming the whole production
- preliminary drawings of your ideas for at least two costumes
- completed designs for at least two costumes
- costings for the costumes designed
- one completed costume, worn in performance
- evidence of understanding health and safety factors
- costume patterns if applicable.

You must show knowledge of:

- the purpose of costume in a production
- how to research necessary costume information, including historical detail
- the use of materials, colours and textures for theatrical effectiveness
- working to a budget, making, hiring and assembling costumes
- the way designs develop through discussion with the director and other designers
- the effects of lighting on colours and fabrics
- the role of the wardrobe supervisor, repairs, quick changes, and other problems.

C Essential resources for the task

If you are to complete this task successfully, you must have:

- a performing group who are presenting a play which gives you suitable opportunities for your design understanding and ideas
- access to suitable materials for producing the costume
- the ability to produce a costume from your design
- the facilities and money for realising the finished costume
- access to relevant research material
- an understanding of what the writer, improvisers or dancers intend
- enough art ability to draw the designs (you can use a template) to communicate ideas.

D What are the possibilities for Costume?

What sort of costume would you like to make?

You may have a clear idea of whether you want to design, for example, a historical costume, an animal costume or a fantasy costume. You may recognise that your dressmaking skills are fairly limited and that you therefore want to design a simpler costume, e.g. a 1920s 'shift', a symbolic costume, or adapt costume pieces already in existence. Remember that the vast majority of stage characters are ordinary people in everyday situations. So, if you want the opportunity to produce something 'different', you must look closely at the plays which are being suggested by the performers. You must also consider what research facilities are available to you if you choose a more unusual character: period costume, in particular, needs very thorough researching. You must also consider how close or far away your audience will be, as this will affect the amount of detail and accuracy needed.

How can you produce the costume?

Many costumes are found: 'recycled' from other people, theatres, charity shops, jumble sales, etc. However, if you simply set out to find a costume, you are not likely to show many skills. You will be showing more if found items are altered and adapted for your particular play and actor. For example, you might change the colour or the sleeves, or create a bustle. Still more skills will be shown by the candidate who makes the costume from scratch, as long as they have the ability to do so! This gives you far greater freedom to produce the costume you think is most suitable: but you must find or make the necessary patterns, buy or find the materials, and show the construction skills necessary. Whatever you decide, you must ensure that you keep within your budget, which is often very low for school and amateur productions!

How can you show the character through the costume?

There are various aspects which must be considered. Most importantly, who they are will obviously affect all your other ideas: a teacher will be very differently costumed from a garage mechanic, or an alien, or Guy Fawkes. What age are they? Young people, or animals, are clothed differently from the adults, or from the elderly. Their class may affect things such as materials, newness, tailoring. Their personal pride may affect the way the clothes are actually worn, their cleanliness and their state of repair. Their country of origin often has an influence: an Innuit would not wear exactly the same as an Italian even in these days of international fashion. What is their status within the play's characters? The more important the role, the more carefully you must think about detail: the good costume will help to direct the audience's attention to the character, whereas the lower status character can be helped to 'fade' into the background a little. What is their purpose? If they are intended to be spokespeople for the play's message, they must be helped to be taken seriously through the right costume. If the audience is expected to laugh at them, then the costume can have more humorous touches.

What about style/genre?

This will have an effect on your design, so you must recognise the essentials of each one. In general terms, the more serious the presentation, the more accurate will be the costume; the more humorous the presentation, the more colourful and stereotyped the costume; the more fantastical the presentation, the more imaginative the costume. Look back at Section A5 (pages 37–45) for more guidance.

What are costume accessories?

These are items such as handbags, jewellery, gloves, shoes – anything the actors *wear* in order to convey their character. These are also the responsibility of the costume designer: so you must consider whether anything is needed for your chosen characters.

E Common faults and pitfalls

During the preparation of your work, in addition to the general points raised on page 158, you need to be aware of some of the very common 'traps' associated with costume design.

- **Producing a costume which is way beyond budget**. You must adapt your first designs and ideas to fit a realistic budget. Do not be tempted to up the budget to fit the costume! Costuming is only one aspect of a production, and you are only producing one completed costume, so you cannot expect to have pots of money for it.

- **Restricting movement**. Often the student has not considered carefully enough what movement and action is expected of the character, so that when the actor comes to wear it they find they cannot do comfortably what is expected of them. Instead of helping the actors, it simply makes them look awkward.

- **Unsuitable costume**. Sometimes candidates costume their characters as though they were dressing themselves; or they only see the character as a middle-aged businesswoman without realising that she is Italian or anorexic; or they fail to research adequately, and have a mix of different historical elements; or they overdress their actor in lots of layers! Sometimes they overlook the fact that there is a quick costume change, needing a costume which is quick and easy to get in and out of: with the result that the audience are kept waiting, or the actor reappears only half-dressed. Make sure that the actor practises, so that you know if there are any problems: buttons on elastic can be wonderful!

- **A costume which draws attention to itself**. A well-designed costume will not draw attention to itself but to the actor, character, situation, etc, and it will make him/her stand out against the scenery.

- **Overlooking health and safety factors**. Your actor must be both safe and comfortable; and sometimes costumes are neither. For example, too long a hemline can cause an actor to trip; too many clothes make for great heat under stage lights; tight clothes make some movement impossible or hazardous; jewellery can catch in other actors' costumes or hair.

- **Lack of unity with other technical areas**. You must always remember that your ideas must fit with the needs of the actor and the lighting, the set, the make-up, etc. You must be prepared to compromise where necessary, so that the costume is brought to life by the lights, or draws attention to the face, or allows sufficient movement in a restricted stage space.

- **Poor time management**. Sometimes candidates spend far too long copying pages of research material, or drawing loads of designs, without leaving enough time actually to produce the costume. Try to recognise how long this will take, and adjust for the time allowed. The performance cannot wait while you finish. It is your job to be ready in sufficient time to allow the actor to rehearse in the costume.

F Possible starters for costume designers

- **Researching different materials.** If you are to produce a good costume, you need to know what properties different materials have. For example, which hang well, are easily worked on, easily washed or dyed? Which are non-iron? Which are inexpensive? Much information you can get from books or the Internet; but you also need to get samples of different materials from shops, old clothes, or your Technology Department, and experiment with them. Try decorating, dyeing, washing, ironing. In general, natural fibres are better for maintenance purposes, for actors' comfort, for hard wear, and for the design process; they tend to hang better, and dye better. Put different pieces together to see what they look like together. And above all, try them under stage lighting to see what will happen to them on stage. Some materials come to life under lights, while others look drab and uninteresting.

- **Working realistically.** For example, is the costume pressed or tatty, threadbare or rich, clean or stained, old or new? Is it fitting or ill-fitting, formal or informal, fashionable or old-fashioned? How can you create a realistic impression? What about wear and tear on a costume? Using a cheese grater or sandpaper can create an excellent impression! What compromises might be made, without spoiling the realism? Try sketching some realistic costumes.

- **Working symbolically.** If you want to symbolise your costume you will probably need to think in simple terms if the audience is to understand. You might use colour: e.g. Death might be in black, and Success in gold; material: e.g. Youth might be in denim, and the Queen of Hearts in velvet; representational items: e.g. an animal might have a head mask and/or a tail, and Fire a brilliant flame-shaped head-dress; shapes and symbols: e.g. bunches of grapes for the God of Wine, and zig-zags for Lightning. Try sketching some symbolic costumes.

- **Experimenting with ornamentation.** Get samples of sequins and jewellery, and try out what they look like on different materials and under different lights. What effects do they give? What sorts of character do they suggest? Experiment with different border patterns and trimmings, and notice how they can change the whole character of a costume. What sorts of character are suggested by the unadorned costume? And what characters when you add the patterns or trimmings? If you have access to appropriate facilities and expertise, try out different artistic techniques such as silk-screen painting, tie-dye or batik work. What sorts of design do they produce? What sorts of material are most suitable? What sorts of character do they suggest?

G Possible written work

1 Personal response to the task:

- how you explored different ideas and possibilities
- what problems you came across in both the design and the realisation
- why you came to your decisions
- how you worked in with the actors and the other designers/technicians
- what compromises you had to make.

2 Research:

- the job of the costume designer in today's theatre
- basic costumes, and how to adapt them to a variety of uses
- theatrical costumes from other cultures, e.g. Japanese Kabuki, Hindu Dance-Drama, Caribbean Mardi Gras
- historical accuracy versus theatrical effect
- presenting animals on stage.

3 Comparisons:

- American Indian costume for *Hiawatha* adapted by Michael Bogdanov
- farcical costume for the Pyramus and Thisbe interlude from *A Midsummer Night's Dream* by Shakespeare
- historical costume for *Murder in the Cathedral* by T. S. Eliot
- three contrasting designs for a lion, e.g. from *Wizard of Oz* by Frank Baum, from the Pyramus and Thisbe interlude from *A Midsummer Night's Dream*, from Chinese Dance/Drama.

Examiners' tip

Your choice of play is very important. You must make sure that your research is thorough so that character, style, status and period are reflected accurately in your designs and completed costume. The finished article must be worn in performance, must be comfortable for the actor to wear, and must communicate important information about the character. You will need to discuss and negotiate with your actor and other members of the group.

Option 8 Make-up

A What is meant by 'Make-up'?

Make-up is the painting of the actor's face. This is done either to counteract the effect of stage lighting on the detail of a face, or to create a special character effect. In both cases, specialist stage make-up is necessary. Make-up also includes any changes to the hair which may be necessary.

B What must be done?

You must complete the following:

- designs of at least two contrasting types of make-up
- notes on methods of using the necessary stage make-up
- practical demonstrations of the two contrasting designs as seen in performance
- evidence of understanding health and safety factors
- costings for the chosen designs.

You must show knowledge of:

- the purpose of make-up in a production
- straight, character and fantasy make-ups
- different types of make-up, and their use
- how to achieve theatrical effectiveness
- the way designs develop through discussion with the director and other designers
- the effects of lighting on the face, colour and design.

C Essential resources for the task

If you are to complete this task successfully, you must have:

- a performing group presenting a play which gives you suitable opportunities for your design understanding and ideas
- access to suitable stage make-up, both in type and choice

- an understanding of what the writer, improvisers or dancers intend
- enough artistic ability to draw the designs, both on paper and on faces!

D What are the possibilities for make-up?

What are the choices for straight make-ups?

Straight make-up is the basic human make-up of foundation, shaping with shadows and highlights, lines emphasising eyes and mouth, and powdering. However, while straight make-up is the most commonly needed, it varies in detail according to the character. For example, the basic foundation and lip colour will be different for different sexes, different ages, different nationalities, different states of health; the shaping will depend on both the character and the actor's actual face structure, and will include such skills as making the face thinner or fatter, and drawing laughter lines and wrinkles around the mouth and/or eyes. Eye make-up will depend on the actor's own eyes, as well as the type of performance –

Dance, for example, lays a different emphasis on eyes, as they are even more important when speech is not used. Remember that other exposed parts of the body may also need making-up – legs, arms and hands, necks, etc – and the hair may also need attention.

What are the choices for character make-ups?

These will include humans who have to have additional features added, such as with facial hair – beards and moustaches; or nose putty – changed nose shapes, warts and moles; or casualty effects, such as wounds, bruises and scars. It will also include any exaggerated forms of human make-up as in cross-gender roles like the Pantomime Dame, and stereotyped make-up, as for mime clowns or geisha girls. It includes make-up for animals, where you will have to consider carefully face shape, essential features, colours, putty and hair. Again, other exposed parts of the body may need making-up, and the hair is very likely to need major alteration in style, colour, length, thickness, etc.

What are the choices for fantasy make-ups?

These will include any non-human characters other than animals, for example, statues, robots, playing-cards, flames, mythical beings, and fantasy characters from literature, such as Frankenstein's monster. They will also include any totally imagined characters, such as fairies, aliens and sci-fi characters. While some fantasy make-ups have certain basic expectations, many give you total freedom to imagine what you want. Other exposed parts of the body may need making-up, and the hair is very likely to need major alteration.

What types of make-up are there?

You must recognise that the first reason for having make-up on stage is to give the actor a face which shows up under stage lights, and from a distance in a large performance space. Ordinary fashion make-up is intended purely to emphasise beauty and hide blemishes: it is not suitable for stage work. The traditional stage make-up is '**greasepaint**' – in sticks and tubes – and is still the most common material. **Creme make-up** – in tubes and cakes – is smoother and less greasy, but also more expensive. It can also be easier to 'overdo' it, because it goes on easily, and you need far less of it. You might prefer to use a **water-based make-up**, which is better for the skin and much easier to get off again, although many students find it more difficult to apply. It is, however, more like painting a picture, and you can achieve finer results, very suitable for when the audience is close to the performers, as in a small studio. Whichever you use, you will need pencils/liners for detail, powder to absorb the grease and perspiration, and extras like hair, putty and wigs for the additional effects.

E Common faults and pitfalls

During the preparation of your work, in addition to the general points raised on page 158, you need to be aware of some of the very common 'traps' associated with make-up.

- **Unhygienic use of materials**. You must clean and maintain your brushes and materials after every use, otherwise you will find it difficult to get the colour you want, and you are in danger of causing skin problems.

- **Failure to test for allergic reactions**. Some people do have allergic reactions to different types of make-up. Remember that the face is very sensitive, and you need to test for adverse reactions before you cause real problems. If you find someone has had a reaction after the first application, you need to consider changing the type of make-up or find a suitable skin protector to be put on under the foundation layer.

- **Lack of thought**. For example, using heavy greasepaint for a studio presentation so that everyone looks artificial and clown-like; using fine water-based make-up in a large performance space so that the effect is little better than an unmade-up face; forgetting that the performer's own skin colour and tone has a great effect on the foundation colour needed; or forgetting about the need to shape with shadows and highlights, or the need to blend one area into another. Whatever you use, try out your design in your acting space; and under lights.

- **Producing a mirror image**. If you are making yourself up, remember that you are looking at your mirror image as you do so. Usually this does not have any significant effect, but with some designs it can produce quite the wrong effect, e.g. on a playing card when the numbers are back-to-front.

- **Only making up the face**. How much of the performer needs to be made up will depend partly on the character and partly on the costume. There is nothing worse than seeing an actor with a wonderful face and an almost white neck. For some characters the performers' own hands will be acceptable, but, for example, for an elderly person with his hands on a stick and therefore clearly seen, young hands distract as much as white necks! Arms, legs, feet and bodies all need consideration in certain roles, so don't get caught out!

- **Lack of unity with other technical areas**. You must always remember that your ideas must fit with the play itself, and with the needs of costume and lighting. There must always be a willingness to compromise when necessary, so that, for example, the make-up and costume add to, and not fight with, each other, and the make-up considers the lighting gels which are being used and compensates for any adverse effects.

- **Poor time management**. Sometimes students forget that the performer must be ready for the performance! Your early experiments will be slow but, once you know exactly what you are doing, you need to practise so that you can complete the face as efficiently as possible: performers hate waiting. The length of time needed will vary according to the complexity of the make-up: but don't try to compete with the four hours needed for the Phantom from *Phantom of the Opera*! In reality, you are allowed to make yourself up for the examination; but you need to show understanding of time management in what you do.

F Possible starters for make-up designers

- **Experiment with make-ups for older people:** e.g. different coloured foundations; making the face thinner and the eyes and cheeks more sunken; lines and wrinkles; moles; hair colouring and thinning; and hands and arms and legs.

- **Experiment with animal make-ups:** e.g. Badger from *Wind in the Willows*; the White Rabbit from *Alice in Wonderland*; Napoleon from *Animal Farm*. When you have decided how you are going to tackle the face, try it on a friend.

- **Experiment with effects:** e.g. moulding putty, using prosthetics, liquid blood, tooth enamel, metallic sprays. Also experiment with everyday objects which can be used to create effects, e.g. rice krispies make good warts, and pasta sheets can be used for large scars. Keep your eyes and imaginations open and try things out – you may create excellent effects at a fraction of the cost. Keep your design ideas simple, so that the finished effect is clear.

- **Experiment with hair**: e.g. changing the colour (without dyeing it!); backcombing and spiking to achieve bulk or shape; adding features such as ringlets; creating a parting; adding creme (water dries out under lights!). Try using wigs and smaller hairpieces: attaching them securely can be a problem on some people's own hair. Practise dressing the wig to create the effect you want. Practise blending the junction of the wig and the performer's hair.
- **Experiment with fantasy make-ups**: e.g. use colour and symbol to draw a design for a water nymph; draw a design for Cobweb from *A Midsummer Night's Dream*; or draw a design for a clock. Once you have drawn your designs, see whether you can transfer them to your own face.

G Possible written work

1 Personal response to the task:

- how you explored different ideas and possibilities
- what problems you came across in both the design and the realisation
- why you came to your decisions
- how you worked in with the actors and the other designers/technicians
- what compromises you had to make.

2 Research:

- the job of the make-up designer in today's theatre
- stage make-up at different historical periods, e.g. medieval, Restoration, Victorian
- stage make-up for different genres/styles, e.g. Commedia dell'arte, Straight, Horror
- stage make-up from different cultures, e.g. Kathakali Dance/Drama, Japanese Kabuki.

3 Comparisons:

- realistic and fantasy characters in *The Tempest* by Shakespeare
- realistic and fantasy characters in *Wizard of Oz* by Frank Baum
- realistic and fantasy characters in *Dr Faustus* by Christopher Marlowe
- three different make-up designs for a queen, e.g. Elizabeth I of England from *Vivat! Vivat Regina!* by Robert Bolt; the Queen of Hearts from *Alice's Adventures in Wonderland* by Lewis Carroll; Jocasta from *Oedipus Rex* by Sophocles.

Examiners' tip

> There is more to stage make-up than pure face-painting! Experimenting and practice is needed. You must give yourself the opportunity to demonstrate your skills both in the designs and the realisations of the two make-ups: so don't choose two teenagers in a modern setting! Make sure that the contrasts give you the chance to show both the basic skills as well as your artistic flair. Remember that the completed work will be seen under stage lighting, and on a costumed actor, so you must consider other technical aspects and be able to negotiate with other members of the group.

Option 9 Properties

A What is meant by 'Properties'?

Properties are any hand-held items that are not costume accessories. They include anything which is carried most of the time, such as a walking stick or a pipe; but also include items which are only used once, perhaps briefly, during the scene, such as a knife to cut the cake, or a bottle of whisky to pour a quick drink. Properties can also include any stage 'furniture', such as a chair, which is moved at some point in a scene.

B What must be done?

You must complete the following:

- a property list for the production to which you are attached
- drawings of the set which show where various props will be put
- diagrams and notes to show how to make two chosen props for the production
- two completed self-made props used in performance
- costings for the chosen props
- evidence of understanding health and safety factors.

You must show knowledge of:

- the purpose of properties in a production
- how to get necessary information on props and on their historical period
- how to make various props
- other possible sources of props
- how to organise the props for a production
- the preparation of a property plot.

C Essential resources for the task

If you are to complete this task successfully, you must have:

- a performing group who are presenting a play which gives you suitable opportunities for your design understanding and ideas
- access to suitable materials for making your props
- facilities for making the chosen props
- access to relevant research material
- enough ability to draw the designs and plans to communicate your ideas
- the ability to produce two props which are as close as possible to the finished designs
- an understanding of what the writer, improvisers or dancers intend
- sufficient space to store the chosen props.

D What are the possibilities for properties?

What about 'everyday' items?

Generally, everyday items can be found easily, so do not waste time making them, unless they have a very special purpose. For example, if the performer needs a cup and saucer, there should be no problem, but if they are going to throw the cup down so that it breaks, then you have to make a cup which will do just that.

What about period items?

Anything which has to be historically accurate may be much more difficult to find. Some items, such as lorgnettes or a snuffbox, may be relatively easy to come by with a little bit of effort; but you may run into problems with value and cost. Some may be very difficult to find, such as an old upright telephone or a tapestry carpet bag. So you may need to consider making period items. Make sure that you do plenty of good research, so that you are quite sure about what they looked like, what materials were used originally, and the details which will convince your audience that your items are the real things!

Making and decorating prop shields for a Greek drama

What about non-realistic props?

This is certainly an area for the good props designer, as these will all have to be made or adapted from existing objects. It will include all fantasy items, such as the White Rabbit's watch in *Alice in Wonderland*, which only tells the days of the month; but also many objects which are used in more representational or symbolic drama, such as Neptune's trident.

Where can props be found?

Obviously, you may have many objects at home, at school, or with friends, but make sure before you borrow them that the owners are not going be upset if, by any chance, they are lost or damaged. All performers should be trained to look after props, but accidents do happen on stage, and it is only fair to warn people lending items. Then there are jumble sales and car boot sales, charity, secondhand and 'junk' shops – although with the increase in interest in recent years, prices have risen dramatically. You can, however, still find bargains.

What about adapting items?

You need to develop your imagination, and keep your eyes open. You also need to be prepared to experiment with different materials and processes in order to get the effect you may want, without going to a lot of expense. For example, using a cheese grater on chair fabrics quickly makes them look more worn and threadbare: but don't be tempted to try that without permission from the owner! Perhaps a character takes an indigestion tablet, and the audience needs to see it fizzing: try something like fizzy Vitamin C tablets.

E Common faults and pitfalls

During the preparation of your work, in addition to the general points raised on page 158, you need to be aware of some of the very common 'traps' associated with properties.

- **Items falling apart**. Remember that props are to be used! Even if they are hardly touched during a performance, they will suffer from the unavoidable wear and tear of rehearsals and storage, however careful you try to be. So do ensure that your work is not going to fall to pieces when it is used – look carefully at both the materials you are using and the way in which you are constructing the props.
- **Items which did not need to be made**. There really is no point in making poor replicas of objects which you use regularly, e.g. teapots, rulers, beer glasses, wallets. So look at what is needed, and choose two objects which show your understanding of props-making.
- **Choosing too big a challenge**. While it is very commendable to choose two props which will show the best of your ability, if you overstretch yourself you may fail to complete the task. First, consider your time limit, and then the size or complexity of the object. Don't decide to make something like Toad's car from *Wind in the Willows* unless

you have plenty of time, space and skill! It is better to tackle something within your capabilities and make an excellent job of it, so be realistic in your choices.

- **'Artistic' props instead of 'theatrical' props**. While this task does use your knowledge and skill in art and technology, some candidates produce real 'works of art'. This may seem to be wonderful, but the extra effort has been wasted if the performance is in a space where the fine detail cannot be seen. Indeed, the effort may even be quite wrong, if the audience stop concentrating on the performers in order to admire the beautiful prop. So, remember you are producing items to help the drama, and while they often have to look realistic, they are, in fact, stage props, so may lack some of the fine detail, or may be sturdier than usual.
- **Poorly finished articles**. At the other extreme are the props which are so roughly made that they would not fool anybody! And sometimes, they are actually dangerous, with edges or corners which will catch on, scratch or cut the performers. Again this shows a lack of understanding of the purpose for which they have been made – and also a lack of awareness of health and safety considerations.

F Possible starters for props designers

Consider how you might produce the following items. Which would you be able to find easily? Which would need you to visit various shops? Which would you need to make? Draw some quick sketches of possible designs.

- **Representational props:** e.g. for a medieval Mummers' play – swords, Doctor's pills and potions, pair of pliers for extracting teeth
- **Realistic props:** e.g. for *A Day in the Death of Joe Egg* by Peter Nichols – a hamster cage, a cowboy painting, a joke spider
- **Pantomime props:** e.g. for *Cinderella* – the glass slipper, a pumpkin, a proclamation scroll
- **Fantasy props:** e.g. for Act 2 of *The Admirable Crichton* by J. M. Barrie – gramophone, clock, fresh-air fan (all made from things to be found on a desert island).

G Possible written work

1 Personal response to the task:

- how you explored different ideas and possibilities
- what problems you came across in both the design and the realisation
- why you came to your decisions
- how you worked in with the actors and the other designers/technicians
- what compromises you had to make.

2 Research:

- the job of the props manager in today's theatre
- historical props
- magicians' and trick props
- mechanical props
- techniques and materials for making props.

3 Comparisons:

- edible props for the witch's cottage in *Hansel and Gretel*
- historical props for the market in *The Doctor and the Devils* by Dylan Thomas
- mechanical props in *Sleuth* by Anthony Shaffer
- three different designs for a heart, e.g. the supposed heart of *Snow White*; a heart for a shadow-play of a piece called *The Operation*; and a robot's heart for a sci-fi presentation called *The Feelings of a Robot*.

Examiners' tip

Remember that the props are going to be used by the actors, so they need to be both safe and robust. Actors can be very clumsy! Don't waste time making props which can be hired or obtained locally. If mechanical props are considered, you might well be able to double enter for the Design and Technology GCSE examination. Larger props are often more successful than smaller, intricate pieces.

Option 10 Masks

A What is meant by 'Masks'?

A mask is a covering which hides the face, or part of the face, of the actor. They may be eye-masks, half-face masks, full-face masks, or full-head masks; and they may be realistic or representational or exaggerated.

Full-face Comedy mask and half-face Commedia dell'arte mask for the character of Harlequin

B What must be done?

You must complete the following:

- diagrams and designs for two contrasting masks, showing how ideas have developed
- notes on using and constructing the masks
- practical demonstration with the two completed masks, seen in performance
- evidence of understanding health and safety considerations.

You must show knowledge of:

- the purpose and use of masks in a production
- the design and construction of different types of masks
- the limitations of different types of masks in performance
- the way designs develop through discussion with the director and other designers
- the relationships with other design aspects.

C Essential resources for the task

If you are to complete this task successfully, you must have:

- a performing group who are presenting a play which gives you suitable opportunities for your design understanding and ideas
- access to relevant resources, and the facilities for making masks

- access to relevant research material
- an understanding of what the writer, improvisers or dancers intend
- enough ability to draw the designs and plans to communicate your ideas
- the ability to produce your masks from your designs.

D What are the possibilities for masks?

What types of masks might you choose?

First of all, the **eye-masks** are much the easiest to make, because they only cover the eye area of the face. **Half-face masks** cover at least the top half of the face, but leave the nose and mouth uncovered, allowing for easy breathing and speech. **Full-face masks** have a much stronger visual impact; but you must remember eye, mouth and breathing holes for the actor! You may also need to think about a wig which can be worn with the mask, although the actor's own hair may be suitable for many roles. **Full-head masks** are obviously the most complicated to design and make, as they cover the whole head. You will have to consider how best to fit them over the head while preventing unnecessary 'wobbling' once they are on. You certainly have to consider the hair, or equivalent (as these are often of characters such as animals), when you use a full-head mask. You might do well to choose two different types of mask to show greater understanding, but this will partly depend on the performing group with which you are working. You must, however, show a contrast of some sort.

What materials might you use?

Eye-masks are usually made from card or felt, or from papier mâché: and they may be decorated with paint or with items such as sequins, old jewellery, or tinfoil. They may be on elastic to fit round the head; or, if stiff, may be fixed to dowelling and held in the hand. All the other masks can be made of papier mâché; although, while the half-face and full-face masks may be shaped on a mould of clay or plasticine, the full-head mask will often need a wire frame to support the extra weight and shape. Again, these may be painted or decorated with a wide variety of materials to gain the impression needed. Whatever materials you use, make sure that the masks are sturdy enough to stand up to rehearsal and performance conditions!

What masks might be best?

This really depends on the presentation being offered, and on your own ability in constructing the masks. However, the following examples provide you with some general guidelines. Eye-masks might be needed if the characters are going to a masked ball, as in *Romeo and Juliet* by William Shakespeare. You might be providing masks for a Greek-style play, such as *The Frogs* by Aristophanes, in which case full-face masks are needed, giving very clear, although exaggerated, impressions of age, character, or feeling. It may be that you are making masks for animals, as for *Noah* by Andre Obey, in which case you will probably be best with full-head masks. However, if the presentation is Dance/Drama, you are less likely to use full-head masks even for animals, as these can become very heavy when dancing: it is more likely that full-face or half-face masks would be used for this. You need to judge the type and style of presentation, as well as the characters, before you can design an appropriate mask.

What about the actors?

Masks can give actors real problems, so you must try to reduce the potential difficulties. For example, some masks may rub unless you give them suitable 'padding' at appropriate points; some may be very heavy unless you use lightweight materials in the construction. Some may become unbearably hot unless you consider some 'ventilation', and may make it difficult for the audience to hear what is being said, unless you think carefully about the size, shape and position of the mouth. Performers may have difficulty in seeing where they are going unless you pay attention to the size, shape and position of the eye-holes. Always remember that while you may wish to provide a real work of art, your job is to aid the actor in his or her performance, so everything you do must come from that starting point.

E Common faults and pitfalls

During the preparation of your work, in addition to the general points raised on page 158, you need to be aware of some of the very common 'traps' associated with masks.

- **Failing to fit properly**. In performance, this can mean that the mask moves around, or the actor may have to adjust it; the actor may not be heard properly, or may not be able to see properly. You must make sure that the mask fits the actor it is intended for, so you need to work closely with them at every stage. Keep checking – and adjust if there are problems!
- **Being unsuitable in style**. For example, having a pantomime-type mask for a straight play; or a wonderfully realistic mask for a representational play; or a frightening mask for an infant audience. Think carefully about the style/genre of the presentation and the audience.
- **Choosing too big a challenge**. While it is very commendable to choose two masks which will show the best of your ability, if you overstretch yourself you may fail to complete the task. First, consider the time limit, and then the complexity of the masks. It is better to tackle something within your capabilities and make an excellent job of it rather than find time has run out with the masks unfinished. Be realistic in your choices.
- **Failing to survive rehearsal conditions**. Your actors must practise with the masks, so that they become completely confident with them. But you must ensure that the masks do not become 'tatty' or broken before the performance: and that the 'ties' do not snap, or break away from the mask itself. So masks must be well constructed and sturdy, even though surface damage may occur. This, however, can be dealt with after each rehearsal or immediately prior to the performance itself.
- **'Artistic' masks instead of 'theatrical' masks**. While this task obviously uses your knowledge and skill in art and technology, some candidates produce real 'works of art'. This may seem to be wonderful, but the effort may be totally misplaced if the audience stops concentrating on the performance in order to admire the wonderful mask. So, recognise that you are producing items to help with the Drama, and compromise accordingly.

F Possible starters for mask designers

- **Simple masks:** made, for example, with paper or card or mod-roc. Experiment to discover the best position, size and shape of holes for the eyes, mouth, nose and ears, and the best position for elastic or ribbon or whatever you may use to tie the mask on. Make notes of decisions you make, so that you can do it 'right' when it matters.
- **Unpainted, neutral masks:** don't worry about character. Just experiment to see how to make them fit the head and feel comfortable; and how to make them practical and sturdy.
- **Decorations:** experiment with glitter, paint, shapes, different materials, etc. Test your experiments under stage lights, and make notes of anything you find is particularly successful, and which you might be glad to use in the future.
- **Animal masks:** experiment with the essential features, the colours, the materials, the shaping, in order to create masks of different animals.

G Possible written work

1 Personal response to the task:

- how you explored and developed different ideas and possibilities
- what problems you came across, both in the design and the realisation
- why you came to your decisions
- how you worked in with the actors and the other designers/technicians
- what compromises you had to make.

2 Research:

- the job of the mask designer in today's theatre
- techniques and materials for making masks
- how different styles/genres use different types of masks
- the use of masks at different historical times
- the use of masks in different theatrical cultures, e.g. Japanese Noh Theatre, Italian Commedia dell'arte.

3 Comparisons:

- full-face masks for Balinese Dance/Drama, e.g. Barong and Rangda
- half-face masks for Commedia dell'arte, e.g. Harlequin and Pierrot
- full-head masks for Chinese Festival masks, e.g. lion and eagle
- three different mask designs for a 'mysterious stranger', e.g. for a romance, for a Dance/Drama, for a western.

Examiners' tip

You will need to find a play in which contrasting masks are used, so close co-operation with your actors is essential. It is important that the masks reflect the overall style of the production. Whatever type of mask you make, it must be effective in performance and must be comfortable, safe and durable! Avoid very fancy and elaborate masks which will not stand up to the demands of the piece. You might also be surprised at how often the obvious needs of seeing and breathing are completely forgotten!

Option 11 Puppets

A What is meant by 'Puppets'?

A puppet is a non-living representation of a character, which has to be worked by human control. It includes glove puppets, marionettes, rod puppets and ventriloquists' dummies.

B What must be done?

You must complete the following:

- various diagrams and designs for a puppet, showing how ideas have developed
- notes on using and constructing the puppet
- notes on achieving characterisation with the puppet
- practical demonstration of the completed puppet in performance
- evidence of understanding health and safety considerations.

You must show knowledge of:

- the purpose and use of puppets in a production
- the design and construction of different types of puppets
- the limitations of different types in performance
- the way designs develop through discussion with the director and other technical designers
- the relationship with other technical design aspects.

C Essential resources for the task

If you are to complete this task successfully, you must have:

- a performing group who are presenting a play which gives you suitable opportunities for your design understanding and ideas
- access to relevant resources, and the facilities for making a puppet
- access to relevant research material
- an understanding of what the writer, improvisers or dancers intend
- enough ability to draw the designs and plans to communicate your ideas
- the ability to produce a completed puppet from your designs.

D What are the possibilities for puppets?

What types of puppets might you choose?

The simplest form of puppet is the **finger puppet**, but it is also the most restricted, as it is so small and is worked by just one finger. A **hand** or **glove puppet** is the most familiar to children, as it is the typical Punch and Judy puppet, and is also often seen in toy shops. It has a firm head and hands, and a loose costume: it covers the whole hand, and is worked by the first finger in the head, and the thumb and second finger in the two hands. A **rod-puppet** is attached to a rod or a set of rods held in the hand; it is usually a rounded figure with full-length costume, although, in **shadow puppets**, it is often a flat two-dimensional figure. A **ventriloquist's dummy** is a scale model of the character, although it has 'floppy' legs so that it can sit easily on the puppeteer's lap. It is worked from the back by internal levers and strings, and it has a mouth and eyes which can open and close. In Japan, you will find **full-size puppets** which need up to three people to support and work them from behind. Another more complicated puppet is the **marionette** or **string-puppet**, which is worked from above by strings attached to various parts of the puppet's body.

What materials might you use?

This will depend on the type of puppet, but whatever you use must be strong enough to survive rehearsals and performances! Wherever you need a firm head, hands and feet, it is likely that you will be using something like papier mâché or wood. The inner construction of a marionette, or any large puppet which has to remain upright, will probably be a mixture of wood and wire; while rod puppets need rods of wood, plastic or metal. A shadow puppet will be made of any dark, fairly rigid material which will cast a clear shadow when lit from behind; traditionally in the Far East this was buffalo hide. Clothes will be made of any material which would be suitable for any stage costume.

What puppets might be best?

This will depend partly on your own 'favourite', but also on a number of other factors. How large will the completed puppet be? How complicated will it be to make? And how long have you got to complete it? How skilful are you at making puppets before you start? In addition, you must obviously make a puppet which fits in with the rest of the group and what they are intending to do: should it be, for example, realistic, historical, symbolic or imaginative; should it be of a particular person or character? Does the story the group is intending to tell lend itself traditionally to a particular type of puppet?

What about the 'puppeteers'?

Do they have any skill with a particular type of puppet? Or are they going to have to learn how to use them? If so, how long will this take? Is it likely that they will be better at using puppets which need working from above (marionettes) or below (glove or rod) or behind (dummies or full-size)? What about the actual stage to be used (or constructed)?

Does the puppet have to be finished before the 'acting' rehearsals?

This is a difficult problem, because ideally the puppet needs to be completed before the puppeteers can get on with the rehearsals. However, you may be able to borrow or make a quick representation of your puppet which can be used in rehearsal. Even though it has no detail – or even the wrong detail – of the character intended, it does give the puppeteer something to practise with. You may also be able to provide the basic puppet very quickly, so that it can be used in rehearsal, while you develop the rest of it and its clothes between rehearsals. The finished puppet must obviously be completed with time enough for the puppeteer to get thoroughly familiar with it and any 'oddities' of working which it may have! Look carefully at the length of time allowed for this project, and try to be realistic in your calculations of how long it will take you.

E Common faults and pitfalls

During the preparation of your work, in addition to the general points raised on page 158, you need to be aware of some of the very common 'traps' associated with puppets.

- **Not being flexible enough for movement**. A puppet must appear to be able to move easily. If you use unsuitably rigid materials, or costumes which are too restrictive, the puppet will not move as freely or as quickly as it should do.

- **Having unsuitable costume**. In addition to costumes which restrict movement, sometimes clothes are too tight, so that stretch creases appear as the puppet is used; or clothes are so long that the puppet gets tied up in its own costume. Sometimes the clothes have no character, because too much time has been spent on perfecting the head, and there is no time left for the costume. Plan carefully so that these problems do not arise.

- **Being unsuitable in style**. For example, having a pantomime-type puppet for a straight play, or a frightening puppet for an infant audience. Think carefully about the style/genre of the presentation and the audience.

- **Choosing too big a challenge**. While it is very commendable to choose a puppet which will show the best of your ability, if you overstretch yourself you may fail to complete the task. First consider the time limit; and then the complexity of the puppet. It is better to tackle something within your capabilities and make an excellent job of it rather than find time has run out before you have finished. Be realistic in your choice.

- **Failing to survive rehearsal conditions**. Your puppeteer must practise with the puppet, so that they become completely confident with it. But you must ensure that the puppet does not become 'tatty' or broken before the performance. So it must be well constructed and sturdy: particularly as many puppets are used for plenty of action, including 'violent' action at times!

- **'Artistic' puppets instead of 'theatrical' puppets**. While this task obviously uses your knowledge and skill in art and technology, some candidates produce real 'works of art'. This may seem to be wonderful, but the effort may be totally misplaced if the audience stops concentrating on the performance in order to admire the wonderful puppet. So recognise that you are producing a puppet to help with the Drama, and compromise accordingly.

F Possible starters for puppet designers

- **Heads:** research ways of making sturdy heads, and experiment with some of the ideas, e.g. using papier mâché, wood, cloth; creating shape to the head, and ears; decorating by using paint or by fixing materials to the head. Find the ones which seem to produce the best results for you, and make notes of your decisions. If you want to do a ventriloquist's dummy, experiment with making mouth and eyes which open and close.

- **Rod-puppets:** fix a lump of something such as clay, play dough or sticky-tack to the end to represent a head, and practise bringing your rod puppet to 'life', remembering that the 'face' of the puppet should be seen. How can you move it to produce different actions and feelings? What are the problems and shortcomings in using a rod puppet? What are the advantages? What themes and styles/genres might be most suitable? Concentrate on any essential design features, such as the ideal length of the rods, the weight of the head, creating the 'front' of the puppet.

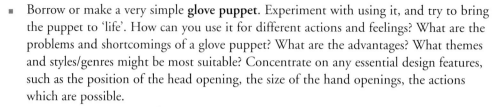

- Borrow or make a very simple **glove puppet**. Experiment with using it, and try to bring the puppet to 'life'. How can you use it for different actions and feelings? What are the problems and shortcomings of a glove puppet? What are the advantages? What themes and styles/genres might be most suitable? Concentrate on any essential design features, such as the position of the head opening, the size of the hand openings, the actions which are possible.
- Borrow a **marionette**. Unless you are used to using these, they can be quite difficult to work in the early stages. So experiment with it, and try to bring the puppet to 'life'. Notice which parts of the body need to have strings attached to create most movement. How can you use it for different actions and feelings? What are the problems and shortcomings of a marionette? What are the advantages? What themes and styles/genres might be most suitable? Concentrate on any essential design features, such as the position and number of strings, the size and layout of the control bars, which strings can be used together.
- **Costume:** experiment with different types of material to see which hang and move well when fixed to a basic puppet. Try adding different types of decoration to the material to see the effects of, for example, glitter, lace or tinfoil. Try to notice how far you need to go in detail to produce a theatrical representation of the character. With all your experiments, try them out under lights, and make notes of anything which seems to work well.

G Possible written work

1 Personal response to the task:

- how you explored different ideas and possibilities
- what problems you came across, both in the design and the realisation
- why you came to your decisions
- how you worked in with the puppeteers and the other designers/technicians
- what compromises you had to make.

2 Research:

- the job of the puppet-maker in the theatre today
- techniques and materials for making different types of puppet
- different puppets through different historical periods
- different puppets in different countries in the world
- puppet theatres and audiences today.

3 Comparisons:

- Javanese rod/shadow puppets, especially for the Ramayana and Mahabharata
- Punch and Judy glove puppets
- life-size puppets used in *The Lion King*
- three different designs for puppets of a devil, e.g. for a religious play, for a melodrama, for a shadow play.

Examiners' tip

It can be difficult finding a scene in which puppets are involved, so there needs to be very close collaboration with your group throughout the whole process. You need to agree on the style, type and function, and to recognise the advantages and constraints of different types of puppet. And don't forget that the puppeteer will need plenty of rehearsal time to get used to it!

Option 12 Lighting

A What is meant by 'Lighting'?

Lighting is the provision of any sources of light, whether from hanging or standing lanterns, or from table-lamps, candles, Christmas lights, etc.

Lighted setting for thrust staging of *Our Country's Good* by Timberlake Wertenbaker. This uses wide-angle parcans to light the voile banners with entrances and exits; and profile spots for the central acting area. The wood shavings not only create an interesting and appropriate floor-covering: but also prevent the reflection of light from a polished wooden floor

B What must be done?

You must complete the following:

- rigging diagrams for your performance space
- a working lighting plot/cue-sheet
- an annotated script
- evidence of understanding health and safety factors
- a demonstration of lighting your chosen performance.

You must show knowledge of:

- the purpose of stage lighting in a production
- different types of lantern and lamp and their technical uses
- focusing, angling, wiring and patching
- the operation of switchboard and dimmer packs
- use of colour filters, gobos, special effects lanterns – and their effect on actors, set, costume and make-up
- preparing a lighting plot.

C Essential resources for the task

If you are to complete this task successfully, you must have:

- a performing group presenting a play which gives you suitable opportunities for your design understanding and ideas
- access to sufficient and suitable lighting equipment
- the constant adult supervision which is needed on health and safety grounds
- the ability to create total blackout when needed
- access to relevant research material
- an understanding of what the writer, improvisers or dancers intend.

D What are the possibilities for lighting?

How can you help the audience to see what is happening?

The first priority for any lighting designer is to ensure that the actors and their set can be seen. Only then can you consider any special effects. You need to define the acting space for the audience by adequate and suitable general lighting – e.g. by the use of floods or soft-edged spots – although this will not necessarily be the whole stage space, nor necessarily full intensity of light. Perhaps the audience need to focus on one character or one key moment. This can be done by using areas of greater intensity or different types of lantern.

What about the use of colour?

Most students love using colour, but be wary of over-using it because it can have the wrong effect, especially when it makes everything look artificial! And remember that white is a colour – often the most suitable colour. Altering the intensity may be sufficient to take any unwanted 'glare' out of the light. However, the use of gels immediately alters the impression on the audience; and you need to experiment with them to understand the effects they can have. With pale gels, the effect on the audience is subtle and often subconscious, but helpful to the mood and atmosphere, e.g. a pale rose creates a feeling of warmth and well-being, whereas a steel tint underlines threat and confrontation. Lighting characters with different colours from different sides can make faces look less 'flat' and more interesting. There are also situations when stronger colours are needed, e.g. in a non-realistic scene, or a traditional melodrama. However, resist the temptation to use a different colour in every lantern! Select just two or three which complement the set and costume.

How about other design elements?

A good lighting designer can help to enhance not only the actors but also the set, costume and make-up; a bad one can 'kill' the other elements. You must work with the other designers throughout if you are to be aware of colours, textures and characteristics which they are using, so that you can help to 'bring them to life'.

What about special effects?

There is a tremendous range of possible effects, but some will only be available to you if your centre has suitable equipment. If they do, then experiment with gobos, mirror balls, colour wheels, strobes, ultraviolet light, projected images and lighting animation. Find out what your centre is capable of, and be prepared to use its resources to the full – provided the effects are relevant to your piece of work!

E Common faults and pitfalls

During the preparation of your work, in addition to the general points raised on page 158, you need to be aware of some of the very common 'traps' associated with stage lighting.

- **Inadequate resources**. Sometimes candidates try to offer this option when the centre only has four or five lanterns. While this may be sufficient for their everyday purposes, it is not enough for the depth of understanding and expertise which this examination demands.
- **Unavailability of resources**. You need to check that the equipment you want to use is, in fact, going to be available to you. Check that it has not been earmarked for Sixth Form exams, or for lending out to another school, just at the time when you want to use it; and that the performance space itself is not being used as an examination room at the time when you need to be rigging and patching. Also check that your school's health and safety rules do, in fact, allow you personally to use the equipment needed.
- **Insufficient light**. All too often, lighting designers ask their audience to watch the performance in semi-darkness! Eyes get tired, and with that, minds switch off, because it is just too much trouble to concentrate. You must make sure that actors' faces can be seen properly, so that expression can be understood. If you want to create a feeling of semi-darkness, this can be done as the scene begins, but then you should gradually increase the intensity of the light – in such a way that the audience is unaware of the change. They then just think that their eyes

have got accustomed to the darkness: and you have succeeded in creating the *impression* you wanted.

- **Lack of understanding of specific lanterns**. You must ensure that you know exactly what lanterns and models you are using, and learn through your teacher, research and experimentation, exactly what each can do, including how far their beams will reach. Otherwise you will soon find yourself using the wrong lantern in the wrong place or for the wrong purpose.
- **Inappropriate use of colour**. It really is pretty grim to watch a play in, for example, a green light just because it is set in a wood. It is just as bad as sitting in semi-darkness, especially when green kills so many other colours on the stage. Again, you need to think about how to create an impression of a woodland as the scene opens, but then to adjust the contribution of white light after the first few seconds. Sometimes the wrong colour is used for the atmosphere of the piece, or for the colour or texture of the set, costume or make-up, so that it spoils the whole effect.
- **Inability to create total blackout**. This is a great shame if a total blackout is needed for the effect of the piece, as it can distract from that effect. If the problem occurs between scenes, then consider the possibility of scene-changing in full-light in role: this can be extremely effective if it is well done – and practised as much as the rest of the action!

F Possible starters for lighting designers

- **Experiment with different lanterns**. Compare the areas of light from flood and spotlights, and the 'spilling' of unwanted light. Look at hard-edged and soft-edged spots; at floor lighting, footlighting, follow spotting; at the use of gobos, irises, barndoors and other effects. Make a note of any conclusions you come to, so that you can always pick the right lantern for the right occasion.
- **Use the control board**. Learn to alter the intensity of the beam and to cross-fade; to use a timer, a pre-set and programmable boards; to understand the dimmer packs and patching.
- **Experiment with the use of colour**. Try to create different moods and atmospheres with the use of colours; the time of day or of year; different weather effects; different locations. Think about the gels being used, the balance between different colours, the intensity of different colours, the type of lantern and lamp being used, and the direction of beam. Make a note of any particularly good effects so that you can use them at a future date.
- **Work from a cue-sheet**. Cues may be visual, such as 'M. stands up'; spoken, such as 'R. says: Come here!'; or sound, such as 'as *The Wedding March* begins'. They need to be accurate, and the performers have to understand that they must keep to any cues given. You need to know whether you are bringing the lights up, fading them, cross-fading or blacking-out; whether changes are sudden, gradual, on a timer, etc; and what the final intensity of each lantern is to be. There is a photocopiable blank cue-sheet in Appendix 7 (page 247).

G Possible written work

1 Personal response to the task:

- how you explored different ideas and possibilities
- what problems you came across, both in the design and the realisation
- why you came to your decisions
- how you worked in with the actors and the other designers/technicians
- what compromises you had to make.

2 Research:

- the job of the lighting designer in today's theatre
- the development of stage lighting through different historical periods
- today's use of technology
- different ways of lighting a production, including different styles
- *Son et Lumière* presentations.

3 Comparisons:

- a fantasy scene such as the jewel cave in *Aladdin*
- a melodrama such as *Maria Marten/Murder in the Red Barn* by Constance Cox
- a play with flashbacks such as *Ernie's Incredible Illucinations* by Alan Ayckbourn
- three different lighting designs for the opening witch scene from *Macbeth* by Shakespeare, e.g. to help communicate threat; to help communicate power; for a Dance/Drama presentation.

Lighting: rigging and controls of a theatre-in-the-round production

Examiners' tip

Always remember that the first requirement of stage lighting is to light the actors. Creation of mood, time and atmosphere is important, but the audience must be able to see the performers. Make sure that both the chosen play and the resources and rules of your centre give you the opportunity to show your creativity as well as your ability to rig, focus and control equipment. It is perhaps not a good idea to offer lighting if these demands cannot be met!

Option 13 Sound

A What is meant by 'Sound'?

Sound includes any sounds which are not made directly by the performers themselves.

B What must be done?

You must complete the following:

- a sound plot for your production
- an annotated script or running-order, and cue-sheet
- any necessary diagrams
- evidence of understanding health and safety factors
- a practical demonstration of sound effects in performance
- evidence of controlling sound at appropriate levels for background and/or dramatic effects.

You must show knowledge of:

- the purpose of sound in a production
- the use of sound quality to create atmosphere
- the use of 'live', directional and recorded sound
- the ability to record, mix, splice and edit.

C Essential resources for the task

If you are to complete this task successfully, you must have:

- a performing group presenting a play which gives you suitable opportunities for your design understanding and ideas
- access to suitable and adequate resources, including for recording and editing
- access to relevant research material
- the ability to produce the necessary sound effects
- an understanding of what the writer, improvisers or dancers intend

D What are the possibilities for sound?

How can sound help a dramatic presentation?

Sometimes a sound is a necessary part of the scene, e.g. a telephone ringing or a knock on a door. But sound can also set the scene and create mood and atmosphere. This is often done with music – as with TV programmes – but there are times when other sounds will be more suitable, e.g. the sounds of a murder taking place during a blackout, or the sounds in a playground to suggest the play's setting. If you do use music, however, realise that classical music gives you a much greater choice! Pop music may occasionally be right, e.g. for a disco, or if the words and mood fit the piece, but music without words is often much better for creating the right atmosphere.

Sound can be used, too, to create a feeling of historical period or of a different culture, e.g. the use of the right musical instruments might suggest an Elizabethan court or an Arabian market; the use of the right film news commentary might suggest a World War II setting or the Notting Hill Carnival. Sound very easily establishes the location of the piece, e.g. by the sea, or in a busy street; the weather, e.g. rain or wind; and the time of day, e.g. dawn chorus or owls hooting.

Why is directional sound important?

If you are to help the effect of the performance, any sound you provide must appear to come from the right place on stage. To have a door stage right, and the sound of a doorbell stage left does not help credibility! Directional sound can sometimes be a major problem, and you may need to discuss with the actors and set designers how you can compromise to make, for example, the sound of the radio come from the radio on stage.

When would 'live' sounds be most suitable?

Any sound which can easily be made backstage, without taking away the effect from what is happening on stage, should be done live, especially if it is a sound of short duration, e.g. a knock on the door or a wolf whistle. Other sounds which are easy to make and which do not take up valuable space backstage can also be 'live', e.g. a trumpet call or a clock chiming.

What about recorded sound?

If the sound is to go on over a long time, it is probably easier to record it, e.g. the playing of romantic music during a meal in a restaurant. It will also be necessary to record any sound which you cannot easily reproduce backstage, e.g. a train coming into a station. However, with all recorded sound, you must make the quality as good as you possibly can. The audience should not hear the recorder being switched on and off each time; neither should it be obvious from the sound quality that this is not a 'live' sound. Remember that it is the audience who hear it, and you need to sit in the audience space and listen whilst someone else works the recorder. If it doesn't convince you, do something about it!

How can you produce the sound wanted?

Obviously it may be easy to produce a sound because it is simple, e.g. rolling dried peas in a drum to create rain; or because you can use electronic equipment such as microphones, voice synthesisers and CDs. But there are times when you have got to use your imagination and experiment with all sort of likely and unlikely objects, e.g. sawing through a cabbage is good for cutting off someone's head! Take time to make sounds with anything available – and don't forget to try making them in unlikely situations, such as too close to a microphone. For example, if you agitate water gently in a plastic bucket, and record it close-up, you will manage a very good sound of water lapping on the shore, or against a boat. Producing sound effects for fantasy productions can be great fun!

E Common faults and pitfalls

During the preparation of your work, in addition to the general points raised on page 158, you need to be aware of some of the very common 'traps' associated with sound.

- **Coming from the wrong place.** The sound must appear to come from the right place on stage, if the audience is to believe in it. Look again at the information given under 'Why is directional sound important?' above.
- **Being too loud.** Many students forget that the sound is there to help the action, not to replace it! If it drowns out what is being said, or if it becomes too loud for comfort, then the audience will become restless and noisy themselves. You must allow the actors to be heard: and you must avoid giving your audience headaches! Always check the volume by going into the audience position to listen to proposed levels of sound.
- **Trailing cables.** Think about health and safety considerations! Obviously, try to avoid such hazards, although they are sometimes unavoidable – in which case they *must* be secured.
- **Failure to edit or cue tapes properly.** It is awful when performers and audience have to wait while the tape runs on to the right place, or when one sound slides noisily into the next. Such mistakes usually cause unwanted laughter from the audience, so make sure that you prepare your tape properly beforehand.
- **Over-dependence on commercially-produced tapes.** Such tapes can sometimes be a godsend, because they include just the sound you need, especially when it is something unusual or atmospheric. However, the recordings are often of the wrong length for what you need, and they may need editing. Sometimes students use a recording when a live sound would be better, e.g. the sound of footsteps offstage. Certainly use commercial tapes, but be fully aware of their shortcomings.
- **Producing historically incorrect sounds.** In a piece where period equipment is being used, do make sure that the sound you produce is right for the time. The old Bakelite, ring-dial telephones had a very different sound from today's phones, just as the sounds of Elizabethan music and instruments were very different from today's. Make sure that you do your research properly, so that you can avoid such mistakes.

F Possible starters for sound designers

- **Listen to music.** Play different pieces of orchestral and instrumental music to discover pieces which suggest different moods, atmospheres, locations, historical periods or places in the world. It often helps to sit with your eyes shut, or in a darkened room: your imagination and 'inner eyes' work much better when you cut out anything which may distract you. Experiment with distorting music or mixing music for effect. Make a note of any pieces which have dramatic possibilities, and how they might be used: you will never remember when you need to find something quickly!
- **Create your own sounds.** Again you need to be able to use your imagination. You will be surprised at how simple ideas are often very effective. Opening and closing metal filing cabinet drawers can be a substitute for opening and closing cell doors. Find different objects – and experiment! Try crushing tissue paper near a microphone to create fire; crushing a handful of old recording tape near the mike to create footsteps in the forest; or crushing a bag of flour near the mike to create footsteps in the snow. Again, make notes of anything which seems to be successful: you will never remember exactly what you used or what you did, when the time comes.

- **Work from a cue-sheet.** Cues may be visual, such as 'M. stands up'; spoken, such as 'R. says: Come here!'; or lighting, such as 'when the lights cross-fade'. They need to be accurate, and the performers have to understand that they must keep to any cues given. You also need to know the length of time needed for each sound; whether they are to be sudden, gradually increased or decreased; and what volume they need to reach. You must know which of the sounds you are making 'live' and which are recorded; and where backstage each sound is going to be made in order for the direction to be correct. There is a photocopiable blank cue-sheet in Appendix 8 (page 248).

Note

> You should be aware of copyright restrictions on all music and recordings, and how these will apply to your choices, especially if you are giving a public performance.

G Possible written work

1 Personal response to the task:

- how you explored different ideas and possibilities
- what problems you came across, both in the design and the realisation
- why you came to your decisions
- how you worked in with the actors and the other designers/technicians
- what compromises you had to make.

2 Research:

- the job of the sound designer in today's theatre
- ways of creating different sound effects
- ways of recording different sound effects and the equipment available
- different styles of music and their possible uses
- *Son et Lumière* presentations
- copyright restrictions on music and recordings.

3 Comparisons:

- railway station sounds for *The Ghost Train* by Arnold Ridley
- school sounds and others for *Forty Years On* by Alan Bennett
- music and other sounds for *84 Charing Cross Road* by Helene Hanff
- three different sounds for creating the impression of a winter's night.

Examiners' tip

> Make sure that the scene chosen is appropriate for your needs, and that sound is not just an 'add on' which just distracts from the drama. Try to use both live and recorded sound, and make sure that it is historically accurate, directionally correct, and does not drown out any speech on stage. You must show your skill in an actual performance, so you must work very closely with your actors and other technicians throughout. Accurate timing of sound effects is essential, and this can only be achieved by constant rehearsal.

Option 14 Stage management

A What is meant by 'Stage management'?

This is the organisation and control of everything which happens backstage, and everything needed on stage, during a performance.

B What must be done?

You must complete the following:

- a prompt copy/stage manager's book
- evidence of understanding health and safety factors
- rehearsal schedules
- preparation of the acting area for rehearsal and performance
- a demonstration of 'running the show' during an actual performance
- the organisation of the backstage area and personnel.

You must show knowledge of:

- the responsibilities of a stage manager before, during and after the show
- all backstage equipment
- how to get the best from your backstage team.

C Essential resources for the task

If you are to complete this task successfully, you must have:

- a performing group who are presenting a play which gives you suitable opportunities for your understanding and ideas – a very short performance will often not enable you to cover many of the necessary aspects of the job
- an understanding of all technical equipment
- the ability to stand in for absentee technicians or performers
- an ability to organise people and resources
- an ability to get people to work as a team for the good of the production
- an ability to thrive on challenge
- access to relevant research material
- an understanding of what the writer, improvisers or dancers intend.

D What are the possibilities for stage management?

What organisational opportunities are there?

The stage manager is responsible for managing the performers, the technicians, the performance and the performance space. This means that you must be able to organise both people and objects. You need to encourage responsibility in the rest of the team and a commitment to produce the best of which you are all capable; and you need to be able to see how resources can best be organised to make the most of what is available to you. You also have to ensure that deadlines are met: e.g. that the actors arrive at rehearsal at the right time and in the right place, and that essential props appear when they are needed.

What about rehearsals?

You are also responsible for organising rehearsal schedules, and for seeing that your teams attend. If they don't, you will have to cover for them. Obviously you must be realistic in your schedules, and take people's other commitments into consideration, but you also need to be able to lead compromises when they have to be made. Bear in mind that not everyone will necessarily be needed at every rehearsal, so be flexible where you can. Perhaps one of the actors does not appear at all in the section of the play due to be rehearsed on Monday; or actors are not going to be made-up on Wednesday; or the lighting resources are being used by another group on Friday. However, once the commitment is made to a particular day, you need to make sure that everyone needed is there. You also need to get the space ready for rehearsal, and see that the technical team are ready for the day's scene, so that you can start without wasting time. You are responsible during the rehearsal for making sure that everything goes as smoothly as possible, and for making notes of any decisions which are made in connection with both the acting and the technical sides. After the rehearsal, you will see that the space and resources are left properly, and that any costumes, props and sound tapes are checked and stored securely.

What about erecting and striking the set?

The stage manager will organise the team who erect the set, move furniture and props during the performance, and who take it all down at the end of the performance. In reality, within a school this is usually the performers, who double up as the 'stage team'; but one of your jobs will be to organise how all this is done, and by whom. It often needs as much rehearsal as the piece itself, if you are going to make the changes smooth and quick. You must know exactly where everything goes, where everything is needed, and who is going to use it. You will also check it all to make sure that no repairs are needed.

What about cueing the production?

Every performance needs to run as smoothly as possible, and sometimes this means that the stage manager has to warn people when things are about to be needed: for example, in a long production, to give actors a five-minute warning of their next entrance; or to warn the sound technician of a visual cue which is about to come up. In order to do this, you must know exactly what happens when, and be able to see ahead whilst the performance is actually going on. Your stage manager's book or prompt copy will have all this information.

How good is your knowledge of the technical side?

While you may not be as much of an expert in any individual aspect, you must have a good working knowledge of lighting, scenery, props, sound, masks, costume and make-up. You must know what is possible for those designers and technicians, so that they are not asked to do the impossible. You must be able to make suggestions on improving the effectiveness of what they are suggesting or demonstrating, and know how to achieve those improvements. You must be able to see how they can each help the effectiveness of the others, and, equally, how they can spoil what the others are trying to achieve if compromises are not made. There may be occasions when you will actually need to operate equipment, so you will need to be competent.

What about health and safety?

Again, you have to be able to think for everyone. So you need to have a good working knowledge of essential considerations in every department of production – both acting and technical – and must be able to think for and with the technicians. You need to have your eyes open at all times for potential hazards – with the ability to solve problems when they arise. The health and safety of the whole production is, in the end, down to you!

E Common faults and pitfalls

During the preparation of your work, in addition to the general points raised on page 158, you need to be aware of some of the very common 'traps' associated with stage management.

- **An incomplete prompt copy/stage manager's book**. If you have failed to keep a note of everything which happens during the piece, you can be fairly sure that you will forget something in the pressure of the performance, and that is where things begin to go wrong! If you find that your book has a lot of reminders all together, then it may be worth colour-coding your notes, e.g. red for actors, blue for lights, green for sound, so that you can understand them at a glance.
- **Poor teamwork**. This can mean disaster for a performance, if, for example, some people have lost interest, or can't be bothered, or just want to show how good they are, never mind anyone else! Then, instead of everything working together to produce an effective presentation, the work becomes bitty and unbalanced – and very obvious to the audience. If, therefore, you have problems in the team, you have to do everything you can to sort it out well before the performance itself: not always an easy task, but don't consider stage management if you don't like that sort of challenge!
- **Miscueing parts of the piece**. This may be due to a poor prompt copy/stage manager's book; to lack of rehearsal or preparation; or to the stress on the day. Whatever the cause, it can throw the actors and the technical team, and can, again, be the cause of disaster taking over. You must be very clear in your own mind exactly what has to be cued, and you must concentrate on giving the cue at the right moment!

F Possible starters for stage managers

- **Draw up a possible rehearsal schedule.** Remember to check the location for each rehearsal, the availability of the room, the availability of the actors and the designers/technicians, the frequency of rehearsals. What problems have occurred? How can you best overcome them?
- **Prepare a prompt copy/stage manager's book** for the extract of *The Ruined Abbey* on page 28. On it, note all the possible moves by the actors; props needed; any lighting changes; sound cues; and any other information which will help you to run the show efficiently.
- **Prepare a sketch plan of the acting space** you are most familiar with, and show on it any essential set/furniture which you might need for *The Ruined Abbey*.
- **Prepare a sketch plan of the backstage space** for *The Ruined Abbey*. Mark on it the following: the position of actors' entries or exits; the positions of any essential backstage technicians; the position of any live or directional sound effects; the position of any props, and any costume needed for quick changes; and anything else which you feel you might need to take into consideration.

Stage manager's plan of the stage area for a GCSE presentation of *The Burglary*:

(Lighting desk at rear of audience)

House-lights off style diagram:

- Lighting Stand for streetlamp + chime bars for clock
- Window flat
- Props 2
- Sound
- Audio Trolley
- Curtains
- Plant stand + plant
- Display cabinet + contents
- Trolley + drinks
- Door Flat (kitchen)
- Armchair
- Sofa + cushions
- Door Flat (Hall)
- Armchair + squeaky toy
- Coffee table + plant + radio
- Nest of tables + books
- Props 3
- Props 1
- Magazine rack + magazines + papers
- Screen
- Screen

A U D I E N C E

Stage manager's Prompt Copy for the opening of a GCSE presentation of *The Burglary*:

Introduction: 'With cat-like tread' from The Pirates of Penzance by Gilbert & Sullivan
House-lights off
Darkness
Silence
Streetlight on (preset 1)   *rucksack with tools*

silhouetted   Burglar 1 appears outside the window. Hands explore the frame, and then
gently open the window. B1 climbs in, looks around, goes through hall door.
silhouetted   Burglar 2 appears outside window. Throws large bag through open window.   *torch & bag*
B2 shines torch

B2   (*stage whisper*) Hey, mate. Where've you gone? Help me up!

B1 re-enters and rushes to the window.

B1   (*hissing*) Shut it, you fool! Do you want to wake someone?

B2   Well, give me a hand then.

Lights rise gradually (timer)   B1   You'll never get in there. Go to the front door – I've just unlocked it. Come in that way – but for goodness' sake, don't make a sound. (*Watches through the window as B2 goes to front door. Then looks at kitchen door and moves towards it.*) *B1 closes curtains*

clock chimes   B2   *enters through the hall door, just as a grandfather clock in the hallway*   *B2 tiptoe*   *chimes midnight.* *B2 trips over feet – falls flat on face*

B1   Can't you do anything quietly? *Threatening towards B2*

B2   Hey, you can't blame me for that! You didn't hear me come through the front door, did you? *B1 lifts B2 by scruff to chair UC*

B1   Well, you've made up for it now. Just sit down there – and don't you dare move. *B1 shuts hall door*

B2   OK, Boss. Just as you say.

B1   Good. I'm just going to look through here. (*Exits through the kitchen door.*)

Radio sound   B2   *sits down and looks round. Sees the radio, and turns it on just as B1 re-enters* *Radio* *from the kitchen, carrying food and drink.* *2 cans Coke, 2 meat pies, 2 pkts crisps*

Lights (2)

G Possible written work

1 Personal response to the task:

- how you explored different ideas and possibilities
- what problems you came across, both in the planning and the realisation
- why you came to your decisions
- how you worked in with the actors and the other designers/technicians
- what compromises you had to make.

2 Research:

- the job of the stage manager in today's theatre
- the role of the stage manager at different historical times
- health and safety considerations.

3 Comparisons:

- for Act 1 of *The Lion, The Witch and the Wardrobe* by C. S. Lewis, adapted by Glynn Robins
- for Act 2 of *Absurd Person Singular* by Alan Ayckbourn
- for any of the *Farndale Avenue Townswomen's Guild* scripts
- the different problems/solutions/skills you have needed in stage managing two different performances; or the difference for the actors between having a specific stage manager and having to organise all the work themselves.

Examiners' tip

Being a successful stage manager is not easy and you will need to remain calm and objective both before and during a performance. Ideally, the piece which you stage manage will involve not only actors but also other technicians and backstage hands, so that your organisational skills can be demonstrated fully. You must be able to work constructively throughout and, once the presentation begins, must be prepared to deal effectively with any problem which arises! Remember that the best stage managers are unobtrusive, magnificently organised backstage and their word is law! It is a vast undertaking and unless you know you can cope with the responsibility and stress – don't even consider the job!

Preparing for the Written Examination

Using this section of the book

This section will help you to recognise what you have to do in the exam. If you work carefully through the material in sections A, B and C you will gain the practical experience on which you can base your answers.

D1 Getting to know the written paper

When do you sit the written paper?

You will sit your exam in the summer term at the end of your Drama course.

What does the written paper ask you to do?

- The most important thing to remember is that Drama GCSE is a practical subject and that the examiner will expect you to show that you have gained knowledge and understanding of practical skills.
- If you have studied set plays, you will have to show that you can apply what you have learnt to selected scenes. You will be asked to take a practical point of view.
- If you have studied live productions you have seen, you will be asked to show that you are able to appreciate and judge the work and skills of others.

What kind of things do you have to know?

You will be asked to show your knowledge and understanding of practical drama work you have done in class or seen on stage. By the end of your course you will be able to talk confidently about many of the following:

- characterisation
- voice – volume, accent, pace, timing, emotional range
- physical qualities – movement, posture, gesture, facial expression
- visual qualities – costume, make-up, properties
- design qualities – scale, shape, colour, texture
- use of scenery, lighting, sound
- social context and style/genre
- awareness of health and safety factors.

How is it assessed?

Out of 40 marks for each question you can gain up to:

- 20 marks for understanding the practical skills
- 10 marks for response to plays and other kinds of drama
- 10 marks for analysing and evaluating.

Remember

> Your final grade will be based on your practical marks and your written examination marks added together.

What will the paper look like?

On the opposite page there is an example of the front page of the Drama exam paper. It contains important instructions and information that you will need to know before you start to write your answer. The technical term is **rubric**. Always read the **rubric** carefully, even if you think you know what it contains.

D1.1 activity

Look at the example of an exam paper opposite. Read the page twice carefully.
Now cover it up and answer the following questions.

1 What are you expected to bring into the exam room for Section A?

2 What are you allowed to bring in for Section B?

3 How much time do you have to complete the paper?

4 How many questions must you answer?

5 Can you answer questions from the same section?

6 Can you use diagrams or sketches to help make your answer clearer?

7 Where must you write your rough work?

8 What must you do if you don't want the examiner to mark part of what you have written?

9 Can you keep your notes for Section B?

10 How many marks are awarded for each question?

Check your answers. How well did you do?

7–10 Excellent! You have a good memory for detail.

4–6 Good. You have remembered the main points but it shows you that you need to check the rubric even after you have read it through.

0–3 Don't worry. You are probably being too keen. Calm down and read it slowly. The real paper will not be such a surprise when you see it.

How will the paper be set out?

There will be two sections.

■ Section A is based on the six set plays.
■ Section B is based on visits to live productions.

What kind of questions will be set in Section A?

In Section A there will be six questions, one on each set play. Within each question there will be a choice.

■ Part (a) which asks you to answer as a performer.
■ Part (b) which asks you to answer as a designer or technician.

Each question will offer a short selected scene of about four pages from the set play and you will be asked how you would perform a role in that section or how you would present the scene using your own design or technical skill.

D

General Certificate of Secondary Education

ASSESSMENT and
QUALIFICATIONS
ALLIANCE

Date when you sit the paper.

DRAMA: (3241)

Dateline

Tells you what you will need to have and what you can use in the actual exam. Read with care.

In addition to this paper you will require:
- a 12-page answer book;
- plain text(s) of the selected play(s) for Section A;
- personal notes for Section B.

How much time you have. Divide this by the number of questions to see how long to spend on each answer.

What you MUST do. Read with care.

Time allowed: 2 hours

Instructions

Important! You answer **two** – no more, no less.

- Answer **two** questions, to be chosen from Questions 1 to 10.

- You may choose two questions from the same Section, but you must use a different play in answer to each question. In Section B you must not write about productions of plays that have been set for study in Section A.

How many questions and where from.

- You may support your answers with sketches or diagrams if you wish.

Useful for design candidates.

- Do all rough work in the answer book. Cross through any work you do not want marked.

Warning! Take note.

- Your personal notes for Section B must be handed to the invigilators at the end of the examination.

Useful to know. Helps you plan.

Be ready to hand in your notes. The examiner will wish to see them.

Information

- The maximum mark for this paper is 80.

These marks can make a huge difference to your grade.

- All questions carry 40 marks.

- You will be assessed on your ability to present relevant information in an appropriate form and to ensure that your handwriting is legible and that your spelling, punctuation and grammar are accurate so that meaning is clear.

This is important. You must make sure that the examiner can read and understand what you have written. Make sure you spell technical terms correctly.

Divide your time equally to use the time most efficiently.

What kind of questions will be set in Section B?

In Section B there will be four questions.

You will have to write about a live performance of a complete scripted play that you have seen and studied. This *must not* be one of the six set plays.

There will be a choice to write about performances, design or a combination of both.

Do you have to answer a question from each section?

You may choose two questions from the same section if you wish, but *you must use a different play* in answer to each question.

*In **Section B** you must not write about a play that has been set for study in Section A.* This is to make sure that during the course you have studied at least two complete plays.

What kind of notes can you take into the exam?

For **Section A**, you can take plain copies of the plays you have studied into the exam. This means that there should be no notes on any of the pages. If you have made notes in your texts you must make sure they have been removed before you go into the examination room.

For **Section B** you are allowed to take in up to two sides of an A4 sheet of paper of personal notes on each production you have seen and wish to write about.

'Personal notes' means notes that you yourself have made and not handouts given by your teacher or any published material. They may be handwritten or word-processed and should be in the form of bullet points (see the note-taking part of Section A7 on pages 54–7) and not full sentences or essays you have previously written.

'You may open your exam papers'

When you are allowed to turn the page in the exam, first read the rubric at the top of the page. It is a good idea to look at it now so that you are familiar with what you will have to do.

SECTION A: SET PLAYS

EITHER answer **two** questions from this Section **OR** answer **one** question from this Section and **one** question from Section B.

If you choose two questions from this Section, your answers must be on **different** set plays.

At the beginning of your answer, you must give the name of the publisher of the edition you are using in the examination room.

You will notice that you have to name the publisher of the edition of the play you are using for your answer. This is to help the examiner check your references.

- You will find the publisher's name on the cover, spine or title page.
- Get into the habit of naming the publisher on every essay you write so that you remember to do so in the exam.
- For example, set play, *Twelfth Night*, The Players' Shakespeare, Heinemann.

Reading time

D1.2 activities

1 Test your **reading time** by selecting a scene of about four pages from a play you are studying for Drama.

- A typical question might ask for 'Act 2 – to the bottom of the fourth page'.
- Time yourself finding the selected scene in your copy of the play.
- Write down the result. Now read the selected scene carefully. How long did it take you? The result will be your reading time for one question only.
- Remember, you will also need time to read the front page of the paper and time to check your answer at the end.

2 Ask your teacher if you may see a copy of the Specimen Paper and Mark Scheme books published for teachers by AQA. Look at Section B. Then:

- Check your notes and see which questions you could attempt to answer. Work out your reading time.
- Turn to the Mark Scheme and look up the questions you have chosen. You will find that there is a list of points an examiner would expect to find.
- Copy them down and tick the ones you have already recognised.
- Highlight the points you still have to cover. Follow them up by asking your teacher for advice: or share ideas with the others in your group.
- Realise that the examiners' list does not necessarily cover *all* the possible points that can be made. You may be able to think of some that have not been included.

Improving your examination technique

In any written examination, the main skill required is to communicate to the examiner the information that has been asked for in the question, as fully and as clearly as possible in the time available. You will have to mention as many points as you can, and then justify and explain why you have included them. Here are some general ways in which you can improve your examination technique.

- Read the question carefully to see what the examiner wants from you.
- Know what you want to say.
- Have a clear idea of the most effective order in which to say what you have to say (refer to Section A7 Written Techniques on pages 52–62).
- Explain what, how, and why.
- Support everything you write with reasons, examples and details.
- Plan your answer.

You must remember to draw a line through your plan to show that it is not part of your answer. It is helpful to plan how to answer questions before you sit the paper, and the following advice will help you to do this.

Drama is a practical examination

So the written paper expects you to take a practical approach.

Each year there will be a choice of six set plays available for study. To answer questions on this section you will need to have studied one or more from a practical point of view.

Many candidates gain disappointing grades simply because they choose to answer a question on a play they have not studied in Drama.

You will have learnt a range of Drama skills and will have been shown how to apply them to written scripts. You will also have learnt to understand and use the specialist vocabulary that goes with your skills. The written paper will give you an opportunity to demonstrate what you have learnt.

Presenting your set plays

It is always useful to design for or perform your set plays and this is the best way to study them. You may wish to perform a scene with members of your group or act out the whole play as a school production as your Acting Option, or include extracts in your Devised Thematic Option.

By working on the play you will soon discover the problems that face the performer or the designer and you will be forced to find practical solutions. If other groups are working on the same play, you will be able to share ideas and observe how others might tackle the same problem with different solutions.

Always make full notes of what practical things you did, how you did them, and why. You may find it helpful to look back at the section on note-taking in A7 (pages 54–7).

Examiners' tip

Things that seem obvious to you and which you take for granted may well be points that the examiner can reward. You must include them in your answers if the examiner is to give you credit for knowing or understanding. You could earn up to 40% of your total marks for your answers in the Written Paper – so make sure that you set out to win as many as possible for yourself.

Written paper: set plays

The next two sections will make use of the following extract.

If you do not know the play, don't worry, just try the activities and then see how what you have learnt can be applied to set plays that you have studied.

If you have access to a copy of the play on CD Rom, you could print out your own copy of the scene and write your notes directly on it.

Macbeth by William Shakespeare, Act 5 Scene 1

Enter a DOCTOR OF PHYSIC *and a* WAITING-GENTLEWOMAN.

	DOCTOR	I have two nights watched with you, but can perceive no truth in your report. When was it she last walked?
	GENTLE.	Since his majesty went into the field I have seen her rise from her bed, throw her nightgown upon her, unlock her closet, take forth paper, fold it, write upon 't, read it, afterwards seal it, and again return to bed, yet all this while in a most fast sleep.
5		
	DOCTOR	A great perturbation in nature, to receive at once the benefit of sleep and do the effects of watching. In this slumbery agitation besides her walking and other actual performances, what at any time have you heard her say?
10	GENTLE.	That, Sir, which I will not report after her.
	DOCTOR	You may to me; and 'tis most meet you should.
	GENTLE.	Neither to you nor to anyone, having no witness to confirm my speech.

Enter LADY MACBETH *with a taper.*

15		Lo you, here she comes. This is her very guise, and, upon my life, fast asleep.
		Observe her. Stand close.
	DOCTOR	How came she by that light?
	GENTLE.	Why, it stood by her. She has light by her continually. 'Tis her command.
20	DOCTOR	You see, her eyes are open.
	GENTLE.	Ay, but their sense are shut.
	DOCTOR	What is it she does now? Look how she rubs her hands.
	GENTLE.	It is an accustomed action with her, to seem thus washing her hands. I have known her continue in this a quarter of an hour.
25	L. MACBETH	Yet, here's a spot.
	DOCTOR	Hark, she speaks. I will set down what comes from her to satisfy my remembrance the more strongly.
30	L. MACBETH	Out, damned spot; out, I say. One, two – why then 'tis time to do't. Hell is murky. Fie, my lord, fie, a soldier and afeard? What need we fear who knows it when none can call our power to account? Yet who would have thought the old man to have had so much blood in him?

	DOCTOR	Do you mark that?
35	L. MACBETH	The Thane of Fife had a wife. Where is she now? What, will these hands ne'er be clean? No more o' that, my lord, no more o' that. You mar all this with starting.
	DOCTOR	Go to, go to. You have known what you should not.
	GENTLE.	She has spoke what she should not, I am sure of that. Heaven
40		knows what she has known.
	L. MACBETH	Here's the smell of blood still. All the perfumes of Arabia will not sweeten this little hand. O, O, O!
	DOCTOR	What a sigh is there! The heart is sorely charged.
	GENTLE.	I would not have such a heart in my bosom for the dignity of
45		the whole body.
	DOCTOR	Well, well, well.
	GENTLE.	Pray God it be, Sir.
	DOCTOR	This disease is beyond my practice. Yet I have known those which have walked in their sleep who have died holily in their
50		beds.
	L. MACBETH	Wash your hands, put on your nightgown, look not so pale. I tell you yet again, Banquo's buried. He cannot come out on's grave.
	DOCTOR	Even so?
55	L. MACBETH	To bed, to bed. There's knocking at the gate. Come, come, come, come, give me your hand. What's done cannot be undone. To bed, to bed, to bed. (*Exit.*)
	DOCTOR	Will she now go to bed?
	GENTLE.	Directly.
60	DOCTOR	Foul whisp'rings are abroad. Unnatural deeds Do breed unnatural troubles; infected minds To their deaf pillows will discharge their secrets. More needs she the divine than the physician. God, God forgive us all! Look after her.
65		Remove from her the means of all annoyance, And still keep eyes upon her. So, good night. My mind she has mated, and amazed my sight. I think, but dare not speak.
	GENTLE.	Good night, good doctor.

Exeunt.

Before you work through the next section here are some points to ask yourself.

Have I studied a set play?

- If the answer is 'No' you will need to go straight to **Section B** questions on the exam paper. (Look at Section D4, page 218.)
- If the answer is 'Yes' then go to **Section A** questions on the exam paper and ask yourself:

Have I worked on it as a performer or as a designer?

- If **performer**, look only at **part (a)** of the question. (Look at Section D2, page 207.)
- If **designer**, look only at **part (b)** of the question. (Look at Section D3, page 211.)

D2 Set plays – performance questions

Sample question

SHAKESPEARE: Macbeth

(a) *Selected scene: Act 5 Scene 1. The Sleepwalking Scene.*

*Discuss, in detail, how you would wish to play **either** The Doctor **or** Lady Macbeth in the selected scene. You will need to refer to voice, movement, gesture and facial expression, as well as to how your chosen character responds on stage.*

D2.1 activities

1 Read the question carefully. Notice the key words '**discuss**', '**detail**', '**how**', and '**would**'. They will appear elsewhere in the written exam questions so it is important to know exactly what you are expected to do.

Discuss – You are expected to write about a wide range of aspects of both the character and the scene. You must give reasons for your answer and justify the points you are making.

Detail – You must give details to support or justify your comments. Don't just say *The Doctor would be very professional in this scene*. It may well be true but it does not say how he is professional or why or when.

How – You will need to explain how you would move, speak, gesture and change your facial expressions. You will also need to say **when** your chosen character carries out the actions you are describing and **why** you think the character would react in the way you describe.

Would – This asks you to suggest how you might perform the part. For example, *I would play the Doctor with authority* or *As Lady Macbeth I would sigh deeply as I rubbed my hands vigorously.*

2 In the exam you will be working against the clock so you will need to practise finding scenes quickly and without panic. Remember to give yourself sufficient time for reading, planning, writing and checking your answer.

Time yourself on turning back to the extract from *Macbeth* on page 205 and on reading it through. In the exam you will have to find the selected scene in your book. If you have a copy of *Macbeth* you may wish to experiment with finding the scene. Notice how long it takes just turning pages.

Once you have found the selected scene, read the question again and check that you are answering the right question on the right scene.

What do you have to do?

The question asks you to write about how you would play the part of either the *Doctor* or *Lady Macbeth* in the scene you have just read.

First, you need to decide upon which character you will choose. It is usually best to pick a character you have played or have wanted to play because then you will have some background knowledge to draw upon. If you have been able to read a play, interpret a character, and perform it to an audience you will have the skills and knowledge to enable you to answer the question.

It is possible that the examiner will select a section of the play which is less familiar to you, or choose a character that you have not prepared for. If this happens, do not despair! The examiner is looking for evidence that you know about, and understand, the process of playing a character.

For the sake of this exercise, let us decide to choose the Doctor as the subject of our answer. As you may know, he does not appear elsewhere in the play.

How do you get started?

Preparation for the written paper starts with your practical work on the set texts. You should make notes during rehearsals.

Useful tip

If you are not allowed to write in your books, consider the following.

- Interleave the section you are working on with plain paper. Be careful to number the sheets as you do so in case they fall out.
- Use large Post-it sheets and fix them with the gummed edge tucked closely into the spine of the book. Again, number them!
- Have two copies, one for practical work and one for the exam.
- If you have to write in your copy, use pencil and leave the rubbing out until just a few days before the exam. Re-read your notes as you rub them out to fix them in your mind.

The following activities will give you an idea of what kinds of notes you will need. Read through the *Macbeth* extract and then work through the activities.

The scene

At the beginning of the scene it is night-time. The Doctor and the Gentlewoman are in Lady Macbeth's rooms in the castle. They have already been waiting and watching secretly for two nights because the Gentlewoman is worried about Lady Macbeth and has called in the Doctor to see her mistress sleepwalk.

D2.2 activities

1 Prepare brief notes in answer to the following prompt questions.
- Where is the scene set? When?
- How does the character enter?
- What is the character doing?
- Why is the character there?
- Who else is present?
- What is their status?
- How do they react to each other?
- What action is there?
- How do they exit?

You can use these questions as prompts for almost any scene from any play.

2 Choose the words which most closely fit the Doctor's attitude and manner changes during the scene.

cheerful	nervous	aggressive
embarrassed	irritated	calm
anxious	patronising	suspicious
dismissive	shocked	intense
thoughtful	reassuring	professional
concerned	pompous	

- Write each word you have chosen on a small Post-it note. This will help you remember any change that happens.
- Now arrange the words and stick them on your script in the relevant places. You should try to arrange them to show when the change happens. Remember, some changes will happen gradually.
- Look at lines 1–14. Identify the Doctor's manner or attitude in his first three speeches.
- Think about how you as an actor would show this to an audience through body movements, voice and facial expressions.
- On your Post-it notes add how you would stand, move, speak and react.

Developing the work

If you worked carefully through the scene you will have some material from which to start planning your essay.

A basic plan of how to write a Drama essay

Introduction

- **This will tell the examiner what your answer will focus upon.**

  In the selected scene, Act 5 Scene 1 from Macbeth, I would like to play the part of the Doctor. As the scene opens we hear that he and the Gentlewoman have been waiting in vain to see Lady Macbeth walk in her sleep.

Point

- **Make a clear statement of your idea.**

  The Doctor is probably irritated and is feeling that his time is being wasted.

Justification

- **You need to give a reason for why you think your point is true.**

  The two of them have been waiting for two nights and nothing has happened so far.

Evidence

- **Always support your answer with evidence in the form of references to the script. You can do this by:**
  - quoting a short section – *'Look how she rubs her hands.'*
  - giving a line reference – *Lady Macbeth should rub her hands* (line 23).
  - general reference – *The section where the Doctor observes that Lady Macbeth is rubbing her hands.*

Example

- **This is the heart of your answer – the part where you demonstrate how the point you have made could be shown on stage through performance skills. You will need to cover as many details as possible and give reasons for your suggestions.**

  To show this, I would stand in a haughty, upright way and possibly fold my arms to show that I was creating a barrier between myself and the Gentlewoman. My face would be frowning in disbelief and I would say the words carefully and in measured tones because the Doctor is a professional man and a scientist who wants to get to the truth. Because the play is set in Scotland and because Edinburgh University has produced doctors for hundreds of years, I would give him a refined Edinburgh accent. It would be appropriate for both him and the Gentlewoman to speak almost in whispers because, effectively, they are spying on Lady Macbeth.

Continue this process throughout your essay ■ **You will need to keep to the same pattern, picking up points as you progress.**

Conclusion

- This can be almost as difficult as getting started, as you will want to find a way of summing up the main points you have been making. At this point you should check back to the question to make absolutely sure you have answered it. It may also be useful to refer back to the beginning to show how the character has changed or developed from the start of the selected scene.

  At the end of the scene the Doctor is no longer the professional person in charge of the situation. He would shrink off the stage, a much worried and troubled man, 'I think, but dare not speak' (line 68).

1 Read the answer under **Example** (page 209) and notice each time the word 'because' is used and how it supports the details.

Note down other ways of saying 'because' in the passage.

2 Read the statements below then try to act them out yourself, or ask a partner to do it.

At the start of the scene the Doctor uses body language to show that he does not believe the Gentlewoman.

The Gentlewoman replies to the Doctor using lots of big hand movements.

Notice how these descriptions are too vague and give little idea of what might be happening. Next time you are describing how you would move on stage consider how someone else would interpret your instructions, and give sufficient detail.

3 It is useful to think of your essay as being a set of instructions on how to play the part in a particular scene. When you have completed the first draft of your first essay, ask someone in your group to act out the examples you have given.

- Note what the actor finds difficult to perform or what looks silly.
- Note what has been missed out.
- Go back to your essay and try and find a way to put it right.

Reminders

- In the exam you will have to remember to identify the question you have chosen to answer. When you are sure of your choice, write the number and part (a) clearly in the left-hand margin. Many candidates fail to do this and leave the examiner to guess what is to be marked. Get into the habit of numbering.
- Start at the beginning and be methodical. This helps you to order your thoughts and to write clearly.
- Always answer the question that is set. This may mean having to check back to the question from time to time as you are writing. If you do not answer what has been asked, the examiner cannot give you credit for what you have written.
- Attention to detail demonstrates knowledge and thought.

Examiners' tip

Many candidates fall into the trap of making statements that are too vague or general to earn themselves marks. Don't expect the examiner to do your work for you. Remember the basic plan:

Introduction

> **Point**
> **Justification**
> **Evidence**
> **Example**

Conclusion

This approach can be applied to any essay on any character in any play.
Remember the plan and keep it simple!

D3 Set plays – design questions

Sample question

SHAKESPEARE: Macbeth

(b) *Selected scene: Act 5 Scene 1. The Sleepwalking Scene.*

Discuss, in detail, how one area of design might add to the overall effectiveness of the selected scene. In your answer you will have to show how your ideas relate to other aspects of design.

D3.1   activity

Read the question carefully. Notice the key words '**discuss**', '**detail**', '**how**' and '**might**'. They will appear elsewhere in the written exam questions so it is important to know exactly what you are expected to do.

Discuss – You are expected to write about your own particular area of design. You also need to refer to other design aspects of the scene and must give reasons for your answer to justify the points you make.

Detail – You must give details to support or justify your comments.

How – You will need to explain how you would use your chosen technical skill to design for this scene. You will also need to say **why** you are making your suggestions, and may need to say **when** something occurs.

Might – Imagine that the facilities available to you will be ideal. Be practical in your ideas, but do not feel that you have to limit yourself to the facilities you work with in real life. For example, *I would design a set based on a medieval Scottish castle, and use a revolve to change scenes smoothly and effectively.*

What do you have to do?

One way of preparing yourself for the question is to put yourself in the place of the examiner who will have a mark scheme which will set out the main points to reward. You will be expected to include some of the following:

- style of production
- choice of period
- costumes, fabrics, textures, colours
- use of space and levels
- make-up, puppets or masks
- lighting, colours, intensity, plot, special effects – it is night, indoors, there is reference to 'a taper' so expect mention of candlelight, shadows, gloom
- sounds – perhaps owl cry to establish night and link with murder scene 'It was the cry of owl', which is made explicit by Lady Macbeth's speeches
- properties 'How came she by that light?' – and their management – if Lady Macbeth has to wash her hands in mime, where does she put the taper?
- awareness of health and safety factors.

There is a considerable amount of material that could be included in your answer. If you are attempting these questions, you will have studied and used at least one technical design skill in your practical work. That will be your main area of expertise and will be your starting point.

In any area of design you will know that you have to work closely with other designers because the overall effect will depend upon every aspect fitting together in harmony. You will need to show that you understand this 'unity' and that you have some knowledge of how your design area fits in with those of others.

For the purposes of this exercise we will choose lighting as the subject of our answer.

How do you get started?

Preparation for the written paper starts with your practical work on the set plays and you should make notes on possible design ideas.

Useful tips

If you are not allowed to write in your books, consider the following.

- Interleave the section you are working on with plain paper. Be careful to number the sheets as you do so in case they fall out.
- Some people find it useful to use large Post-it sheets and fix them with the gummed edge tucked closely into the spine of the book. Again, number them!
- Have two copies, one for practical work and one for the exam.
- If you have to write in your copy, use pencil, and leave the rubbing out until just a few days before the exam. Read your notes as you rub them out to fix them in your mind.

The following activities will give you an idea of what kinds of notes you will need. Read through the *Macbeth* extract and then work through the activities.

The scene

At the beginning of the scene it is night-time. The Doctor and the Gentlewoman are in Lady Macbeth's rooms in the castle. They have already been waiting and watching secretly for two nights because the Gentlewoman is worried about Lady Macbeth and has called in the Doctor to see her mistress sleepwalk.

Example of partially completed spider diagram for design questions

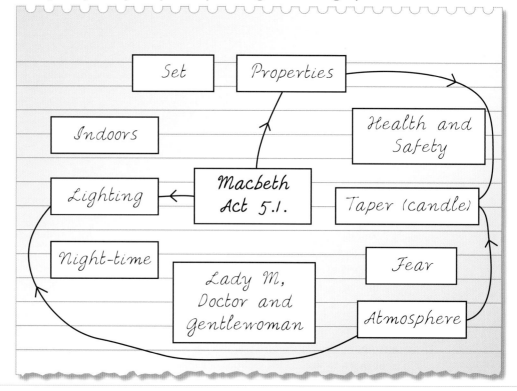

D3.2 activities

1   Prepare brief notes in answer to the following prompt questions.

- When was the play written?
- When was the play set?
- What period would you wish to place it in? Why?
- Where is the scene set? Indoors? Outdoors? What difference might this make?

- What properties will be required?
- How will they be used?
- What furniture and/or set dressing will be required?
- How will they be used and what will be their function?

- What style has been adopted for the production? Why?
- How will this affect your designs?
- What time of day, year, is it set?
- What is the mood or atmosphere the scene needs to convey?

- What opportunities are there for using masks or puppets?
- How might they be used?
- What opportunities are there for sound effects?
- Are there any health and safety implications?

- Who appears in the scene?
- What needs to be shown about their character, status or age?
- What make-up is needed?

You can use these questions as prompts for almost any scene from any play.

2   From the list of questions, choose five you think you could answer easily.

A spider diagram (opposite) is a useful way of organising your ideas because you can show how different elements relate to each other. Draw a spider diagram to help you answer the five chosen questions.

When you have completed your diagram choose one box and see how you can link it up with others. For example:

The atmosphere of fear can be created by suitable lighting effects, e.g. by the use of a flickering taper to suggest candlelight.

Developing the work

If you worked carefully through the scene you will have some material from which to start planning your essay.

A basic plan of how to write a Drama essay

Introduction
- **This will tell the examiner what your answer will focus upon.**

  I would like to design the lighting for the selected scene, Act 5 Scene 1 from Macbeth. The scene is set in an atmosphere of gloom and fear in a room in Macbeth's castle.

Point
- **Make a clear statement of your idea.**

  The atmosphere can be emphasised by creating the impression of candlelight.

Justification
- **You need to give a reason for why you think your point is true.**

  We are told that Lady Macbeth is holding a candle when she enters.

Evidence
- **Always support your answer with evidence in the form of references to the script.**

  You can do this by:
  - quoting a short section – *'Enter Lady Macbeth with a taper'*
  - giving a line reference – *The Doctor's comment in line 18*
  - general reference – *The section where Lady Macbeth enters holding a candle.*

Example
- **This is the heart of your answer – the part where you demonstrate to the examiner how the point you have made could be shown on stage through design skills. You will need to cover as many details as possible and give reasons for your suggestions.**

  When Lady Macbeth enters there should be a slight increase in the levels of light, because she is an important character and needs to be seen. Not only is what she says in this scene important to the plot, but also she is carrying a taper or candle, 'Enter Lady Macbeth with a taper'. Candlelight is very atmospheric and can also help reinforce the fact that the scene is set at night. However, there is a safety problem in that naked flames are a safety hazard on stage even when all scenery and drapes are fireproofed. It would be safer if the props department could provide a battery-operated candle as it is possible to obtain these with realistic flicker effects. When Lady Macbeth enters it would be possible to raise gradually the level of light in her acting area. I would use a lantern with a fresnel lens to give a soft focus effect and use a warm colour filter to contrast with the ice-blue moonlight effect I am already using with a castle window gobo.

Continue this process throughout your essay
- **You will need to keep to the same pattern, picking up points as you progress.**

Conclusion
- **This can be almost as difficult as getting started, as you will want to find a way of summing-up the main points you have been making. It may also be useful to refer back to the beginning to show how your design ideas have developed from the start of the selected scene.**

  By the end of the scene the audience should share a feeling of fear, with the lights fading gradually into complete darkness as the Doctor and Gentlewoman leave.

D3.3 activity

Read the answer under **Example** (opposite) and notice the following points.

- The candidate shows a clear understanding of the lighting needs for this scene. The actors need to be seen by the audience and there is need for a special atmosphere because it is night and the writer says Lady Macbeth is carrying a light.
- There is an awareness of health and safety issues – naked flames are dangerous on stage – and the candidate offers a safe alternative in the form of a battery-powered artificial candle that flickers realistically.

- There is reference to colour filters, lanterns, lenses and gobos, and how these might be used effectively in the selected scene.

The answer is detailed, knowledgeable, and is directly related to the question, with each point supported with reasons and appropriate evidence.

Sketches and diagrams

- You are allowed to support your answer with sketches or diagrams if you wish.
- Keep your drawings clear and appropriate – they should help the examiner understand the point you are trying to make.
- Always label any sketch or diagram as you may gain marks for the information you are giving.
- Colour your sketches or diagrams if doing so helps make the point clearer but remember that this is a Drama exam and not an Art exam. Do not spend too much time on your drawing – it is meant to support your answer, not replace it. It is better to indicate colours by simple labels than either not to mention them at all or to lose valuable writing time as you colour in too carefully.
- You will not be allowed to take copies of your sketches or diagrams into the exam. Prepare for this by planning your drawings in advance. Practise drawing them in spare moments – make them replace your usual doodles! See how quickly and accurately you can set down a whole variety of designs.
- If you are doing lighting, plan lighting rigs using standard symbols for the different lanterns you would use.
- If you wish to include a diagram of a set, it is usually more helpful to draw a picture rather than a stage plan. The examiner needs to know what it looked like rather than exactly where the flats and furniture were placed.

Useful tip

Avoid drawing each separate item of clothing like a paper dressing-up doll. It is more important to show the overall effect of your design than what each individual shoe is like.

Example of good informative costume sketch

Lace bed cap covering her hair. This will draw attention to her face and will help make her look drawn and severe. Her make-up will be pale with shadows under her eyes from lack of sleep. 'You see her eyes are open . . .'

The narrow gold band shows that she is Queen. She has a royal emblem embroidered on her sark.

She is wearing a linen sark or shift. It is an undergarment that people also wore to bed in medieval times. It shows that she does not know that anyone can see her, and that she has just got up out of bed.

It is shapeless to contrast with the closely fitted and sexy dress I designed for her in Act 1 Scene 5 where she was able to manipulate Macbeth. The style also links with the Witches who I have dressed in sarks. It suggests that she has now become totally under their influence.

White is a useful colour as it will make her appear like a ghost – she is herself haunted by her past – and it will take colour from the lights and could turn red as she recalls the murder of Duncan.

Simple plain neck with drawstring.

The sleeves are short to draw attention to her hands as she repeatedly enacts washing them.

The bracelet and the ring are symbols of royalty, and contrast with her simple garment.

She is wearing simple slippers to protect the actress's feet from splinters. If Lady Macbeth was able to pick up a taper in her sleep, she could also have worn slippers to avoid having to walk on the cold stone floors of the castle.

The hem is raised at the front to reveal her bare legs and feet. This will make her appear vulnerable in contrast to her earlier scenes. The raised hem is also for safety as she will be less likely to trip.

Costume for Lady Macbeth Act 5 Scene 1. Notice how the candidate has managed to include detailed labels which can be explained and justified in the written answer

Reminders

- In the exam you will have to remember to identify the question you have chosen to answer. When you are sure of your choice, write the number and part (b) clearly in the left-hand margin. Many candidates fail to do this and leave the examiner to guess what is to be marked. Get into the habit of numbering.
- Start at the beginning and be methodical. This helps you to order your thoughts and to write clearly.
- Attention to detail demonstrates knowledge and thought.
- Sketches and diagrams often help to make your ideas clearer.
- You need to show how your design skill relates to those of others.
- Remember the basic plan suggested here:

Introduction

> **Points**
> **Justification**
> **Evidence**
> **Examples**

Conclusion

This approach can be applied to any essay for any design aspect of any play.
Remember the plan and keep it simple!

Examiners' tip

> Always answer the question that is set. This may mean having to check back to the question from time to time as you are writing. The examiner has to work to a mark scheme. If you do not answer what has been asked, the examiner will not be able to give you any credit for what you have written.

D4 Response to live productions

What do you have to do?

There will be four questions in this section on live performances of plays that you have seen. These will cover the following:

- performance
- design
- a combination of performance and design
- overall effectiveness.

Remember, all questions are worth the same number of marks.

You will have to state the name of the play, and where you saw the live production, at the beginning of each answer in this section.

Are there any restrictions as to what play you write about?

The production you choose must be:

- a live performance. You may not write about a video you have seen!
- a complete full-length play. It cannot be an extract from a longer play.
- a scripted play and not an improvisation.

You should have access to the script.

You should have studied the play before or after your theatre visit.

*You may not write in **Section B** about any play that is set for **Section A** of this exam.*

What is the point of analysing live productions?

Understanding how and why a production makes its impact can make visiting the theatre an even more pleasurable experience. After a year or two of studying Drama you should be both informed and critical. You should be able to make judgements as to what is successful and what is not. Your opinions might differ from those of your friends. The important thing is being able to defend these points with evidence based on knowledge and understanding.

When you go to a live production the overall impression can be overwhelming. It is impossible for anyone (even the examiner!) to take in every single aspect of a live production at just one visit. Every area of a production works with others to achieve the overall effect. When you sit in the audience it is difficult to know what points you should remember and note down. This section will help you to find your way towards being able to write an answer that will help you gain marks for knowledge and understanding.

How can you prepare?

- Gain some personal knowledge of performance and/or design skills by doing them yourself. Whatever your personal level of skill you will soon know enough to recognise the strengths and weaknesses of others. Look back at Section A Developing your skills, to refresh your memory of technical terms used in performance and design.
- Make useful notes on your theatre visits. The prompt sheet on 'Response to live performance' in Appendix 6 (pages 241–6) suggests what to look out for.
- Important! Show consideration for other theatregoers. Do not try to fill in the form while you are watching the show. You'll miss important details, miss out on the experience of the production and be forever hated by those who have gone to enjoy the show. Write it down in the interval or after the final curtain.

- Share what you have seen with others. Talk about it on the way home or next day. Discussion with others is the best way to refresh your memory and make clear in your mind the main points of the production. Note down any extra details you cover.
- Read your notes carefully and reduce them to two sides of A4, in preparation for your exam. If you have access to a word processor you can easily edit your notes by cutting and pasting, and you will have a range of colours to use for highlighting important areas.

From your notes, memories and practical experience you will have a good idea as to the areas of the production which you can discuss in greatest detail. This should help you decide which questions you should attempt.

Questions on performance aspects

As part of your course you will have performed in a piece of practical work. You should, therefore, have some knowledge and understanding of audience reaction and the skills which an actor must bring to any role.

Sample question

> Leader. This tells you the area on which to focus.

Choose a production you have seen during your course where you were impressed by the quality of the acting.

*Discuss, in detail, the performances by **two** actors that most impressed you. You will need to give details of particular scenes or sections where the acting impressed you. You will need to include references to voice, movement, characterisation and relationships created on stage.*

(40 marks)

D4.1   activity

Notice that the question is divided into two paragraphs.

- The first paragraph is the leader and sets out the area you need to think about.
- Look at the first paragraph leader and pick out the key words.
- Ask yourself the following question: 'Which production have I seen that best fits the requirements of the question?' You will need to have in mind a play seen recently in which at least two of the actors gave what you felt were impressive performances.
- Having made your choice, look again at the second paragraph.
- Notice that there are three sentences.
- Pick the sentence which states what you have to do.

- In this instance it is the first sentence. Note the words 'Discuss', 'detail', '**two** actors' and 'most impressed you'. These tell you where to focus your answer.
- The other two 'support sentences' give you helpful hints as to what the examiner will be looking for.
- 'Give details of particular scenes or sections.' Don't be general: give examples by referring to a particular scene and then stating what was done, why and how.
- 'You will need to include references to voice, movement, characterisation and relationships created on stage.' These are all areas you will have worked on as a performer. Use this as a checklist.

Reminders

Discuss – You are expected to write about a wide range of aspects both of the character and the scene. You must give reasons for your answer to justify the points you make.

Detail – You must give details to support or justify your comments.

Performances – This tells you to concentrate on the acting. But if this was significantly affected by the costumes, set, lighting or sound you would need to mention these and say how the acting was affected.

Two actors – This specifies the number of performers you need to write about in detail. Note that the word 'actors' refers to both female and male performers.

Most impressed you – This directs you towards the aspect the examiner wants you to write about. You are asked to discuss not just any impressive performance but just the two that were most impressive *in your opinion*.

Useful tips

- Analyse the questions. It may be helpful to write down key words until you are confident that you know for certain what the examiner wants from you.
- Make sure you are certain what the question is asking before you start writing.
- Always remember that the examiner may not have seen the production you are describing so make your descriptions clear.
- What may seem obvious to you still needs to be set down and made clear, otherwise the examiner will not know that you know the basics.

What should you include in the answer to a performance question?

The point of the exam is to find out what you know and understand. Make sure you find ways to tell the examiner. You will be expected to write about:

- audience reaction
- the chosen characters' age and status
- use of voice, including accent, pitch, tone, emphasis (see Section A3)
- use of body and movement, gesture, posture (see Section A3)
- facial expression (see Section A3)
- interaction with others on stage
- characterisation (see Sections A2 and A3).

Your task in the exam is to:

- provide as many references to these points as you can in the time available
- support your points with examples and details.

How to gain marks

Marks awarded will not just depend upon the number of points that you are able to include, but also on the breadth and range of your knowledge and understanding.

To do this you will need to be constantly answering for yourself the key questions:

- **Who?**
- **Where?**
- **How?**
- **When?**
- **Why?**
- **What?**

D4.2   activity

- Look at an essay you have written as part of your Drama course.
- Identify each statement you have made.
- Ask yourself the key questions at the bottom of page 220 about each statement.
- Answer the key questions by giving examples and details from the production.

You will soon find that a short essay, which originally perhaps gained a low mark, is now much longer and is covering a wider range of points than before. It will bring you better marks.

In order to gain a high mark, you will have to:

- give a sound and competent discussion
- refer to as many points as possible from the 'what should you include …' list (opposite)
- show a high level of sensitivity, and awareness of the performance skills displayed by your chosen actors
- show depth, detail and understanding.

Questions on design aspects

Sample question

Choose a production you have seen during your course that demonstrated the skills of designers in an effective way.

Discuss, in detail, one scene or section that you found particularly effective. You will need to refer to the way in which the design elements helped make the production more effective.

D4.3   activity

- Re-read activity D4.1
- Re-read the sample question above.
- Find the leader sentence.
- Note down the key words.
- Think of a play you have seen which best fits what the question is asking for.

- Look at the next paragraph.
- Find the sentence that states what you have to do.
- Note down the key words.

- Look at the support sentence for reminders of how to improve your answer.
- What kind of scene are you being asked to look at?
- What are you asked to do?

Useful tip

You will be able to recall a number of scenes or sections of plays that you have seen where the design was effective. Choose a scene which particularly stands out in your memory. If there is a choice of scene, pick the one which gives you the widest range of aspects to write about.

What should you include in the answer to a design question?

You will be expected to refer to some of the following:

- style of the production
- communication of period or place
- set design

- costumes, fabrics, textures, colours
- use of space and levels
- make-up, puppets or masks
- lighting, colours, intensity, plot, special effects
- properties and their use and management
- use of music.

Spider diagram as a planning tool

Using a spider diagram you will be able to see at a glance the range and spread of your responses to the production.

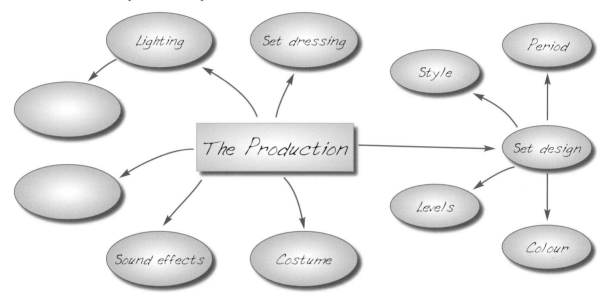

As you build your diagram you will notice links and relationships. The costume design will have links with period and style and will be affected by lighting and set design. Note the links and answer the questions 'How?' and 'Why?'

You may wish to complete the blanks above and extend the links for yourself.

D4.4 activity

- Choose a play you have seen as part of your course and select a scene that you found particularly effective.
- Read through your notes and produce a spider diagram to help you organise them.

- Try to find examples and details to support the points you have noted.
- Write them down.

Example of how to use your sketches

A group of students went to their local theatre to see a touring production of *The Woman in Black*, a ghost play, adapted by Stephen Mallatratt from the book by Susan Hill. Many of them were a bit surprised when they entered the auditorium and saw, instead of the closed red velvet tabs (stage curtains), a rather bleak stage.

Below is a drawing of the set made by one of the students. Notice the following.

- The quality of the drawing is less important than the details that are included, and the labels clearly explain what each aspect is.

- This is not intended to be part of an essay, so there is use of a personal shorthand.
- The sketch shows the main details as a reminder of the staging.
- There is an indication of colour and materials as well as the mention of effects.

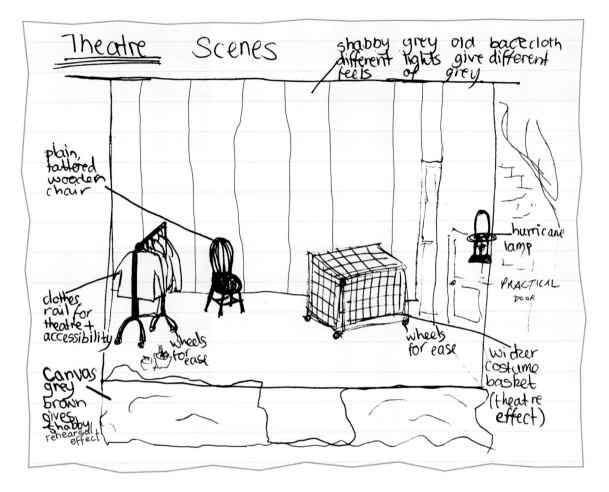

'Wheels for ease' is there to remind her that the basket and the clothes rack are moved about the stage by the actors, and wheels give ease of movement. 'Practical door' means that the door is not painted on the scenery but is practical, i.e. it is capable of being used. The use of this door is important later in the play when it represents the interior of Eel Marsh House

The student's description of the set

The backcloth was drab grey and there were three flats downstage left. The one furthermost upstage was reversed, showing its wooden frame. The centre flat contained what was later revealed to be a practical panelled interior door with a wooden architrave. The downstage flat was painted to depict a brick wall upon which hung an unlit hurricane lamp. A grey drape hung bunched up over the top edge.

The stage itself was empty apart from a wooden bentwood chair and wicker costume basket set centre stage. Stage right was a rail of costumes and downstage of this a couple of paint kettles with brushes protruding from them.

Along the front of the stage, and hanging over into the orchestra pit, lay a greyish brown canvas backdrop or stagecloth which looked as if it had been casually dumped there.

The stage was lit dimly by what appeared to be working lights and this added to the overall drab and uninviting impression of a stage in a theatre that was 'between productions'.

Notice how much information can be conveyed in a simple sketch and notes.

Notice also how the description is systematic and covers details of:

- set, including colours, materials, style and construction
- furniture
- set-dressing
- lighting
- atmosphere.

To gain higher marks the answer would have to go on to say:

- **how** the set was used
- **why** the individual aspects were included
- **when** they were used
- **where** they were used
- **who** used them
- **what** effect was created.

Questions on overall effectiveness

At this point, having looked at some detail at both performance and design aspects of live theatre visits, it will be useful to examine how both performance and design elements can be brought together in answers on overall effectiveness.

Sample question

Choose a production you have seen during your course which made a strong emotional impact on you.

Discuss, in detail, one scene or section that made an impact on you. You will need to refer to the activity on stage, the audience reaction, possible lighting, sound, set design or costume.

D4.5 activity

Read the question carefully and ask:

- What is the question asking?
- What play have you seen that best fits the description in the leader sentence?

- What help are you given in the support sentence?
- What scene or section of that play gives you the widest amount of material to use in your answer?

How to use your notes

Example of student notes on *The Woman in Black*

Aspects you will need to include	Notes of your responses
the emotional impact	Eerie and disturbing. Fear for safety of dog, Spider. Steady increase in tension.
style of production	Semi-naturalistic. The play is set on the stage of an empty theatre and the story is told through flashbacks using theatrical effects.
communication of period or place	Place through drab, grey drapes and scruffy flats and stage. Period through costumes and set (late Victorian)
set design	See sketch. Interior of a 'dark' theatre. Grey backcloth (gauze), flats DSL, one with practical door. Staircase and nursery furniture behind gauze.
costumes, fabrics, textures, colours	Lawyer in black jacket, waistcoat, pin-striped trousers, wing collar. Tweeds when visiting Eel Marsh House. Actor in tweed suit, tweed overcoat, black wide-brimmed hat. The woman in black dress with crinoline, black bonnet and veil.
use of space and levels	Stage on one level but raked. Staircase USK used by woman. Action in this scene upstage behind gauze and downstage centre.
make-up, puppets or masks	Woman: white make-up to give ghostly impression. Eyes appear sunken, skin stretched tight.
lighting, colours, intensity, plot, special effects	Evening, house interior downstage. Fade to blackout. Spotlight on closed door. Lights on area behind gauze upstage as Kipps switches on lights. Blackout. Dawn effect - pink.
properties and their use and management	Costumes on rail used for quick changes. Prop basket used as desk, pony trap, altar. Torch. Candle.
movement on stage	Hands to mouth as speaking trumpet when calling. Suggests anxiety by rapid head movements. Breaks into a run on the spot in slow motion facing audience. Reaches, arms outstretched, crouching towards Spider.
use of music and/or sound effects	Wind, howling. Child's cry. Chilling and eerie whistle. Sounds of gulls and seabirds to set place. Pony and trap. Kipps' feet, running.
audience reaction	Everyone gasped when they heard the whistle offstage. I felt a shiver go down my spine when I saw the woman in black.

The **notes of your responses** provide a useful framework for your essay.

- Read through your own notes and your sheets recording your response to live performances (see Appendix 6). Often just the sight of the sheet you used to make your original notes will spur your memory.

- Draw a spider diagram, this time including both performance *and* design.
- Write a paragraph of about five or six lines on one aspect of the production you saw.

In order to gain a high mark you will need to:

- include as many points as you can
- discuss the points in a sound and competent manner, showing that you know what you are talking about and are able to back up your comments with examples and evidence
- be sensitive to, and aware of, the design and performance skills demonstrated in the scene you are discussing.

Careful preparation and a calm approach on the day of the exam can really push your marks up.

Avoiding common faults and pitfalls

Examiners are experienced teachers who have prepared candidates for the exam in their own centres. Many are also parents who have seen their own children worrying about their exams. They are human beings who want you to do well. To avoid common faults and pitfalls, take the following advice.

- **Be specific.** Avoid comments like *the lighting was basic* as it conveys very little. Explain what effects were created, how they were achieved and why they were needed.
- **Think about what you are writing.** *The scene had dark lights in it* obviously does not make sense, yet every year dozens of candidates write it in their answers. Presumably the candidates meant that the lights were dimmed.
- **Justify the points you make.** *The acting was brilliant* tells the reader nothing if it is not supported by reasons (Why?), and examples (How?).
- **Keep to the point.** You waste valuable time if you tell the story of the play you are supposed to be discussing. Get down to practical details.

Countdown to the written examination

During the course

- You will be engaged in practical work – learn your skills thoroughly.
- Make careful notes during your practical work and later as homework.
- Work your way through the activity suggestions in this section of the book.

During your revision period

- Check the date and time of the exam and make a note of it in a prominent place where you won't forget. This sounds obvious, but many candidates have to be telephoned by their centres because they forget or get the date wrong.
- Convert your notes for Section B of the exam paper into two sides of A4 bullet point notes.
- Look through old essays, especially those for mock exams, and try to spot your weak points. Note down how you could improve them.

- Re-read your set texts, reminding yourself of all your notes; and try to visualise what you or your friends did when you performed the scene or section.
- Mix manageable amounts of Drama revision with revision for other subjects. You will be more likely to absorb and remember details.

Two or three days before the exam

- Take the plunge and remove your notes from the set text you intend to take into the examination room. Try to visualise and recall what you had written.
- Read through your A4 notes for Section B questions.

The night before the exam

- Read through your notes and glance through your texts just to refresh your memory.
- Have a relaxing evening and go to bed at a reasonable time.
- If your exam is in the morning, set your alarm!

The morning of the exam

- Get up with time to spare – having to rush causes panic and confusion.
- Have a good breakfast – your brain can't work on nothing!
- Don't forget to take your A4 notes and/or texts.

The exam itself

- You will have been given instructions as to what you must do by your centre.
- While you wait for answer books and question papers, relax your shoulders. Roll them forward and back, without drawing attention to yourself. Breathe in deeply and slowly. Breathe out to a mental count of four.
- When you are given the instruction to begin, read the rubric on the front cover carefully. Turn to the section you have chosen and read the questions carefully.
- Read them again. Think about what is asked of you and what you want to say.
- If it is helpful, jot down a brief plan in your answer book.
- Re-read your chosen question, glance carefully through your notes and begin.
- Remember to name the edition you are using for Section A answers.
- State the name of the play and where you saw the live performance for Section B answers.
- Part way through your answer, just check again that you *are* answering the question appropriately. It is better to cross it out and start again than to risk losing all your marks.
- Keep checking the time and make sure you have time to answer both questions.
- Read through your answers and, if necessary, correct your spellings.

Examiners' tip

> Always answer from a position of strength. If you know a lot about skills in one area of production, and have at your fingertips both a good understanding and the technical terms, do not decide at the last minute to write an essay on an area you have not studied.

Remember

Everyone wants to see you do well, and that includes the examiners and the authors of this book. If you have done your best then you can be proud of yourself.

Best of Luck!

Appendices

Introduction

The following appendices contain various forms which you can use to help you keep track of what you are doing, and which will help you to improve your work. Each of them can be downloaded from www.heinemann.co.uk/secondary/drama, and can then be photocopied if you so wish.

Appendix 1

This gives some **assessment guidelines**. It is designed to help you to recognise your levels of achievement in different areas of presenting work; and to help you to see what you need to do to improve your levels.

Appendix 2

This is a **rehearsal log-sheet**. It is designed to help you to keep good notes of what you are doing in each rehearsal; and to help you to identify what still needs to be done.

Appendix 3

This is a **performance self-assessment sheet**. It is designed to help you to think in greater detail about various aspects of your performance; and to help you to evaluate the level of success which you achieved.

Appendix 4

This is a **technical self-evaluation sheet**. Like the performance sheet, it is designed to help you to think about various aspects of your presentation in greater detail; and to help you evaluate the levels of success you achieved.

Appendix 5

This is an **audience evaluation sheet**. It is designed for you to give to members of your audience so that they may indicate how your performance came across to them; or you may prefer to ask them the questions, and write down notes of what they have to say.

Appendix 6

This is a sheet for recording your **response to live scripted performances** which you see during the course. These may be professional, amateur or school; but they need to give you sufficient opportunity and information to be able to write a full-length essay on them in your final written exam. You need to make sure you know beforehand what you are wanting to look out for; and then you should record your thoughts, opinions and reasons during the interval or as soon as you can after the performance. If you leave it more than a day or two, you will not remember the detail which will bring you the marks in the exam. Notice that the sheets ask you to evaluate both the acting and the technical aspects of production.

Appendix 7

This is a **lighting cue-sheet**. It is designed to help you organise and record the lighting choices you have made and to be used in performance. It should be completed in such a way that another person could operate the lighting without you having to be there.

Appendix 8

This is a **sound cue-sheet**. It is designed to help you organise and record the sound choices you have made and to be used in the performance. Like the lighting cue-sheet, it should be completed so that another person could operate the sound without you being there.

Appendix 9

This is a **make-up design sheet**. This sheet will allow you to create designs and record the decisions you have made. You could use more than one sheet to show the different stages in the application of the make-up or links to comparisons you have made.

Appendix 10

This is a **costume design sheet**. This sheet will allow you to create designs and to record decisions you have made. You could use more than one sheet to show different layers of the costume or links to comparisons you have made.

Appendix 1 Assessment guidelines

Under each of the following headings there are five levels of performance. The **first** deals with candidates who generally have difficulties; the **second** with those who manage to show their ability every now and then, but who are not able to do this all the time. The **third** deals with those who show ability, although there are still some obvious weaknesses in what they do; the **fourth** with those who can present a confident and competent performance; and the **fifth** with those who can produce that extra 'something', that creativity and originality which brings the performance to life, and makes it a real delight to watch.

Look at each section, and try to identify which definition applies best to you. This may not be the same level for each aspect of presentation, so look carefully at each of them. Tick the box opposite the definition which seems to describe your level of attainment best.

When you have done this, look at what is needed for you to reach the next level up in one or two of the aspects, and concentrate on raising your standards in those before going on to another one.

As far as showing ideas and understanding is concerned, do you tick box

1 Find it difficult to come up with ideas about the play and the acting? ☐
2 Manage to come up with ideas, although they are often very ordinary? ☐
3 Show some creative ideas? ☐
4 Show creative ideas, with sensitivity to mood and atmosphere? ☐
5 Show a high level of creativity and originality, and a thorough
   understanding of how to create mood and atmosphere? ☐

As far as your voice is concerned, do you

1 Find it difficult to be heard, or to use your voice suitably for your
   character and situation? ☐
2 Manage occasionally to use your voice suitably for your character and situation? ☐
3 Use your voice suitably for your character and situation? ☐
4 Show good control of pace, pitch, pause, volume, tone and other vocal qualities? ☐
5 Show an excellent command of pace, pitch, pause, projection, tone, rhythm
   and other vocal qualities? ☐

As far as the use of your body and movement are concerned, do you

1 Find it difficult to use your body, movement and space in a suitable way
   for your character and situation? ☐
2 Manage occasionally to use your body, movement and space suitably
   for your character and situation? ☐
3 Use your body, movement and space suitably for your character and situation? ☐
4 Show good control of body movement, facial expression, gesture and use of space? ☐
5 Show an excellent command of body, face, gesture and space? ☐

As far as role is concerned, do you

1 Find it difficult to act out a believable character? ☐
2 Manage to create a suitable character some of the time, but find it difficult
   to maintain it? ☐
3 Create and sustain a character who is suitable for the play? ☐
4 Create a character who is appropriate and believable? ☐
5 Create a role with sensitivity, originality and flair? ☐

As far as the audience is concerned, do you   tick box

1   Find it difficult to act in a suitable way for them?   ☐
2   Manage occasionally to act in a suitable way for them?   ☐
3   Act in a generally suitable way for them?   ☐
4   Show an obvious awareness of them?   ☐
5   Show an excellent rapport with them?   ☐

As far as working with your group is concerned, do you

1   Find it difficult to work with the others?   ☐
2   Manage to co-operate reasonably well with the rest of the group?   ☐
3   Work well in your group and respond to others' ideas and directing?   ☐
4   Respond positively and helpfully to others in the group?   ☐
5   Show a strong commitment to the group and its success?   ☐

As far as solving problems is concerned, do you

1   Find it difficult to suggest ways to overcome difficulties?   ☐
2   Manage occasionally to suggest suitable solutions?   ☐
3   Succeed in suggesting suitable solutions most of the time?   ☐
4   Show real insight and understanding?   ☐
5   Show a high level of theatrical insight and understanding?   ☐

As far as using technical skills in constructing artefacts is concerned, do you

1   Find it difficult to use the materials to make your artefact?   ☐
2   Manage to show limited skills in using different materials in
    making your artefact?   ☐
3   Manage to show reasonable skills in the use of materials needed to
    make your artefact?   ☐
4   Show well-developed skills in using necessary materials?   ☐
5   Show technical expertise in the constructing of your artefact?   ☐

As far as using technical equipment is concerned, do you

1   Find it difficult to use the equipment correctly?   ☐
2   Manage to show a limited skill in using the necessary equipment?   ☐
3   Manage to show reasonable skill in using the necessary equipment?   ☐
4   Show well-developed skills and understanding in using necessary equipment?   ☐
5   Show a high level of expertise in the use of necessary equipment?   ☐

As far as producing work suitable for a theatrical presentation is concerned, do you

1   Find it difficult to present work which is theatrically suitable?   ☐
2   Manage to show some understanding of what is needed for a
    theatrical presentation?   ☐
3   Manage to produce work which has some theatrical impact?   ☐
4   Produce work which is both practicable and effective for a theatre?   ☐
5   Produce work which shows a thorough understanding of the needs
    of an effective theatrical presentation?   ☐

As far as communicating your intentions and designs is concerned, do you

1   Find it difficult to communicate your ideas and intentions to other people?   ☐
2   Manage to communicate your ideas with some success?   ☐
3   Manage to communicate your ideas successfully?   ☐
4   Communicate your ideas in a relevant, successful and effective manner?   ☐
5   Communicate your ideas in a manner which excites and delights?   ☐

Appendix 2 Rehearsal log-sheet

Name

Date

Rehearsal number

Working title

Option

Agreed aim for the session:

Research activities or research used in the session:

Time management:

What was achieved:

What needs to be done:

Time left to performance:

Activities undertaken:

Detail and polishing achieved:

Diagrams of blocking or stage choreography:

Technical or design ideas arising from the session:

Agreed changes made from last session:

Personal development of role/character/involvement:

Appendix 3 Performance self-assessment sheet

Name	Date

Coursework Option

Title of piece

Brief description of the piece of work:

Description of role/character/function:

Vocal skills used:

Volume ....

Pace ....

Pitch ....

Tone ....

Accent ....

Pause ....

Silence ....

Vocal mannerism ....

Overall vocal evaluation ....

....

....

....

....

....

Physical skills used:

Movement ....

Posture ....

Gesture ....

Stillness ....

Mannerism ....

Facial expression ....

Body expression ....

Use of space ....

Overall physical evaluation ....

....

....

....

....

....

Creation of mood and atmosphere:

Relationship/interaction with the audience:

Quality of group work in the performance:

Rehearsal ideas/techniques that worked in performance:

Successful elements or moments in the performance:

Areas to develop in the next performance or piece of work:

Appendix 4 Technical self-evaluation sheet

Name	Date

Option	Title of piece

Brief description of your task:

What were your design objectives or the intended effect on the audience?

Demands of the text or piece of work:

Equipment used:

Technical skills or techniques used:

Use of the performance space:

Realisation of plans and diagrams:

Successful design elements:

Successful operation elements:

Areas for development in the next performance or piece of work:

Appendix 5 Audience evaluation sheet

Name

Date

Others in the group

Title of piece

Brief description of the story or narrative as you understood it:

Description of the roles/characters:

Evaluation of vocal skills used:

e.g. Volume Pace Pitch Tone Pause Accent Silence Mannerism

Evaluation of physical skills used:

e.g. Movement   Posture   Gesture   Facial expression
Stillness   Mannerism   Use of space

Did you feel that a sense of mood and atmosphere was created in the piece?

Successful moments of tension/comedy/suspense/tragedy/climax:

Evaluation of group performance techniques used:

e.g. Banners   Chorus   Counterpoint   Flashback   Monologue   Narration   Physical theatre   Repetition and echo   Slow motion   Synchronised movement

Evaluation of the overall impact the piece made on you:

Areas that you would suggest for development:

Appendix 6 Response to live performance

Name

Date of performance

Title of play:

Playwright

Theatre 'company'

Venue

Role played:

Acting notes: you should review at least two actors, so that you can quote from contrasting performances.
You will obviously need to photocopy the acting sheets for each actor reviewed.

Write a brief account of what the character did in the play:

What were the character's main relationships in the performance and how did the actor show them?

Identify key moments in which the actor played an important part in the story or action of the play:

Vocal performance techniques used:

Which techniques?   When/How?

Physical/movement techniques used by the actor:

Which techniques?   When/How?

How well did the actor use the performance space?

How did the actor contribute to the creation of mood and atmosphere?

How effective was the overall characterisation?

If you were either directing or acting the part, what changes would you have made, and why?

Technical notes:

Draw a front view of the stage.

Draw a ground plan or overhead view of the stage. Show entrances and exits, important pieces of scenery, different levels; and the position of the audience.

Communication of period or time through the set:

Use of different levels in the set design:

How the set created mood and atmosphere:

Communication of location through the set:

Use of colour/texture/fabric on the set:

Set dressing:

Overall creation of performance space:

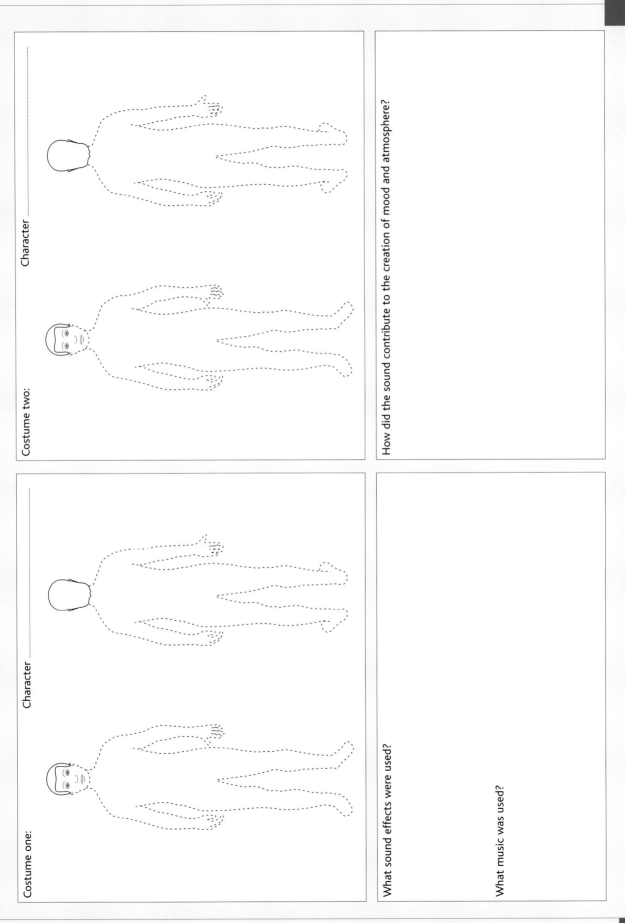

Costume one:

Character _____

Costume two:

Character _____

What sound effects were used?

What music was used?

How did the sound contribute to the creation of mood and atmosphere?

How well were the actors lit?

How did the lighting contribute to the creation of mood and atmosphere?

If you were in charge of the technical design, what would you have changed, and why?

Lighting equipment used:

Use of colour in the lighting:

What did the overall technical elements communicate?

Appendix 7 Lighting cue-sheet

Sheet number

Requirements:

Name ....

Title of performance ....

Operator ....

CUE NUMBER	ACTION	DURATION	FADERS/AREAS	INTENSITY	CUE

Appendix 8 Sound cue-sheet

Sheet number

Requirements:

Name

Title of performance

Operator

CUE NUMBER	ACTION	DURATION	TITLE	VOLUME	CUE

Appendix 9 Make-up design sheet

Name:

Date:

Performance:

Character:

Relevant details of character to be considered:

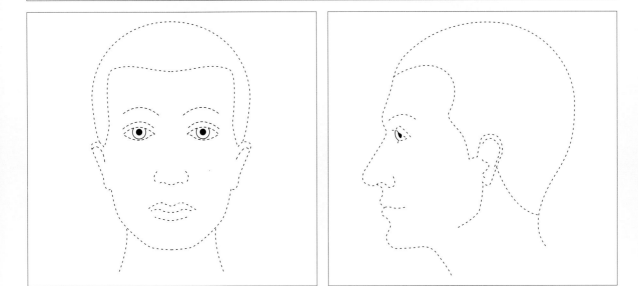

Base:

Highlights:

Shadows:

Eye:

Mouth:

Nose:

Cheek:

Powder:

Hair:

Prosthetics:

Additional notes:

Appendix 10 Costume design sheet

Name:	Date:

Performance:

Character:	Actor:

Relevant character details to be considered:

Front

Back

Torso:

Legs:

Feet/hands:

Head/hair:

Accessories:

Extra notes:

UNIVERSITY OF WOLVERHAMPTON
LEARNING & INFORMATION SERVICES